MICROSOFT® OFFICE FOR TEACHERS

SECOND EDITION

Patricia J. Fewell
EASTERN ILLINOIS UNIVERSITY

William J. Gibbs
DUQUESNE UNIVERSITY

PEARSON

Merrill
Prentice Hall

Upper Saddle River, New Jersey
Columbus, Ohio

Library of Congress Cataloging-in-Publication Data
Fewell, Patricia J.
  Microsoft Office for teachers / Patricia J. Fewell, William J. Gibbs.—2nd ed.
    p. cm.
  Includes bibliographical references and index.
  ISBN 0-13-119376-7
  1. Microsoft Office. 2. Microsoft Excel (Computer file) 3. Microsoft Word. 4. Microsoft
PowerPoint (Computer file) 5. Microsoft Access. 6. Teachers—In-service training. I.
Gibbs, William J. II. Title.
HF5548.4.M525F49 2006
005.5′024′37—dc22

                                                                                    2005041545

Vice President and Executive Publisher: Jeffery W. Johnston
Executive Editor: Debra A. Stollenwerk
Assistant Editor: Elisa Rogers
Editorial Assistant: Mary Morrill
Production Editor: Kris Roach/Alexandrina B. Wolf
Production Coordination: Carlisle Publishers Services
Design Coordinator: Diane C. Lorenzo
Cover Designer: Jeff Vanik
Cover Image: Corbis
Production Manager: Susan Hannahs
Director of Marketing: Ann Castel Davis
Marketing Manager: Darcy Betts Prybella
Marketing Coordinator: Brian Mounts

This book was set in Gill Sans by Carlisle Communications, Ltd. It was printed and bound by Banta Book Group. The cover was printed by Coral Graphic Services, Inc.

Pearson Education Ltd.
Pearson Education Singapore Pte. Ltd.
Pearson Education Canada, Ltd.
Pearson Education—Japan

Pearson Education Australia Pty. Limited
Pearson Education North Asia Ltd.
Pearson Educación de Mexico, S.A. de C.V
Pearson Education Malaysia Pte. Ltd.

10 9 8 7 6 5 4 3 2
ISBN: 0-13-119376-7

This book is dedicated to our families

Earl and Joy Longman and the Longman gang

Annette, Lauren, and Liam Gibbs

James and Helen Gibbs.

ABOUT THE AUTHORS

Patricia J. Fewell

Patricia is Professor of secondary education and foundations at Eastern Illinois University. She received her Ed.D. in 1988 from Illinois State University. A certified K–12 media specialist, she is currently teaching introductory educational media for preservice teachers, as well as data management for graduate students. Dr. Fewell has served as president of the division of educational media management of the Association for Education Communications and Technology (AECT) and as secretary/treasurer for the AECT Board of Directors; she currently serves as secretary for the Education Communications and Technology Foundation (ECT) Board. She gives presentations on technology applications in the classroom at state, national, and international conferences.

William J. Gibbs

Dr. Gibbs is an Associate Professor in the Department of Interactive Media at Duquesne University. In 1992 he received his Ph.D. from Pennsylvania State University. Dr. Gibbs teaches courses in instructional design, courseware authoring, and multimedia. He has given presentations on topics related to instructional technology at state, national, and international conferences and has published a number of articles in this area.

Preface

Conceptual Framework

In this book, computers and associated software are presented as tools or means to accomplish tasks in instruction, learning, and classroom management. From this perspective, we examine various types of computer software, including word processing, presentation, database, spreadsheet, and telecommunication applications. Each category is presented as part of the Microsoft Office suite comprised of Word, PowerPoint, Access, Excel, Outlook, and Publisher, as well as through a combination or integration of the Office products. We offer specific instructions and recommendations for using these products in the classroom and provide teachers with a starting point to develop their technological knowledge and integrate technology into the curriculum.

Teachers are busy and often do not have time to learn new software applications. Word processing, databases, and spreadsheets can improve work efficiency, expand the range of tasks performed, improve accuracy and effectiveness, and reduce the amount of time needed to perform routine tasks. However, the initial time needed to learn these applications can be an obstacle for some teachers. We address this issue in three ways. First, we present a visually illustrated and nontechnical approach to learning the Microsoft Office 2003 suite. The book includes screen-captures supplemented with text descriptions, work templates, and exercises to help teachers learn and use these applications without the frustration often experienced when studying intensive technical manuals. Second, we believe it is useful to build on the suggestions and work of others, so we have created work templates (e.g., sample newsletter, grade book, etc.) and exercises that demonstrate the usefulness of the Microsoft Office suite and the diversity of its applications. Teachers can quickly and easily tailor these templates and ex-

ercises to meet their specific needs. Third, the book focuses on various tasks—such as creating grade books, newsletters, and posters, or making presentations to parent groups or the school board—as a catalyst for learning the Microsoft Office suite.

For example, many preservice teachers need to know how to create a class newsletter, store student records, calculate test scores, and help students create an electronic presentation: word processing, database, spreadsheet, and presentation development skills are fundamental to these tasks. The activities in this book focus on these tasks to cultivate basic computer proficiency. Using nontechnical and graphically illustrated "how-to" procedures, teachers and students accomplish real-world, computer-based tasks and develop skills in word processing, database management, using spreadsheets, and making presentations.

This book is written for teachers with very basic computing skills, such as opening, creating, and closing files and operating a mouse. The activities described in the book require a computer capable of running Microsoft Office 2003.

Organization of the Text

Chapter 1 introduces the text and offers information on state and national technology standards for teachers and students related to integrating technology in the classroom.

Chapter 2 addresses the Microsoft Office 2003 interface, including toolbars, menu options, and working with Windows. It also presents steps for configuring toolbars and using the Office Assistant.

Chapter 3 discusses word processing, including creating a new Microsoft Word document and modifying an existing one. It focuses on creating a book report, a Web page document, and a newsletter. Using the chapter activities, students create word processing documents. They use the copy, cut, paste, and formatting options as well as WordArt and Clip Art to create a document with columns resembling a newsletter.

Chapter 4 introduces Microsoft PowerPoint. It focuses on the fundamentals and how they apply to developing a presentation. Using the example of a student research team reporting on weather conditions, the chapter outlines the steps in creating a presentation. It discusses slide layout, design, importing graphics and Clip Art, and printing a presentation and saving it as a Web page.

Chapter 5 focuses on Excel fundamentals and their application to classroom learning activities. It presents step-by-step instructions for creating workbooks, editing and manipulating data in worksheets. Activities include creating a workbook, entering data into a worksheet, editing data calculating data, and charting data.

Chapter 6 presents detailed instructions for creating, entering information and searching a database using the Wizard and the Access editor. It also shows how to save files, prepare mail, merge documents, and print reports.

Chapter 7 presents basic e-mail concepts and presents procedures for composing, sending, reviewing, receiving, organizing, and deleting e-mail in Microsoft Outlook, as well as using Contacts, Journals, and Calendars.

Chapter 8 discusses preparing brochures, postcards, and flyers with Publisher software using many of the same processes used in Word.

Chapter 9, Integrating Office 2003, builds on the previous chapters and presents readers with ideas on integrating the various Office products to increase work efficiency and enhance the quality of materials created.

Although the chapters are related, they can be used independently and out of sequence. Teachers who want students to create a monthly newsletter will find Chapters 3 and 8 useful; teachers who want students to create book report presentations or perform analyses on data will find Chapters 4, 5, and 9 informative.

Accompanying CD

The accompanying CD contains all of the examples presented in the book and other materials that may be created using the Office suite. You will find examples and exercises in the Examples folder and the Let Me Try folder. Refer to the example on the CD as you follow the text helps facilitate your understanding of the topic being presented. All exercises, activities, and examples in the text that have a corresponding file on the accompanying CD-ROM are called out in the text with an instruction line and are identified by the CD icon. Readers are encouraged to refer to the CD-ROM as they read the section.

Features of the Book

Advance Organizers

Each chapter begins with a set of advance organizers to prepare readers for the main topics. They include the following:

- Chapter outline
- Learning objectives
- Technical terms
- Overview, which provides the rationale for the topics and discusses their use

Show Me

Each chapter presents step-by-step instructions for manipulating the technical aspects of various application, such as writing a letter in Microsoft Word. Using text and graphics, the steps necessary to accomplish this task as well as the rationale for performing specific software functions are illustrated.

Let Me Try

Let Me Try exercises are embedded throughout the chapters so readers can practice the concepts learned. These exercises (1) offer guided practice for operating the software and (2) produce outcomes, such as a database field, a Word document, and a PowerPoint presentation that teachers can use. The Let Me Try exercises are based on daily instructional and managerial tasks, which include creating grade books with Excel, class newsletters with Word or Publisher, and/or student research reports in PowerPoint presentations. In some cases, templates and examples to support the Let Me Try exercises are provided on the accompanying CD.

New to This Edition

- ***Chapter on Publisher 2003.*** Chapter 8 presents Microsoft Publisher 2003, a desktop publishing software that allows teachers to create, customize, and publish professional communications material. Because teachers are communicating with other teachers, schools, students, and parents in new and innovative ways, it is essential to provide them with another resource for creating professional-looking materials to communicate their messages. This provides teachers greater flexibility in developing newsletters, posters, and promotional flyers, and other materials.

- ***Chapter on Integrating Office.*** The first edition provided essential fundamentals of using the Office products as independent applications. However, because of the various ways these applications are used and combined, a chapter devoted solely to integrating the Office products was necessary. Chapter 9 discusses procedures for inserting PowerPoint slides and Excel charts in Word documents and embedding and linking files from one application to another.

- ***Expanded Let Me Try Exercises and Examples.*** Additional Let Me Try exercises and examples have been added to the chapters and to the CD. Throughout the text, references to materials on the CD have been added to direct the reader to additional digital resources.

- ***Glossary.*** A glossary of terms has been added so that readers may refer to terminology presented in the chapters.

Acknowledgments

A number of the ideas within this text were conceived or provided by classroom teachers to whom we are most grateful. We would like to especially thank the teachers at the Prairieland Elementary School for their ideas. Bridgette Belasli graciously provided work samples that proved most useful and helped us develop practical examples. Terry Hyder spent many hours reviewing drafts of the text. Her suggestions were invaluable, and we greatly appreciate her efforts. We also thank Debbie Stollenwerk and Dan Parker for their support of our ideas and the insights they provided along the way. They were always encouraging and helpful.

The following reviewers also provided invaluable advice: Cathy Cavanaugh, University of North Florida; Gayle V. Davidson-Shivers, University of South Alabama; Mary Ann Demuynck, Texas Woman's University; Charles D. Dickens, Tennessee State University; Cheryl Foltz, Southwest Baptist University; Michael Land, Midwestern State University; and Nancy Maushak, Texas Tech University.

Mostly, we thank our families for their understanding and support as we developed this book. Earl Longman, Joy Longman, and Suzanne Schertz; and Annette Gibbs, Lauren Gibbs, Liam Gibbs, and James and Helen Gibbs, your encouragement made this book possible.

BRIEF CONTENTS

CONTENTS

CHAPTER 6 ACCESS 2003   134

CHAPTER 7 OUTLOOK 2003   163

CHAPTER 8 PUBLISHER 2003   184

CHAPTER 9 INTEGRATING OFFICE 2003   208

APPENDIX A WINDOWS   A1

APPENDIX B MACINTOSH   B1

GLOSSARY   G1

INDEX   I1

1 TECHNOLOGY AND THE CLASSROOM

CHAPTER OUTLINE

LEARNING OBJECTIVES

At the completion of this chapter you will be able to:
- Identify the ISTE standards for teachers
- Note technology standards for students
- Be aware of copyright issues
- Be aware of acceptable use policies (AUPs) in school districts
- Identify teacher production activities
- Identify student production activities
- Identify how Microsoft Office products help teachers integrate technology

TECHNICAL TERMS

The following are terms that you will encounter in the chapter and with which you will become familiar:

ISTE **(International Society for Technology in Education)**
NCATE **(National Council for the Accreditation of Teacher Education)**
Acceptable use policies
Copyright

1

CHAPTER OVERVIEW

This chapter discusses the contents of this text and provides an overview of its structure and scope. It offers information regarding technology standards for teachers and students that can serve to establish a context for integrating technology in the classroom. In addition, the chapter presents an overview of acceptable use policies and copyright law.

About This Book and Using Technology

In order to comply with the International Society for Technology in Education (ISTE) and the National Council for the Accreditation of Teacher Education (NCATE) standards, teachers, including preservice teachers, must possess computer skills beyond the basics. In today's educational environment, there is constant pressure for teachers to become technologically competent because of increased access to computing, networking, and communications technologies, among other reasons.

The effective use and integration of technology into teaching and learning is a complex process. Teachers, not technologists, should direct this integration. The acquisition and configuration of sophisticated computing and networking systems is essential for technology integration. It is shortsighted, however, to perceive hardware and software as the only requisites to successful integration and utilization. As Earle (2002) points out, it is comparatively straightforward to situate computing hardware in physical locations. However, it is another matter to integrate technology into teaching, learning, and the curriculum, which should be at the heart of all technology integration efforts. Schools must invest in technology training and development for teachers. Teachers need fundamental understanding of technology and its uses prior to successful implementation or integration of that technology in the classroom. They must have the opportunity to learn about appropriate and effective uses of technology and practice using computers, software, and other communication devices. Additionally, schools and teachers must seek innovative ways to foster teachers' willingness to invest the time and energy needed to use technology effectively.

This book serves as a supplement to computer application texts used in colleges of education for preservice and kindergarten through grade 12 teachers interested in enhancing their computer skills. Using examples and exercises based on the work teachers and students routinely perform each day in the classroom, it provides a technological foundation for beginning students (preservice teachers) to guide them to more advanced skill levels. This introduction to technology should serve as an initial step for teachers as they begin using and integrating technology in their classes.

Expectations of Teachers

Many teachers struggle with how to effectively use computers and software not merely as tools to facilitate the presentation of information but as conduits with which students can construct their own knowledge. The expectation for teachers to integrate technology into the classroom is high. Teachers are expected not only to use technology for class management but also to facilitate and support the curriculum, which can be challenging.

Each state has specific standards for teachers to follow when implementing technology in the curriculum. Many states have adapted or adopted the ISTE standards which has been a leader in the field for establishing technology standards. As teachers begin to integrate technology into their classes, the standards provide an invaluable resource to guide their efforts.

Addressing the development of student knowledge and skills to meet these standards is beyond the scope of this book. However, the text gives specific illustrations for using and integrating the Office products in the classroom environment, which will provide you with the knowledge and skills to meet many of the standards.

The following section includes performance indicators developed by ISTE.

ISTE National Educational Technology Standards (NETS) and Performance Indicators for Teachers*

All classroom teachers should be prepared to meet the following standards and performance indicators.

I. Technology Operations and Concepts

Teachers demonstrate a sound understanding of technology operations and concepts.
Teachers should:

A. Demonstrate introductory knowledge, skills, and understanding of concepts related to technology (as described in the ISTE *National Educational Technology Standards for Students*).

B. Demonstrate continual growth in technology knowledge and skills to stay abreast of current and emerging technologies.

II. Planning and Designing Learning Environments and Experiences

Teachers plan and design effective learning environments and experiences supported by technology.
Teachers should:

A. Design developmentally appropriate learning opportunities that apply technology-enhanced instructional strategies to support the diverse needs of learners.

B. Apply current research on teaching and learning with technology when planning learning environments and experiences.

C. Identify and locate technology resources and evaluate them for accuracy and suitability.

D. Plan for management of technology resources within the context of learning activities.

E. Plan strategies to manage student learning in a technology-enhanced environment.

III. Teaching, Learning, and the Curriculum

Teachers implement curriculum plans that include methods and strategies for applying technology to maximize student learning.
Teachers should:

A. Facilitate technology-enhanced experiences that best address "best practices" research and support content standards and student technology standards.

B. Use technology to support learner-centered strategies that address the diverse needs of students.

C. Apply technology to develop students' higher order skills and creativity.

D. Manage student learning activities in a technology-enhanced environment.

*Reprinted with permission from the National Educational Technology Standards for Teachers, copyright 2002 ISTE (International Society for Technology in Education). Phone: (800) 336-5191 (United States and Canada) or (541) 302-3777 (international). E-mail: iste@iste.org. All rights reserved. Permission does not constitute an endorsement by ISTE. For more information about the NETS project, contact Lajean Thomas, Director, NETS Project, (318) 257-3923, lthomas@latech.edu.

IV. Assessment and Evaluation

Teachers apply technology to facilitate a variety of effective assessment and evaluation strategies.

Teachers should:

A. Apply technology in assessing student learning of subject matter using a variety of assessment techniques.

B. Use technology resources to collect and analyze data, interpret results, and communicate findings to improve instructional practice and maximize student learning.

C. Apply multiple methods of evaluation to determine students' appropriate use of technology resources for learning, communication, and productivity.

V. Productivity and Professional Practice

Teachers use technology to enhance their productivity and professional practice.

Teachers should:

A. Use technology resources to engage in ongoing professional development and lifelong learning.

B. Continually evaluate and reflect on professional practice to make informed decisions regarding the use of technology in support of student learning.

C. Apply technology to increase productivity.

D. Use technology to communicate and collaborate with peers, parents, and the larger community in order to nurture student learning.

VI. Social, Ethical, Legal, and Human Issues

Teachers understand the social, ethical, legal, and human issues surrounding the use of technology in pre-K–12 schools and apply that understanding in practice.

Teachers should:

A. Model and teach legal and ethical practice related to technology use.

B. Apply technology resources to enable and empower learners with diverse backgrounds, characteristics, and abilities.

C. Identify and use technology resources that affirm diversity.

D. Promote safe and healthy use of technology resources.

E. Facilitate equitable access to technology resources for all students.

Expectations of Students

Because technology is now an integral part of the curriculum, learning standards have been developed throughout the nation. For instance, ISTE developed technology standards for students that focus on the following areas:

A Basic operations and concepts
B. Social, ethical, and human issues
C. Technology productivity tools
D. Technology communications tools
E. Technology research tools
F. Technology problem-solving and decision-making tools (ISTE, 1998)

States can adopt the ISTE standards as-is or can use these basic areas to develop their own standards in order to establish expectations for technology proficiency.

The Microsoft Office suite offers many tools with which to create innovative assignments, activities, and exercises that engage students as they use and apply technology. As you become familiar with the concepts presented in this book, you will be able to utilize the standards to cultivate your own technical proficiency.

Copyright in the Classroom

As noted in both the ISTE standards for teachers and for students, teachers are expected to "model and teach legal and ethical practice related to technology use." Central to modeling expectations is appropriate respect for and use of copyright laws. Copyright law is a set of federal laws pertaining to the legal right to use original works. These laws set forth rights and conditions regarding how an individual may copy materials. The Copyright Act of 1976 established fair use, or guidelines that allow educators to use and copy certain copyrighted materials for nonprofit educational purposes (Section 107 of the U.S. Copyright Law defines fair use). Copyright issues can be convoluted, particularly when materials are for use on the Web and other computer-based media. School districts provide teachers with specific guidelines for using copyrighted materials in their classes. It is in your best interest to ascertain and adhere to the policies advocated by your school. The following items are general recommendations to follow when contemplating using copyrighted materials:

- When computer software is intended for one computer, it should be used only on one computer.
- If the picture, video, audio, text (etc.) you would like to use does not belong to you personally, ask permission from the individual or entity that produced the materials.
- Never download material from the Internet unless it specifically says "copyright free." Even if the material is copyright free, you must cite the source when you reuse it.

Acceptable Use Policies

To further address the issue of ethical use of computers, computer software, the Internet, and the World Wide Web, many schools have acceptable use policies. Acceptable use policies (AUPs) are agreements among students, parents/guardians, teachers, administrators, and staff that govern the use of school and school district computers, networks, and the Internet. Acceptable use policies vary greatly from school district to school district. Some schools have separate AUPs for students, teachers, and staff personnel. Many AUPs include the following: a list of rules dealing with copyright issues; a list of rules covering online safety and release of personal information; a list of rules concerning access to objectionable Internet sites; a notice that use of school computers, networks, and the Internet is a privilege, not a right; a statement of how individuals should behave when using the computer facilities; and a statement of what kind of disciplinary action and cancellation of privileges could take place if the AUPs are not followed. As a teacher it is your responsibility to monitor student use of the computers in your classroom and school. Also, you have a responsibility for abiding by the acceptable use policies set out by your school district.

Teacher Production of Materials

Throughout this text, examples are provided for how your students can use the Office products. Office can also be used by teachers for many classroom management tasks (e.g., grading, materials inventory, and so on). The following tables are organized according to Office products, and they present some examples of how to use Office to increase effectiveness and productivity.

Teacher Activity Charts

Word

Instruction/Learning		Classroom Management	
Create lesson plans	Individual educational plans	Worksheets	Class letterhead
Make activity flyers	Thematic units	Field trip permission letters	Letters to parents/ guardians
Develop testing materials	Activity directions	School reports	List of class rules

PowerPoint

Instruction/Learning		Classroom Management	
Teacher presentations	Graphic handouts	Teacher in-service presentations	Presentations to the school board
Advance organizers for lessons	Presentations saved to the World Wide Web	Parent–teacher conference overview	Conference presentations

Excel

Instruction/Learning		Classroom Management	
Graph special project incomes	Graph student achievement	Assessment checklists	Book orders
Monitor numerical data trends	Data analysis	Attendance chart	Lunch/milk counts
Represent data in graphical form	Testing hypotheses	Classroom budget	Grade book Attendance chart

Access

Instruction/Learning		Classroom Management	
Keep records of readings related notes, and citations	Thematic units support material database	Monitor classroom books	Student and parent/ guardian information
List curriculum content objectives	Store teaching activities and strategies	Monitor classroom videotapes/DVD	Classroom inventory

Outlook

Instruction/Learning		Classroom Management	
Cross-cultural e-mail exchanges	Set calendar to help with lesson plans	Maintain a to-do list using Tasks	Use Contacts list to send e-mails or start letters
Appointment book	Corresponding with experts	Send/receive e-mail to/ from parents and students	Journal keeps track of daily activities and classroom events
Personal journals		Send attachments with pictures and printed materials to absent students	Calendar sets teacher/ parent/student appointments

Student Production of Materials

Word

Instruction/Learning	
Write book reports	Create Web pages
Creative writing: stories and poetry that can be illustrated	Develop newsletters about historical topics
Writing process: notes, outline, rough draft, editing, final copy	Create story problems for math
Keeping a journal of science experiments	Design letterhead and stationery

PowerPoint

Instruction/Learning	
Present a research project	Post a presentation to the Web
Create picture books by printing individual slides	Team teach researched concepts
Use presentation outline to start a written report	Create science experiment reports
Create hyperlinks to other reports or Web pages	Create book reports

Excel

Instruction/Learning	
Chart local rainfall	Project grades
Answer "what-if" questions	Create budgets for fictitious businesses
Create timelines	Analyze data using estimation and prediction
Create daylight hour chart	Compare and chart fast food calorie counts

Access

Instruction/Learning	
Create state information database	Create a database of addresses
Create a database of local trees	Create U.S. presidents database
Create a "books read" database	Create a famous persons database
Create a database of resources for a report	Create a database of "rectangles," "squares," or other basic geometric shapes

Outlook

Instruction/Learning	
Create a timeline of what happened on this date in history	Using e-mail, ask scientists or physicians about research projects
Set calendar with class assignments and due dates	Keep a to-do list of class activities
Keep a journal of reading by month	Using contacts, create a list of local senators and representatives

TYING IT ALL TOGETHER

This chapter provides an overview of the book and presents standards that set expectations for how teachers should integrate technology in the classroom and how students should use the technology. As you work through the book, you will likely find many useful opportunities to use the Office products to enhance your teaching and learning activities, while at the same time identifying ways to help your students meet established technology standards.

REFERENCES

Earle, R. S. (2002). The integration of instructional technology into public education: Promises and challenges. *Educational Technology, 42*(1), 5–13. [Online]. Available: http://www.electroniccampus.org/student/srecinfo/publications/Principles_2000.pdf [November 2004].

International Society for Technology in Education (ISTE) NETS Project. (June 1998). *National education technology standards for students* (pp. 5–6). [Online]. Available: http://cnets.iste.org/students/s-stands.html [February 2004].

2 Getting Started with Office

Chapter Outline

1. Learning Objectives
2. Technical Terms
3. Chapter Overview
4. Working with Microsoft Office Suite
   a. Opening Office Applications
      1) New Document Task Pane
      2) Main Menu Toolbar
      3) Standard Toolbar
   b. Office Assistant
   c. Formatting Toolbar
5. Tying It All Together

Learning Objectives

At the completion of this chapter you will be able to:
- Use the commands found on the Office menu bar
- Use the icons on the standard toolbar
- Modify the viewable toolbars on the screen
- Move toolbars around the edge of the screen
- Go to the Help menu or the Office Assistant feature

Technical Terms

The following are terms that you will encounter in the chapter and with which you will become familiar:

Commands

Expanded menu

Shortcut menus

Chapter Overview

This chapter provides an introduction to the toolbars, menus, and functions that are available in the Microsoft Office suite. Each Office application has additional components in the toolbars and menus unique to that program. After studying this chapter, you will be able to customize your toolbar and use basic commands common to all the Office products.

Working with Microsoft Office Suite

The Microsoft Office suite may include any or all of the following products: Word, Excel, PowerPoint, Access, Publisher, and Outlook. Most standard editions of Office for Windows include these products. All of them have toolbars, menus, and help information that function similarly from product to product, which makes working with the applications easier. To access the toolbars, menu items, and help information, the Office program (e.g., Word) must be open.

Opening Office Applications

To open any of the Office applications, click the Start button on the Windows taskbar. On the Start menu, move the mouse pointer to *Programs* and the Programs submenu appears. Move the mouse pointer to *Microsoft Office* and the Microsoft Office submenu appears. Click the Microsoft application that you want to open. *Note:* Depending on how you installed Office 2003, the menu items for the applications may be placed in various locations on the Start menu. In most cases, they can be found under *Programs* or under *Programs* within the Microsoft Office folder (see Figure 2.1).

1. To open a new Word document, for example, you need to open the Word 2003 application.

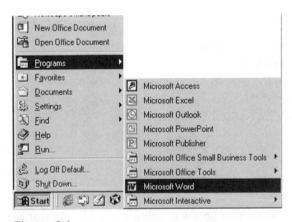

Figure 2.1
Opening Microsoft Word

2. Once Word has been opened, its features (e.g., toolbars, menus, and so on) become available. Typically, by default there is a main menu bar, standard toolbar, a formatting toolbar, and a New Document task pane (see Figure 2.2). Other toolbars may be added as you need them. Most of these features and the interface used to access them are standard across all Office products.

Main menu bar

Standard
toolbar

New
Document
task
pane

Formatting
toolbar

Status
bar

Figure 2.2
The screen components

New Document Task Pane

The New Document task pane appears by default on the right side of the screen in most Office products. The pane allows you to open a document, create a new document, open a new document from an existing document, or open a new document from a template. The task pane may also contain other task options unique to the Office product you have open (see Figure 2.3).

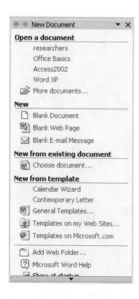

Figure 2.3
New Document
task pane

Main Menu Toolbar

Typically, a main menu toolbar is located at the top of the screen. This toolbar contains a listing of words (menu items) and icons that identify processes or commands that you can activate within the Office product. Several of the toolbar options have pull-down menus that activate once you click them (see Figure 2.4). You only need to click on the toolbar option once, and then, as you pass the mouse pointer over other options, their pull-down menus will be displayed. The double arrows pointing down at the bottom of a pull-down menu indicate that it is an expandable menu. Click the arrows or hold the mouse pointer over them for a few seconds and the menu will expand.

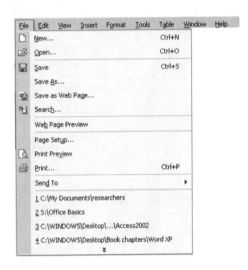

Figure 2.4
Pull-down menu

File

The File menu contains some of the basic commands, such as Open, New (create a new document), Save, and Print, that enable you to work with files. Toward the bottom of the File menu is a list of recently used files, which indicates not only the document title but also the drive to which you saved it. You can quickly open these recently used files by clicking on them. Also, notice that to the right of several items on the pull-down menu there are key-commands. These commands correspond to key strokes that allow you to use the keyboard to accomplish the same task as the pull-down item (see Figure 2.5).

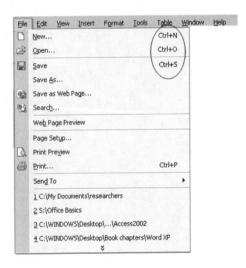

Figure 2.5
Shortcuts

Edit

The Edit menu allows you to manipulate a file or its contents using commands such as Copy, Cut, and Paste. You can copy and paste between Office products, for example, by copying part of a PowerPoint slide and pasting it into a Word document. Find and Replace are also options under the Edit menu that can help you locate or change information in Office products (see Figure 2.6).

Figure 2.6
Edit menu

View

The View menu provides several options for viewing your screen. You can, for example, change how Word displays information on the screen by selecting a View (Normal, Outline) or Layout (Web, Print) option or by using the Zoom feature. The View menu options vary depending on the Office product you are using (see Figure 2.7).

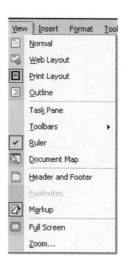

Figure 2.7
View menu

The Toolbars option on the View menu has an arrow, indicating the presence of a submenu. By placing your mouse pointer over the arrow, you are able to see the toolbars that are available. Again, the toolbars available will vary by Office product; generally, the standard and the formatting toolbars will be checked. To view other toolbars, click on the title and a check mark appears indicating that the toolbar will appear on the screen (see Figure 2.8).

Figure 2.8
View toolbars

Insert

The availability of the Insert menu varies depending on the Office product. In Outlook there is no Insert option on the main menu bar. Insert allows you to insert pictures, diagrams, objects, and hyperlinks into a document (see Figure 2.9).

Figure 2.9
Insert menu

Notice that the Picture option on the Insert menu has an arrow indicating the presence of a submenu. This submenu presents a list of options for inserting pictures and graphic objects from a variety of sources (see Figure 2.10).

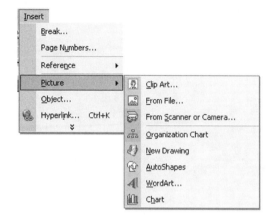

Figure 2.10
Insert Picture menu

Format

The items on the Format pull-down menu vary depending on the Office product you are using. The Format menu provides options to set or change the formatting of the document. In most of the Office programs, you can set the font and style attributes of a document. Outlook does not have a Format option on the main menu bar (see Figure 2.11).

Figure 2.11
Format menu

Tools

All Office products have a Tools menu on the main menu bar. Under the Tools menu you will find the Spelling and Grammar Check and Word Count options, among others. The Office products generally list tools that pertain particularly to that product. For example, the Letters and Mailings option shown in Figure 2.12 is only available in Word. If you are connected to the Internet, you can select *Tools on the Web* and get access to a host of online resources, such as templates or Office help.

Figure 2.12
Tools menu

Table
The Table menu only appears in Word. It gives you the tools to create and modify a table within a Word document (see Figure 2.13).

Figure 2.13
Table menu

Window
The Window menu item allows you to open a document in a new window. You can activate documents that are open. For example, if you have multiple Word documents open, you can switch between them using the Window menu. You can also arrange how document windows appear on your screen.

The Arrange All option arranges all of the windows that you have open on the screen. The Split option splits the screen so you may view different sections of the documents at the same time (e.g., if you have a large spreadsheet in Excel, you may view two sections of it at the same time). Also, you may activate an opened document or open a document that you have recently opened (see Figure 2.14).

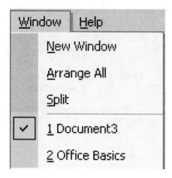

Figure 2.14
Window menu

Help
The Help menu item allows you to find help about the Office product that you currently have open. In Office 2003 the Office Assistant does not open unless you activate it, unlike previous Office versions. Microsoft Office Online provides online help resources when you are connected to the Internet. Activate Product launches the Activation Wizard, used to activate or update information about your copy of Microsoft Office. Word-Perfect Help appears only in Word and provides help for WordPerfect users who are using Word. Detect and Repair automatically finds and fixes errors in the Office product. The About. . . option changes depending on the Office product. For example, in Word this option is titled *About Microsoft Word.* It provides licensing information about the Office product (see Figure 2.15).

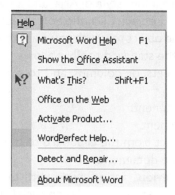

Figure 2.15
Help menu

Standard Toolbar

Typically, the standard toolbar appears below the main menu. It can, however, be moved to any location on the screen. It contains icons that, when clicked, perform many of the functions listed in the main menu, plus some additional functions that connect you to other Office products. If you place the mouse pointer over each icon, its name or function appears (see Figures 2.16 and 2.17).

Figure 2.16
Standard toolbar

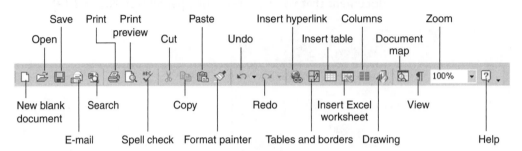

Figure 2.17
Standard toolbar labels

Some of the main options provided on the formatting toolbar include the following:

Copy: Makes a copy of an object (does not remove it from the current document as Cut does) and copies it to the clipboard. The object can be pasted into a document at a later point in time. For example, suppose you want to duplicate a clip art object on a page. Click the object to select it, click *Copy,* and then click *Paste.*

Cut: Cuts or removes an object (e.g., text, clip art, and so on) from the document. The object is copied to the computer's memory or clipboard and can be pasted to another document at a later point in time. For example, suppose you want to remove a clip art object from page 1 and place it in page 3. Click the object to select it, click *Cut,* move the cursor to the desired point on page 3, and then click *Paste.*

E-mail: Sends the contents of the current document as the body of an e-mail message.

Format Painter: Copies information about the currently selected object and applies it to another selected object. For example, suppose that you've formatted a text object (e.g., the title of the page) to a font style of Arial and a size of 36 and want to apply this formatting to another text object. Click the text object (page title) to select it, click *Format Painter,* then click the object to which you want the formatting to apply.

Insert: The Insert portion of the standard toolbar allows you to insert or place hyperlinks, tables, Excel spreadsheets, or columns, and to draw objects into your document.

New: Creates a new blank document.

Open: Opens an existing document.

Paste: Places, or pastes, an object from the clipboard to the current document.

Print: Prints the contents of the document.

Redo Typing: Reverses the previous action made with the Undo Typing command. For example, if you delete a text object and then click *Undo Typing,* the object reappears. Clicking *Redo Typing* makes the object disappear again. In other words, it reverses the previous Undo Typing command. Clicking the downward arrow to the right of the Undo and Redo typing buttons presents a list of recent actions. Using this list, you can select the actions to reverse with the Undo or Redo buttons.

Save: Saves the content of the document currently opened.

Spelling: Checks for spelling errors in the document.

Undo Typing: Reverses the previous action. For example, if you accidentally deleted a text object, click *Undo Typing* and the object will reappear.

The standard toolbar may be resized and repositioned on the screen. To position it in a new location, place the mouse pointer over the bars on the toolbar's left side and drag the mouse to the new location. The toolbar snaps or docks into position when it is dragged to the application window's border. When you drag the toolbar to the middle of the application window, it floats. To resize a floating toolbar, position the mouse pointer on the toolbar's border and drag the border to achieve the desired size (see Figure 2.18).

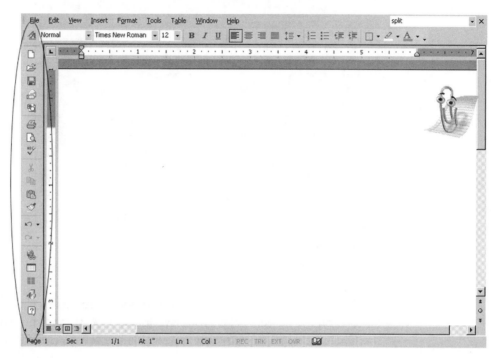

Figure 2.18
Moving the standard toolbar

Office Assistant

The Office Assistant provides help information and hints for working with Office products. You can turn the Assistant off and on and change its appearance. To change Assistant settings, click on the question mark on the standard toolbar or select the *Help* option on the main menu bar. Once the Assistant appears on the screen, click on *Office Assistant* and then click *Options* (see Figure 2.19).

Figure 2.19
Office Assistant

The Office Assistant box opens. The Options tab displays options for turning the Assistant off and on, setting alerts, and other actions that can assist you when using the Office products. To change the appearance of the Assistant, select the Gallery tab (see Figure 2.20).

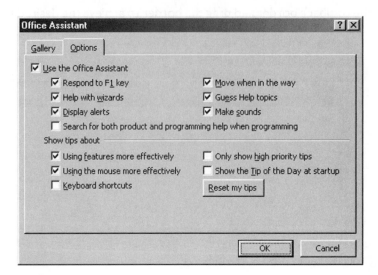

Figure 2.20
Office Assistant graphic

The Gallery allows you to choose different Assistants by clicking the Back and Next buttons on the screen. When you have found an Assistant you would like to use, click the OK button and the Assistant appears on the screen (see Figure 2.21).

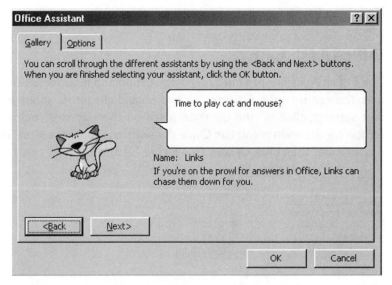

Figure 2.21
Office Assistant graphic

Formatting Toolbar

The formatting toolbar allows you to format text and set attributes (e.g., font style, size, color, and so on). In each of the Office products, options on the formatting toolbar vary;

they correspond to the specific application. Generally, the formatting toolbar options enable you to set or modify text attributes that affect the "look" of the printed text in the document (see Figure 2.22).

Figure 2.22
Formatting toolbar

TYING IT ALL TOGETHER

This chapter gives an overview of the toolbars and options that are available in most of the Office products. As you open the Office products, you will see that the applications have some of the same options, no matter what program you are using. This commonality gives you an interface for using Office and it makes learning the programs easy. But there are some differences in each program, as you will see as you work through the other chapters in this text.

3 WORD 2003

CHAPTER OUTLINE

1. LEARNING OBJECTIVES
2. TECHNICAL TERMS
3. CHAPTER OVERVIEW
4. ABOUT WORD
5. HOW TEACHERS AND STUDENTS MIGHT USE WORD 2003
6. SHOW ME
   a. Creating a Word Document
      1) Opening Word 2003
7. A CHALLENGE USING WORD 2003
8. TYING IT ALL TOGETHER

LEARNING OBJECTIVES

At the completion of this chapter you will be able to:

- Start Word and create a new word processing document
- Navigate the Word workspace
- Spell check a document
- Add clip art to a document
- Cut, copy, and paste in a document
- Format a document
- Insert a hyperlink into a document
- Create a table in a document
- Preview a document for printing
- Undo and redo
- Search for data
- Save material as a Web page

TECHNICAL TERMS

The following are terms that you will encounter in the chapter and with which you will become familiar:

Task pane

Floating toolbars

Formatting

AutoCorrection

Clip art

Hyperlink

Table

CHAPTER OVERVIEW

This chapter provides an introduction to Word 2003. The content focuses on Word fundamentals and how to apply them to a variety of learning activities. Using the example of writing a book report, the chapter's Show Me section presents instructions on how to use many of Word 2003's tools for creating, editing, and manipulating information within a word processing document. The Let Me Try student-oriented exercises provide specific examples with step-by-step instructions for using Word 2003 in learning activities. In addition to the Let Me Try activities, the Challenge section provides stimulating projects for practicing Word 2003. Each one of the illustrations given in this chapter may be found within the "Word" folder inside Example on the CD. You may follow along with the document as you go through the text by pulling it up from the CD. Also, other examples using Word may be found on the CD.

About Word

Microsoft Word is the word processing component of the Microsoft Office suite. It is a productivity tool for you and your students to use. In many ways Word is the electronic typewriter of the computer, but it has many more features than a typewriter. When you open Word, you are literally rolling an "electronic piece of paper" on the screen. With the click of a mouse, you can easily manipulate text material, add graphics to text, check spelling and grammar, and place the words in a column or table format. The finished product may be saved to a disk, printed on a paper, or even saved as a Web page for posting to the World Wide Web. As a teacher who knows how to use Word, you can produce all types of interesting materials and facilitate student production of materials that include photographs, clip art, and graphics.

How Teachers and Students Might Use Word 2003

Teacher Production of Materials

Instruction/Learning	Classroom Management
Create lesson plans	Worksheets
Make activity flyers	Field trip permission letters
Develop testing materials	Letters to parents/guardians
Individual educational plans	School reports
Thematic units	List of class rules
Activity directions	Rubrics for assessment of materials

Student Production of Materials

Instruction/Learning
Write book reports
Creative writing: stories and poetry that may be illustrated
Develop newsletters about historical topics
Writing process: notes, outlines, rough draft, editing, final copy
Create story problems for math
Keep a journal of science experiments
Design letterhead and stationary
Create Web pages

Show Me

Creating a Word Document

Opening Word 2003

1. To create a Word document, you need to open Word 2003 (see Figure 3.1). Click the Start button on the Windows taskbar; move the mouse pointer over *Programs* and the Programs submenu appears. Move the mouse pointer over *Microsoft Office* and the Microsoft Office submenu appears. Click *Microsoft Word* and Word 2003 opens (see Figure 3.2).

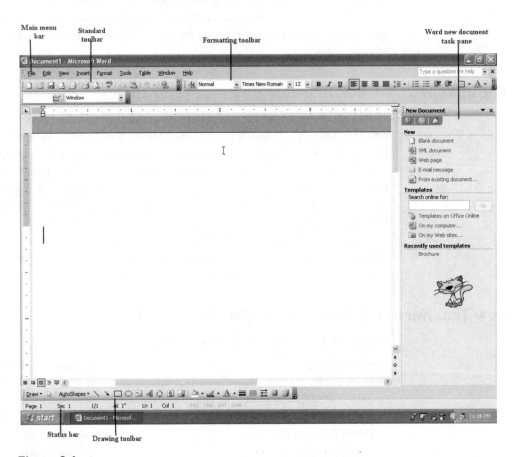

Figure 3.1
The Word workspace

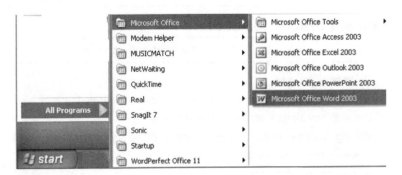

Figure 3.2
Starting Word

2. As an example of the type of project that a student could develop, we will create a book report on *Charlotte's Webb* by E. B. White. For an example of the completed project see "Charlotte book report.doc" on the CD. At the top of the page, type the title of the book, the author, and the byline (your name) on separate lines (press Enter after each item).

3. Place the mouse pointer in front of *Charlotte,* hold the left mouse button down, and drag across the text to highlight it. Release the mouse button and click the Center Text icon (text is automatically left justified) on the formatting toolbar to center the text on the screen (see Figure 3.3).

Figure 3.3
Centering text

4. While the text is still highlighted, click on the Bold icon, select *Arial* font typeface, and increase the text size to 14 points (see Figure 3.4).

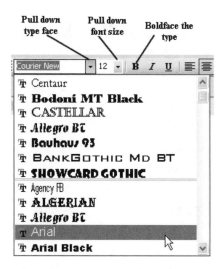

Figure 3.4
Changing font size and style

5. After increasing the type size and changing the style of text, strike Enter twice and click on the Left-Align icon; make sure the typeface is Arial (if it is not, change it to Arial by clicking on the typeface pull-down menu and selecting *Arial*). Select the 10-point typeface. After making these changes, click on the Bold icon to turn off the boldface and set the text to plain, then type several lines about *Charlotte's Web* (see Figure 3.5).

Charlotte's Web
By E. B. White
Reported by Pat Fewell

The main characters of Charlotte's Web are a girl, a pig, a spider, and a rat. The story takes place on a farm where Wilbur, the pig is the runt of the letter, and is saved by Fern when her father wants to kill him. Fern raises Wilbur. He goes to live in the Zuckerman's barn. There he meets Charlotte, the spider, Templeton, the rat and the other farm animals. The story takes place over the summer and Wilbur grows and Charlotte becomes his friend.

In order to save Wilbur, Charlotte weaves spider webs with words in them about Wilbur. The Zuckerman's put Wilbur in a crate and take him to the fair. Wilbur wins a special award. Templeton and Charlotte go to the fair with Wilbur. Charlotte spins a web at the fair that says "humble". She also spins an egg sack. Charlotte is dying as the fair ends, but Wilbur takes her egg sack back to the farm. Wilbur looks after the egg sack and in the spring the eggs hatch.

At the end of the book three of Charlotte's daughters stay with Wilbur while the rest drift away. Wilbur lives a very long life and becomes friends with Charlotte's granddaughters and great-granddaughters.

Figure 3.5
Entering text

6. As you type, the words will wrap to the next line. To leave an extra line of space between the paragraphs, press Enter. To check your spelling and grammar, click on the Spell Check icon, click on Tools, or press F7 on the keyboard. The Spell Check provides options for making spelling corrections (see Figure 3.6).

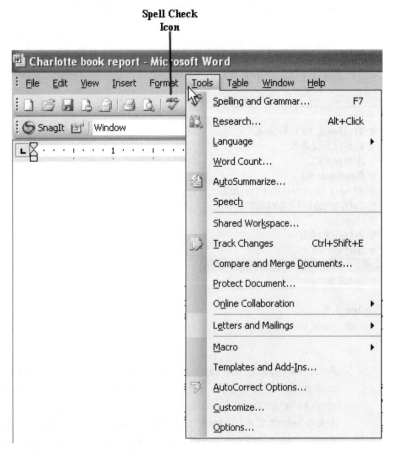

Figure 3.6
Spelling and Grammar Checks

7. After clicking on the Spell Check, the Spelling and Grammar window appears, which you can use to identify spelling and grammar mistakes. If you make a spelling error, the word AutoCorrect feature will automatically recognize errors and make suggestions for corrections. This gives you an opportunity to make corrections, if necessary (see Figure 3.7).

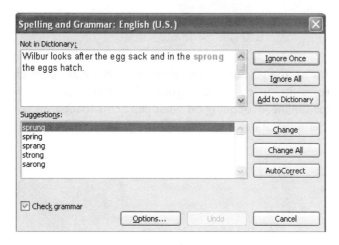

Figure 3.7
Spell Check window

8. At the end of the paragraphs that you have written, press Enter twice. Select *Picture* from the Insert menu and from the Picture submenu, select *Clip Art* (see Figure 3.8).

Figure 3.8
Insert menu

9. Once *Clip Art* is selected, the Insert Clip Art task pane appears on the right side of the Word workspace (see Figure 3.9).

Figure 3.9
Insert Clip Art

10. Click in the *Search text:* box below *Search For* and type in the word *spider* (see Figure 3.10).

Figure 3.10
Search for *spider*

11. Click on the go button. Word will search for available clip art and display pictures of items found (see Figure 3.11). In this case you may have to go to the Clips Online, depending on what clip art is loaded on your computer, to find a spider illustration.

Figure 3.11
Clip art selections

Figure 3.12
Insert selected clip art menu

12. As you place the mouse pointer over a clip art image, information (name of the clip art, its size, and its type) about it appears. Clicking an image inserts it in the document. You can also select *Insert* from the pull-down menu that appears next to the image to insert it (see Figure 3.12). Click the spider picture. The clip art will be placed wherever you had your cursor positioned on the page.

13. Click in the center of the clip art image and a sizing handle will appear on its sides, indicating that it is selected. As you pass the mouse pointer over the selected image's sizing handle, the pointer turns into a double-arrow cursor. Resize the image by placing the mouse pointer over a sizing handle and dragging the pointer until you reach the desired size. Using a corner sizing handle to resize allows for sizing the image proportionally. You may also preserve the image's proportions and keep it centered in the same location by pressing the Control and Shift keys down while dragging the mouse. For this example, click on the sizing handle in the upper right-hand corner of the image, hold the left

mouse button down, and drag the picture down to make it smaller by about half. The sizing handles appear as small black boxes when the image is selected. Depending on the type of image you insert, you may notice that the sizing handles appear as circles with a green circle at the top, which allows you to rotate the object to different angles on the page (see Figure 3.13).

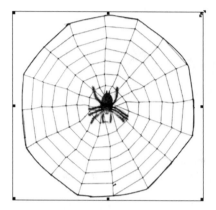

Figure 3.13
Resizing clip art

14. It is a good habit to save your document about every 5 minutes. You can save your changes without changing the document's name or save a variety of versions using different names. To save, click the File menu, then click *Save* or *Save As*. You need to name your document the first time you are saving it. You can save the document to a disk or on the computer's hard drive by selecting the appropriate item in the *Save in:* box on the Save As window (see Figure 3.14).

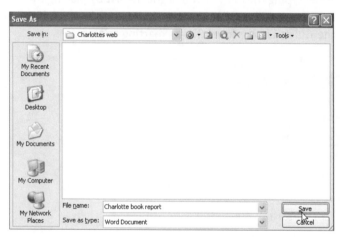

Figure 3.14
Saving a document

15. Text can be inserted next to an illustration by moving the mouse pointer until it becomes a cursor. You may type next to the illustration on the page, labeling the picture. If you would like to have the text next to the picture you may need to modify the text wrap around the clip art. Double-click on the picture and select the Layout tab, then select *Tight Wrapping* style (see Figure 3.15). Type a label for the picture.

Figure 3.15
Format picture

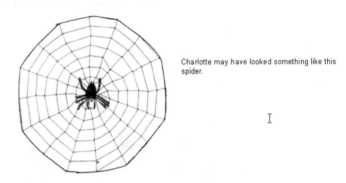

Charlotte may have looked something like this spider.

Figure 3.16
Inserting text into an illustration

16. Move the cursor down the page and press Enter several times to insert blank lines. Select *Picture* from the Insert menu and then click *Clip Art*. Search for a pig on the clip art task pane. Select a pig clip art picture and resize it to fit on one page. Type the following next to the picture: *This is what Wilbur could have looked like*. Save the document.

17. To put some white space between the picture and the text press Enter twice and type the following text: *Some characteristics of Wilbur;* press Enter.

18. Type in the following items and press Enter after each item: *Wilbur likes to eat; Wilbur sleeps a lot; Wilbur is very friendly;* and *Some Pig!*

19. After typing these items, highlight the list by placing the cursor in front of *Wilbur likes to eat* and holding the mouse button down to highlight the list. Then select the Bullet Listing from the formatting toolbar.

Figure 3.17
Formatting menu

20. To change the types of bullets on the list, select *Format* from the main toolbar and select *Bullets and Numbering* from the pull-down menu (see Figure 3.17).

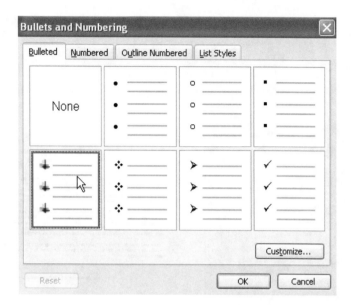

Figure 3.18
Select *Bullets and Numbering*

21. To change the type of bullets of the list, highlight the text then select the first bullet type in the second row; this will change the bullets from the default style to the one selected (see Figure 3.18).

22. To preview the document prior to printing, you can select *Print Preview* on the standard toolbar or select *Print Preview* from the File menu (see Figure 3.19).

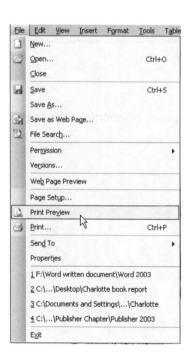

Figure 3.19
File menu; select
Print Preview

23. The Print Preview screen shows you what the page will look like prior to actually printing it. You can zoom in and out to look at specific areas on the page. The cursor turns into a magnifying glass, and by single-clicking with the cursor, you can zoom in and out of the page. Click the Close button to close the Print Preview page (see Figure 3.20).

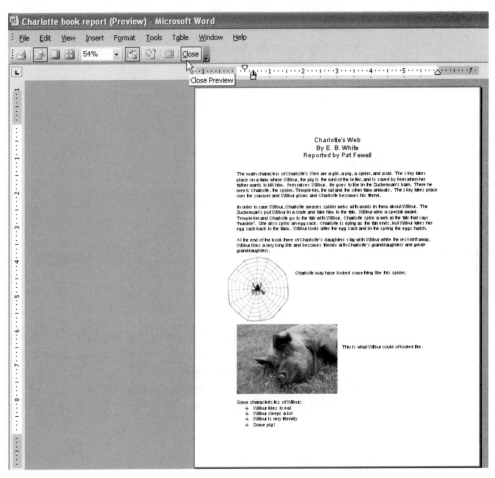

Figure 3.20
Print Preview

24. To change the margins or paper orientation, select *Page Setup* from the File menu (see Figure 3.21).

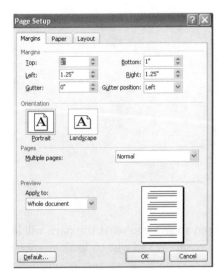

Figure 3.21
Page Setup

25. To print, select *Print* from the File menu. This displays the Print window with several printing options. The Print window, among other things, allows you to select the printer, specify the pages, and specify the number of copies to print. Additionally, you can print the current page, the page the cursor is currently on (if you have multiple-page documents), or use the Zoom feature to print multiple pages on a single sheet (see Figure 3.22). Alternatively, you can click the Print icon on the standard toolbar to automatically print all pages at the default settings. You may also print from the Print Preview screen by clicking on the Printer icon.

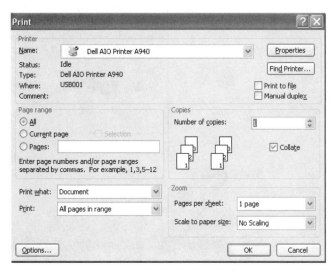

Figure 3.22
Print Document screen

LET ME TRY

So far, we have opened Word 2003 and created a new document that contains centered text, bold text, inserted clip art, and a created list. We also spell checked, saved the document, and previewed printing options.

Suppose your students wanted to make a science page that presents information about one of the characters in *Charlotte's Web*. You want to link the page to the Internet and eventually post it as a Web page. For an example of the completed page, see "Spider Web page.doc" on the CD.

Creating a Science Page to Be Saved as a Web Page

1. Click the Start button on the Windows taskbar. On the Start menu, move the mouse pointer to *Programs;* the Programs submenu appears. Move the pointer to *Word* and click on it.

2. Select *New Document* or *Blank Document* from the New Document task pane or select *New. . .* from the File menu. Because we want to create a printed document, we will open it as a new Word document rather than a blank Web page.

3. Some work on this project requires the formatting, standard, drawing, and Web tools toolbars to be visible. Access these toolbars from the View menu. If they are not already visible on the screen, check the standard, formatting, drawing, and Web tool items (see boxed Figure 3.1).

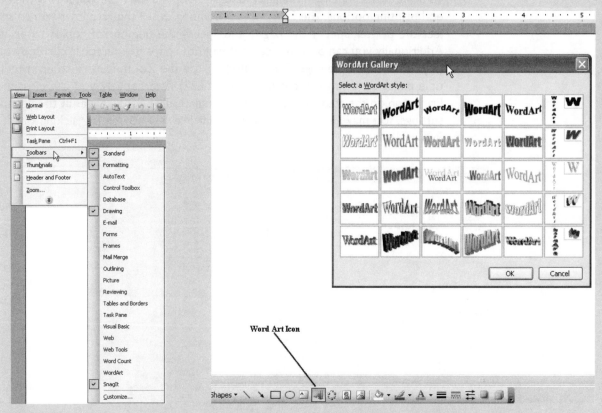

Figure 3.1
Selecting toolbars

Figure 3.2
WordArt icon

4. Press Enter twice to move the cursor down the page. On the drawing toolbar select the WordArt icon to create the title for this page. Click the icon once and the WordArt Gallery appears. Select the type of WordArt you want to use by clicking on the image (see boxed Figure 3.2).
5. Once the type style is selected, type in the words *All About Spiders*. Select 48-point typeface for the lettering and click *OK* (see boxed Figure 3.3).

Figure 3.3
Editing WordArt text

6. The WordArt appears on the page. As with other graphics, you can click on the WordArt and then click on the Center Align icon on the formatting toolbar to center the text.

7. Press Enter twice to add space after the WordArt. The next part of the page will present information about spiders. Select the Align Left icon and type in information in your own words that you find in encyclopedias or on the World Wide Web. Set the text typeface at 12-point Arial.

8. After typing a short paragraph press Enter twice. Select *Insert Table* from the Table menu (see boxed Figure 3.4).

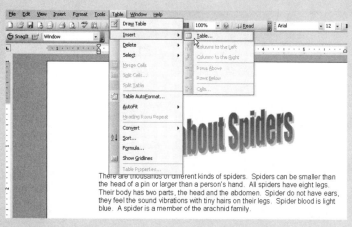

Figure 3.4
Inserting a table

9. Select two rows and two columns for the table properties. Click *OK*. This creates a table at the cursor's location (see boxed Figure 3.5).

10. The cursor will appear in the first cell of the table. To move from cell to cell in the table, press the Tab key on the keyboard. Enter data similar to that in boxed Figure 3.6. To add rows, simply press the Tab key while the cursor is in the right-most cell of the bottom row. Make the labels *Spiders* and *Insects* bold.

11. Click anywhere outside of the table to type outside of the table. Move your mouse pointer to the beginning of the text at the top of the page. Click the

Figure 3.5
Table properties

Spiders	Insects
Eight legs	Six legs
Two-part body	Three-part body
Simple eyes	Complex eyes
No antenna	Antenna

Figure 3.6
Table information

mouse button once. Press Enter twice and select *Insert ClipArt* from the toolbar. Type in the word *spiders* and select a spider from the clip art selection. If you are connected to the Internet you can select clip art from the Web (see boxed Figure 3.7).

12. Resize the spider to about 2 inches by clicking and dragging it. Click on the Align Right icon while the clip art is selected. Double-click on the clip art so there is less white space on the page (see boxed Figure 3.8).

Figure 3.7
Spider clip art from the World Wide Web

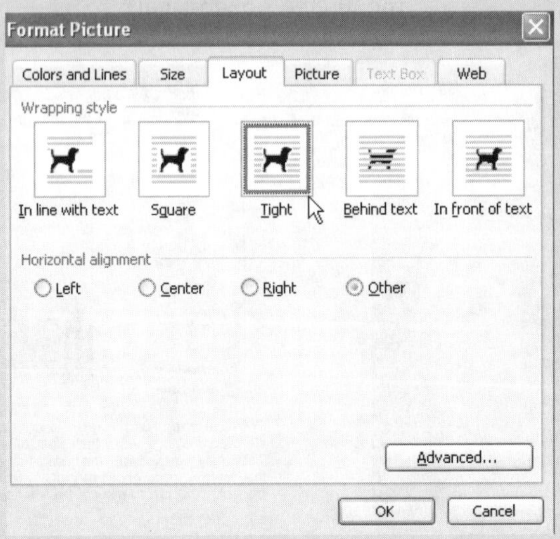

Figure 3.8
Format picture

13. Move down the page, place the mouse pointer below the table, and click one time. This allows you to type on the page in this area. You are going to create a hyperlink to a document on the World Wide Web. Hyperlinks can also link a word or phrase in your document to another document on your computer. For the purposes of this illustration you will be linking to the following Web site: http://www.arachnology.org/. Web site addresses change frequently. If this Web page is not available, go to your favorite search engine and find an appropriate spider Web site. This address must be typed in exactly as printed here to work.

14. To make a hyperlink select the Hyperlink icon from the toolbar. Position your cursor where you want the hyperlink to appear (see boxed Figure 3.9).

15. Type in the text you want displayed as the hyperlink by clicking in the *Text to display:* box. Type *A Great Spider Site.* In the address area, type the URL of the Web

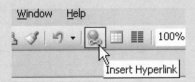

Figure 3.9
Inserting a hyperlink

page, for example, http://www.arachnology.org/. Click *OK* once the information has been typed (see boxed Figure 3.10).

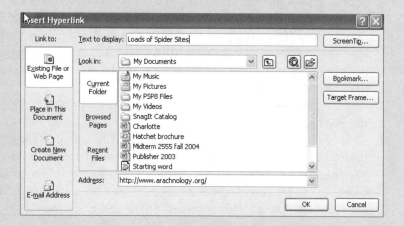

Figure 3.10
Inserting hyperlink information

16. After clicking *OK*, the text appears on the page underlined in blue (see boxed Figure 3.11).

Spiders	Insects
Eight legs	Six legs
Two-part body	Three-part body
Simple eyes	Complex eyes
No antenna	Antenna

A great spider site

Figure 3.11
Hypertext link text

17. To test the link, you must be connected to the Internet. Hold down the Control key on the keyboard and click the hyperlink.
18. To set background effects on the page, select *Background* from the Format menu (see boxed Figure 3.12).

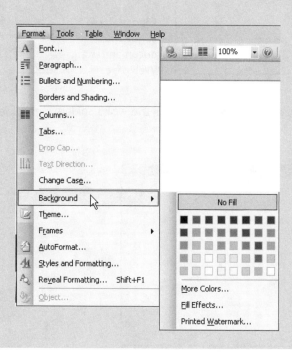

Figure 3.12
Background for a document

19. From the Background options, select *Fill Effects,* then select the Texture tab. Select from one of the textures (a light background is preferred for printing purposes) by clicking on it and then click *OK* (see boxed Figure 3.13).
20. The background is applied to the entire page. To view the page, select the Print Preview icon. If necessary, modify spacing and other document attributes by closing Print Preview and returning to the page. To adjust spacing, click the mouse pointer in the appropriate page location and use the Enter, Delete, or Backspace key to add or delete space.
21. You can print the page if you are connected to a printer by selecting *Print* from the File menu.
22. To save this document select *Save* from the File menu or click the Save icon on the standard toolbar. Save the file on a disk and name it *Spiders.* To save it as a Web page, select *Save as a Web Page* from the File menu. Type a name for the document in the *File name:* box and click *Save* (see boxed Figure 3.14). For an example of the completed Web page see "Spiders.mht" on the CD.

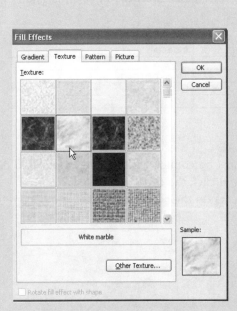

Figure 3.13
Texture background

Figure 3.14
Saving the document as a Web page

23. You will name the Web page by typing the word *Spiders* in the *File name:* box (see boxed Figure 3.15).

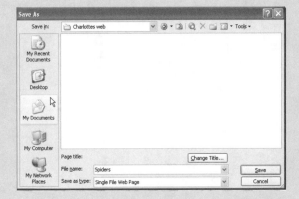

Figure 3.15
Naming the Web page

24. To see how the page looks when posted to the World Wide Web, select *Web Page Preview* from the File menu (see boxed Figure 3.16).

25. Once selected, Word will launch a World Wide Web browser on your computer. The Web page will display as if you are connected to the Internet. If you are not connected to the Internet, you will not be able to check hyperlinks to other Web sites. In order for others to access your page on the Internet, you must publish it to the Web, which requires placing the document(s) on a Web server. Check with your technology specialist to see what resources are available to you for posting documents to the Web (see boxed Figure 3.17).

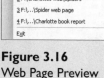

Figure 3.16
Web Page Preview

Figure 3.17
Web browser preview page

LET ME TRY

So far we have created a student book report and a Web page/hyperlinked paper with a table. We can create a newsletter in Word using content from existing documents. For an example of the completed document, see "Newletter Characters of Charlotte.doc" on the CD.

1. Open a new document in Word.
2. Open the *Spiders* Word document that was just created.
3. Highlight the first paragraph of the *Spiders* document and select *Copy* from the Edit menu.
4. On the Windows taskbar, click the button for the new Word document created in step 1 to activate it. Select *Paste* from the Edit menu. This places the paragraph from the *Spiders* document in the new document.
5. Click the mouse pointer at the beginning of the new document and press Enter twice.
6. Move the cursor back to the top of the document and type the title: *Characters of Charlotte's Web*. Highlight the title text, set it in 28-point type, bold, and in a different color from the text. Center the title.

7. Move the cursor down to the line of text that was copied from *Spiders*. Type: *A Little About Charlotte*. Highlight the text you just typed, enlarge it to 14 points, and make it bold.
8. Add another paragraph about Wilbur and pigs.
9. Add a third paragraph about Templeton, the rat.
10. Add a fourth paragraph about Fern, the girl.
11. Insert clip art that relates to Charlotte, Wilbur, and Templeton.
12. Highlight the paragraphs and graphics and click on the Columns icon. A drop-down box appears from which you can set the number of columns. Set two columns by clicking the figure that represents the second column. The text *2 Columns* appears at the bottom of the drop-down box. You should end up with a document similar to that shown in boxed Figure 3.18.

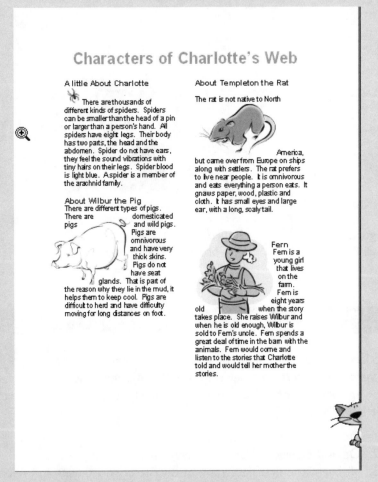

Figure 3.18
Newsletter

LET ME TRY, AGAIN

1. Open a new document in Word.
2. Title the page *Life Cycle of a Spider* in 16-point font, center the text and bold the text.
3. Press the Enter key three times.
4. Select the Insert pull-down menu and select *Diagram* from the pull-down menu.
5. Select *Cycle Diagram* from the chart of diagrams available. The chart will appear where the cursor was located.
6. In the first textbox on the right side of the diagram type the word *Adults* in the textbox; select 22-point text and bold the text.
7. In the second box at the bottom of the diagram select the textbox and type in the word *Eggs*; select 22-point text and bold the text.
8. In the third textbox type in *Spiderlings*; select 22-point text and bold the text.
9. You should end up with a document similar to that shown in boxed Figure 3.19. For an example of the completed document, see "Life Cycle of a Spider.doc" on the CD.

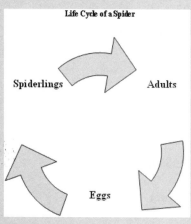

Figure 3.19
Spider life cycle

A CHALLENGE USING WORD 2003

For those who would like a challenge beyond the Let Me Try activities presented in this chapter, try the following exercises.

1. Create an advertisement regarding a speech that a character in a book that you (or your students) have recently read will be giving at your school in the near future.

2. Create a newsletter that your students may send home to their parents regarding activities that have taken place or are going to take place in school next month.

TYING IT ALL TOGETHER

In this chapter, we have created a book report, a Web page with hyperlinks, a newsletter, and a chart—all of which can be produced by students. We have saved documents in Word and Web formats. These are all activities to help you and your students begin creating print and electronic documents. These and other activities will allow students to fulfill some of the ISTE standards for creating work using computer technology.

4 POWERPOINT 2003

CHAPTER OUTLINE

1. LEARNING OBJECTIVES
2. TECHNICAL TERMS
3. CHAPTER OVERVIEW
4. WHAT IS NEW IN POWERPOINT 2003
5. HOW TEACHERS AND STUDENTS MIGHT USE POWERPOINT 2003
6. ABOUT POWERPOINT
7. WORKING WITH POWERPOINT
8. SHOW ME
   a. Starting the Presentation
      1) Opening PowerPoint 2003
      2) Creating a Title Slide and Inserting Text (Slide 1)
      3) Inserting Text into the Title Slide
   b. Adding a Design Template
   c. Inserting Slides and Adding Content
      1) Title Only Slide (Slide 2)
   d. Navigating Between Slides
      1) Title and Text Slide (Slide 3)
   e. Adding Clip Art
      1) Moving Clip Art and Resizing Text Objects
      2) Adding a Title, Text, and Content Slide (Slide 4)
      3) Title Slide (Slide 5)
   f. Modifying Text
      1) Adding a Title, Text, and Content Slide (Slide 6)
      2) Adding a Title and Text Slide (Slide 7)
      3) Adding a Title Only Slide with an Object (Slide 8)
      4) Adding a Chart Slide (Slide 9)
         i. Ordering Data
         ii. Setting the Chart Type
      5) Adding a Title and Text Slide Using the Slide Sorter (Slide 10)
      6) Adding a Text, Title, and Content Slide (Slide 11)
   g. Previewing the PowerPoint Presentation in the Slide Show
   h. Saving the Presentation
      1) Save
      2) Save As
   i. Adding Slide Transitions

42

Learning Objectives

At the completion of this chapter you will be able to:

- Start PowerPoint and create a new presentation
- Navigate the PowerPoint workspace
- Add slides to a presentation in a variety of layouts including title, clip art and text, chart and text
- Add clip art to a slide
- Add slide transitions
- Save a presentation
- Save a presentation as a HyperText Markup Language (HTML) document
- Print a presentation
- Copy a presentation to a CD-ROM

Technical Terms

The following are terms that you will encounter in the chapter and with which you will become familiar:

Slide

Outline tab

Slides tab

Slide Sorter

Design templates

HTML (HyperText Markup Language)

Chapter Overview

This chapter provides an introduction to PowerPoint 2003. It focuses on helping you learn PowerPoint fundamentals and apply them in developing a presentation. The Show Me section presents instructions on how to use many of PowerPoint 2003's tools for creating a slide show. Let Me Try exercises, embedded throughout the chapter, give specific, step-by-step instructions for quickly accomplishing tasks. They also give you opportunities to practice the information presented. You will find additional Let Me Try exercises in the "PowerPoint" folder inside "Let Me Try Exercises" on the CD. Studying the chapter contents and working through the Let Me Try exercises will enable you and your students to develop high-quality presentations suitable for class lectures, student reports and presentations, school board meetings, and other educationally oriented activities.

What Is New In PowerPoint 2003

PowerPoint 2003 has several new features, including an updated viewer, with enhanced output capabilities and no installation required; packaging for CD-ROM; and a new slide show toolbar for navigation during presentations. For additional information about PowerPoint 2003 features, see the *What's New* section of Microsoft Office PowerPoint Help or go to the following Web sites:

- http://msdn.microsoft.com/office/understanding/powerpoint/gettingstarted
- http://www.microsoft.com/office/editions/prodinfo/compare.mspx

How Teachers and Students Might Use PowerPoint 2003

Teacher Production of Materials

Instruction/Learning	Classroom Management
Create a slide show to present photographs, animation, and video to class	Create a slide show to present data related to student performance from year to year
Create a slide show and put it online as a study aid for students	Create a slide show to present innovative ideas and data analysis to teachers, administrators, parents, and the school board

Student Production of Materials

Instruction/Learning
Conduct research and collect multimedia artifacts to be organized and presented in a slide show
Students use PowerPoint as a medium to express their ideas about a particular topic using multimedia
Challenge students to express their ideas graphically and with media other than text using PowerPoint as an integration and media control tool

About PowerPoint

PowerPoint 2003 is a computer application used to create presentation materials. With PowerPoint, you can create electronic slide shows to display on a computer, printed handouts, overhead transparencies, 2-inch-by-2-inch slides, and Web documents. PowerPoint is commonly used to create and display electronic slide show presentations.

There are many ways to use PowerPoint 2003. Teachers can write and present lecture notes and give students printed handouts of the PowerPoint presentation for review and note taking. Teachers and students can create presentations that include multimedia elements such as animation, statistical charts and graphs, photographs, video, and audio to enrich or give emphasis to instructional content. In addition, these presentations can be put on the Web. Media of special school activities may be incorporated into a self-running slide show and displayed at school events. Students can be given research projects that require them to collect and analyze data and to present their findings in a multimedia slide show format. Such a task may cause students to think visually and to collect information of various media (in addition to text) formats and employ them to more fully convey complex concepts. For instance, a student who has researched the rotation of planets in our solar system is likely to have greater impact on his audience using animation or video of planet orbits than if he attempted to explain the information with text or the spoken word. These are only a few applications of PowerPoint. As you become familiar with it, you are likely to find innovative ways to incorporate it into your classroom activities.

Working with PowerPoint

Suppose you assign students the task of creating a school weather station. Divide the class into several Weather Research Teams (WRTs). Students must record the daily high and low temperatures, measure precipitation, and calculate wind speed and direction. You correspond with other geographically dispersed schools and arrange for your students to share and compare weather data with them. Students track weather trends throughout the year and each month report their collection methods and analysis to the class. Your classroom is equipped with a computer and projector, so you encourage students to use PowerPoint to present their findings. PowerPoint can help them create visual slide shows with images, colors, text, and animation effects, among other things.

This chapter focuses on creating a presentation that students use to present their findings to the class. Although the content used here is specific to creating a student report, the steps and procedures are generic and applicable to a variety of presentation types. Feel free to substitute your content and to modify the materials created in this chapter.

The complete PowerPoint presentation (Our Weather Station) and associated files can be found on the accompanying CD-ROM in the PowerPoint folder that is within the Examples folder.

Before developing a presentation, an orientation to the PowerPoint workspace is needed. When opening PowerPoint 2003, you enter the Normal view. It is a workspace comprised of several menus, toolbars, and panes. Figure 4.1 depicts the different areas

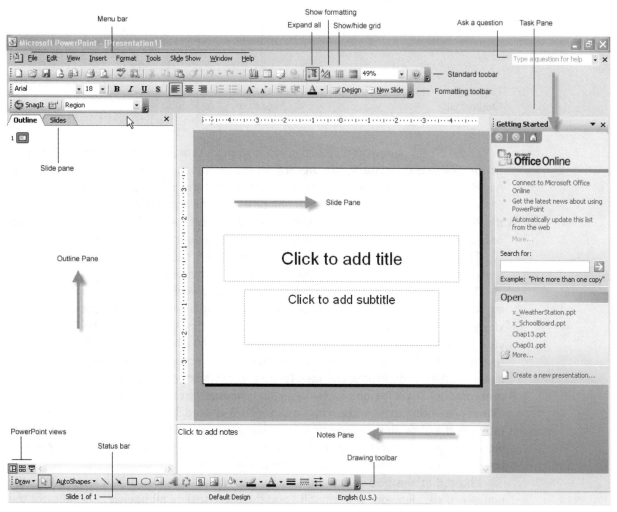

Figure 4.1
The PowerPoint workspace

of the workspace. The top portion of the screen has menus and toolbars, which contain functions and tools to assist in creating a presentation. The middle portion shows four panes—Outline, Slide, Notes, and Task—that divide the PowerPoint workspace. This is the area where most of the slide development work is done. When text, graphics, drawn objects, and so on are added, they appear here and can be arranged and modified to create a professional-looking slide. The size and positioning of the panes vary from view to view. You can adjust the size of each pane by positioning the mouse over the pane border (the cursor changes to double arrows), clicking the left mouse button, and then dragging the pane border to the desired size.

The Outline and Slides tabs display a text outline or miniature slides of your presentation, depending on the tab selected. With the Outline tab selected, you can enter the text for your presentation and organize it in list, paragraph, or slide format (see Figure 4.2). With the Slides tab selected, you see thumbnail images of your slides (see Figure 4.3). When you click on text in the Outline tab or the thumbnails in the Slides tab, the corresponding slide appears in the Slide pane.

Figure 4.2
Outline tab

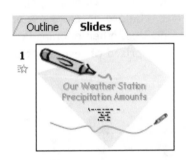

Figure 4.3
Slides tab

In the Notes pane, you type notes about your presentation that remind you of a particular point to be made. When viewing your presentation in the slide show, notes do not display. To view them, click the right mouse button, select *Screen,* and then select *Speaker Notes.* You can add clip art and pictures to your notes pages. Click *Notes Page* on the View menu and then insert objects using the Insert menu. The objects and pictures only appear in the notes page view or when printing your slides with notes.

The task pane displays commonly used commands, such as those for creating a new presentation, applying a design template, and assigning a slide layout.

The lower portion of the screen contains the PowerPoint view buttons, the drawing toolbar (which can be repositioned), and the status bar. PowerPoint provides three views of your presentation: Normal view (with Outline and Slides tabs), Slide Sorter view, and Slide Show. You can switch between views by clicking the buttons on the view toolbar located in the lower left of the PowerPoint screen. The normal view has four panes: Outline, Slide, Notes, and Task. There you can work on all the components of your presentation. The Slide Show displays your presentation without menus and toolbars. When presenting to an audience, the Slide Show is used. You can preview your presentation in the Slide Show at any time by clicking the Slide Show button. The Slide Sorter view displays miniatures of each slide in the presentation. In this view, you can reorder the slide sequence, delete slides, and add transitions.

Located at the bottom of the screen, the status bar gives information about the number of slides in your presentation and the current slide number. It also indicates the design template used for the current slide.

Show Me

Starting the Presentation

Opening PowerPoint 2003

1. Open PowerPoint. Click the Start button on the Windows taskbar. On the Start menu, click *Programs,* move the mouse pointer over *Microsoft Office,* and click *Microsoft PowerPoint 2003.*

   The PowerPoint workspace appears. Depending on your needs, you can begin to enter information on the slide or select from the options listed on the task pane (see Figure 4.4). Note that the Getting Started option on the task pane displays when PowerPoint opens. Click the drop-down arrow to select *New Presentation.* If your task pane does not display, select *Task pane* from the View menu.

Figure 4.4
New Presentation
task pane

2. The options on the task pane include:

   New blank presentation: Opens a new presentation file with one title slide.

   From design template: Displays the Slide Design task pane and enables you to start a new presentation using a design template. The template is applied to each slide.

   From AutoContent wizard: Opens the AutoContent Wizard that takes you through the steps of creating a presentation.

   From existing presentation: Opens an existing presentation with the name *Presentation2* so you can make changes and save a copy of it without altering the original file.

   Photo album: Displays the Photo Album box into which you can place photographs. PowerPoint creates a photo album slide show of the photographs.

   Templates: The templates section of the New Presentation task pane allows you to search for slide templates or access them from your computer or the Web.

   The listings below the Templates section of the task pane present recently opened presentations.

3. Click *blank presentation* to create a new, unformatted presentation. This action creates a new file that contains one blank title slide.

4. You are in PowerPoint's normal view (see Figure 4.1), which has several work areas: Outline tab, Slide tab, Slide pane, and Notes pane. You may find it useful to switch between the Outline and Slide tabs depending on your work needs.

Creating a Title Slide and Inserting Text (Slide 1)

1. Click *blank presentation* and the task pane displays icons depicting slide layout options (see Figure 4.5). PowerPoint categorizes layouts as Text layouts, Content layouts, Text and Content layouts, and Other layouts, and the layouts within these categories include Title Slide, Title Only, Title and Text, Blank, Title and Content, Content, and Title and Chart, among others. A description of each layout displays when you pass the mouse cursor over the corresponding icon. In addition, a bar appears with an insertion arrow that allows you to apply the slide layout to selected slides or to insert a new slide with that layout (see Figure 4.6). Single-click a layout in the task pane and the current slide changes to that layout. You can also scroll through layouts by clicking the up and down scroll arrows on the right side of the task pane.

Figure 4.5
Slide Layout task pane

Figure 4.6
Slide layout

2. The first slide in a presentation is a title slide, which is the layout PowerPoint assigns when you create the presentation. If your layout is not a Title slide, click the Title Slide layout. Figure 4.7 illustrates a title slide layout.

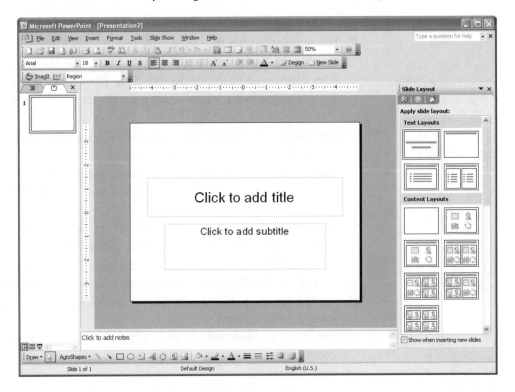

Figure 4.7
Title slide

Inserting Text into the Title Slide

1. You are now in the Normal view of PowerPoint's workspace. You can give the slide a title. On a title slide, there are two textboxes, one for a title and the other for a subtitle (see Figure 4.7).

2. Click inside the textbox labeled *Click to add title* and type the title of the presentation, *Our Weather Station: Precipitation Amounts.* Prior to clicking in the *Click to add title* box, the border is a thin dashed line. Clicking inside the box causes the border to change to a thicker line pattern, indicating that it is selected and you can begin typing. Deselect the textbox by clicking anywhere outside of it.

3. Click inside the *Click to add subtitle* box and type *By the Research Weather Team:* and the students' names to signify that this presentation will be a report about precipitation by the school's weather team.

Adding a Design Template

Design templates consist of predefined colors, layout formats, and font styles that give a presentation a specific look. When applying a design template, each existing slide receives the same treatment, as do all new slides. PowerPoint provides a number of templates that you can apply to a presentation. It is a good idea to add a template when starting the presentation. Otherwise, if you add a template after creating numerous slides, you may need to realign objects and reformat text, depending on the template selected. Select a design template early to ensure the proper positioning and formatting of slide objects.

1. For the weather team's presentation, select a template titled *Quadrant.pot.* Choose *Slide Design* from the Format menu (see Figure 4.8) and a list of designs will display in the task pane. The Quadrant.pot design is located on the task pane under *Available For Use.* If you cannot locate the Quadrant.pot design, click the Browse tool located at the bottom of the task pane. Locate the Presentation Designs folder, which is in the Templates folder located within the Microsoft Office folder. *For your convenience, a blank presentation (Quadrant_Template.ppt) containing the Quadrant.pot template is on the accompanying CD-ROM in the PowerPoint folder within Examples.*

Figure 4.8
Format menu: Slide design

      To remove the design, select the Default Design.pot template under *Available For Use* on the task pane.

2. The slide should now look similar to Figure 4.9.

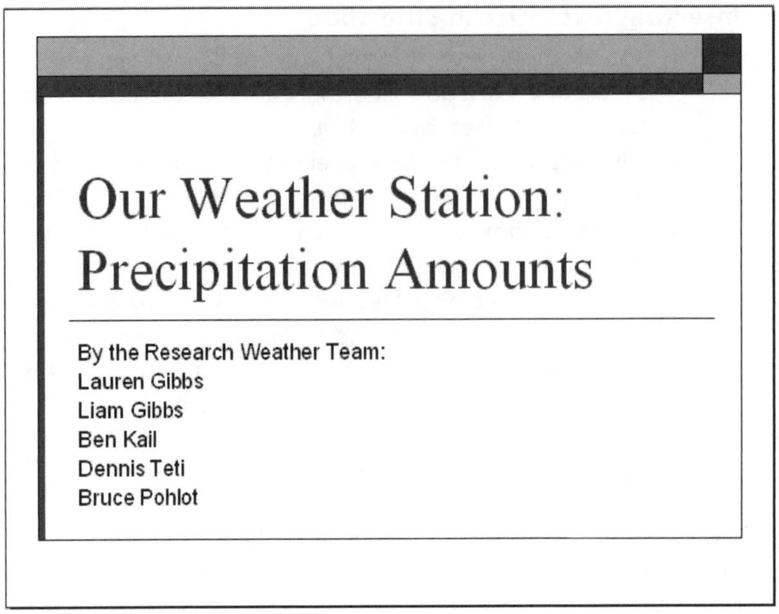

Our Weather Station: Precipitation Amounts

By the Research Weather Team:
Lauren Gibbs
Liam Gibbs
Ben Kail
Dennis Teti
Bruce Pohlot

Figure 4.9
Slide 1

LET ME TRY

At this point, we have created a new presentation that has one title slide. In addition, we added text and a design template to the slide. Let's practice what we have covered so far.

Suppose your principal asked you to deliver a presentation to the school board. The topic is your plan for establishing new graduation requirements. She gives you two days of notice and states emphatically, "dazzle them!" Additionally, she indicates that, "it won't hurt to be high-tech so feel free to use the computer/video projector in the meeting room." As your excitement, and perhaps apprehension, of presenting to the school board rises, you begin to consider all the tasks before you, one of which is creating high-quality, easy-to-understand visuals that illustrate and support the points of your talk. Knowing the room is equipped with a computer/video projector, you decide to develop your visuals using a portable computer (which you will connect to the projector during the presentation) and PowerPoint 2003. PowerPoint will enable you to create a visual slide show with images, colored charts and graphs, text, and animation effects, among other things. The steps for getting started are presented next. *To view a completed version of the school board presentation, open SchoolBoard_ Complete.ppt on the CD-ROM in the PowerPoint folder in Examples. There is also an enhanced version of the presentation (SchoolBoard_Complete.ppt).*

1. Click the Windows Start button. Select *Programs* and move the mouse pointer over *Microsoft Office* and click *Microsoft PowerPoint*. A blank presentation opens with one title slide. If you do not see a blank title slide, then select *Slide Layout* from the Format menu and click *Title Slide*. This action creates one blank presentation that contains one blank title slide.

2. Insert text in the title slide. To enter a title, click inside the *Click to add title* box and type the title of the presentation, *Level Five*. Click anywhere outside the text object to deselect it.

3. Add a subtitle by clicking inside the *Click to add subtitle* box and type *Board Work Session by Lauren Marie Gibbs*.
4. Select *Slide Design* from the Format menu. Apply a template of your choice by clicking its icon on the task pane.

Inserting Slides and Adding Content

Title Only Slide (Slide 2)

A second slide can now be added to the weather station presentation. For this slide, we will choose a *Title Only* layout, which provides a text area for the slide title. The Title Only layout refers to the slide's title and not the title slide of the presentation.

After entering a title, we will create a second textbox in which to type the purpose of the presentation. When we are finished, the slide will look similar to Figure 4.10.

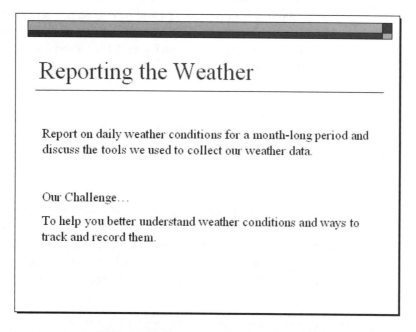

Figure 4.10
Title Only slide

1. There are several ways to add a new slide. Click the New Slide button on the formatting toolbar or select *New Slide* from the Insert menu. You may also use the key combination of CTRL+M.
2. PowerPoint adds a new slide to the presentation and by default assigns it a Title and Text layout. We want the layout to be Title Only, so click the Title Only layout option on the task pane. It is located under *Text Layouts*, the first layout icon on the right side of the task pane (see Figure 4.11).

Figure 4.11
Selecting a Title
Only layout

3. Add a title to slide 2 by clicking inside the *Click to add title* box and typing the following: *Reporting the Weather*. Another way to add a title is by making the Outline tab (on the left side of screen) active. Select the small slide icon that corresponds to slide 2 and type the title (see Figure 4.12). The title appears in the slide pane when typing.

Figure 4.12
Slide title in Outline tab

4. This slide presents the purpose of the presentation. Currently it has one textbox that contains the slide title. We will now create a second textbox for the text describing the presentation's purpose. Create a textbox by selecting the Textbox tool on the drawing toolbar (see Figure 4.13). When you click on the Textbox tool, the mouse cursor changes to the vertical line (see Figure 4.14).

Figure 4.13
Textbox tool

Figure 4.14
Cursor after selecting Textbox tool

5. Place (click) the cursor in the slide pane where you want the textbox to begin. While holding the left mouse button down, drag the cursor to the right side of the slide pane. Release the mouse and a blank textbox appears (see Figure 4.15). By dragging the textbox across the slide, the text wraps to the next line when typing. Alternatively, you could have selected the text tool and simply clicked in

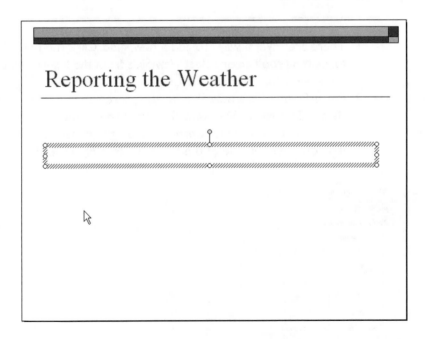

Figure 4.15
Empty textbox

the slide pane and typed. However, the text does not wrap and runs off the slide when using this method.

6. Now, type the purpose of the presentation:

   Report on daily weather conditions for a month-long time period and discuss the tools we used to collect our weather data.

   Our Challenge...

   To help you better understand weather conditions and ways to track and record them.

7. Change the font style and size by clicking the textbox border, then selecting a desired font style and size from the formatting toolbar. When you click a textbox to select it, a border appears with a line pattern (see Figure 4.16), indicating that you can insert or modify text. Clicking the textbox border a second time changes it from a line to a dot pattern (see Figure 4.17). The dot pattern indicates that the contents of the textbox are selected. Any changes (e.g., font size or style) that you make alter the entire contents of the box.

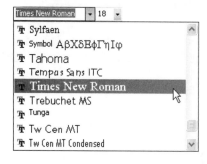

Figure 4.16
Textbox line pattern

Figure 4.17
Textbox dot pattern

8. If you chose the Quadrant.pot design template, PowerPoint assigned the slides a font type of *Times New Roman*. If you want to change the font type, select the textbox and, with the border as a dot pattern, click the small downward arrow in the Font box on the formatting toolbar to display a list of available fonts (see Figure 4.18). Select a font by clicking on the font name.

Figure 4.18
Font type and size

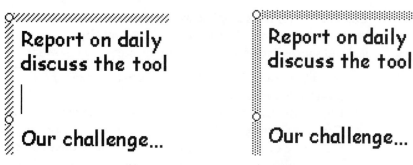

9. To change the font size, click the small downward arrow in the Font Size box, which is located on the right side of the Font Type box (see Figure 4.18). Select a size of 18 or 24 by clicking on the number. Currently, the *Times New Roman* font is set to 18.

10. The slide should look like Figure 4.10.

Navigating Between Slides

We now have two slides and can navigate from one to the other using one of the following methods:

1. Using either the Outline or Slide tab, click on the slide icon that represents the slide to which you want to navigate. The slide appears in the slide pane.
2. In the slide pane, click the scroll bar arrows. The up arrow takes you to the previous slide and the down arrow takes you to the next slide.
3. Use the arrow keys on your keyboard. The right or down arrow moves you forward through the slide show. The left or up arrow moves you back through the slide show.

LET ME TRY

Continuing with the school board presentation example, let's practice what we covered so far. We created a slide with a Title Only layout, created a textbox, and modified and set text attributes. Here are the steps we followed:

1. Add a new slide. Select *New Slide* from the Insert menu.
2. Select *Title Only* on the task pane.
3. Click in the *Click to add title* box and enter the following: *Our Work Here Today. . . .*
4. Create a textbox to place the text describing the presentation's purpose. Select the Textbox tool on the drawing toolbar. The mouse cursor changes to a vertical line when you click on the Textbox tool.
5. With the cursor appearing as a vertical line, click in the slide pane where the text box begins, and while holding the left mouse button down, drag it to the right side of the slide pane. Release the mouse button and a blank textbox appears.
6. Type the purpose of the presentation in the textbox:
   Establish new graduation requirements and standards that ensure high levels of student achievement versus traditional time and attendance requirements.
   Our Challenge. . .
   Invent a new system that prepares ALL graduates for society.
7. With the text box selected and the border as a dot pattern, click the small downward arrow in the Font box on the formatting toolbar. Select *Arial* font by clicking on the font name.
8. With the text box selected and the border as a dot pattern, click the small downward arrow in the Font Size box on the formatting toolbar. Select a text size of 24.

Title and Text Slide (Slide 3)

Now let's add the third slide to the presentation. For this slide, choose a Title and Text layout, which provides text areas for the slide title and a text list. When you enter text into a list, PowerPoint separates it with bullets, check marks, hyphens, and so on. Lists are an easy and useful way to format text on a slide. When we are finished, the slide will look similar to Figure 4.19.

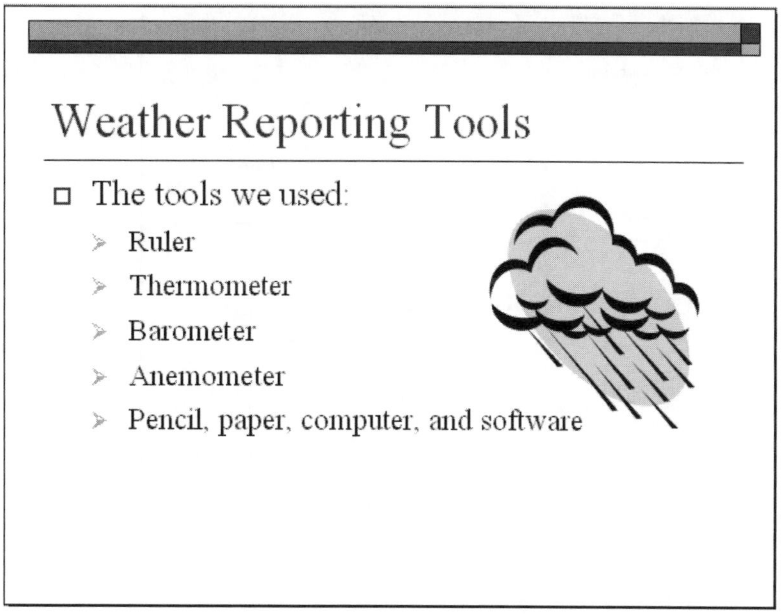

Figure 4.19
Title and Text slide

1. Add a new slide by selecting *New Slide* from the Insert menu. By default, PowerPoint assigns a Title and Text layout, which is the layout we want to use in this example. If your layout is not Title and Text, choose the Title and Text layout option on the task pane.

2. Click in the *Click to add title* box and type the following title: *Weather Reporting Tools*.

3. Click inside the *Click to add text* box and type: *The tools we used:*.

4. Press the Enter key and a bullet character (square) appears on the next line. In Figure 4.19, notice that the first line uses the square bullet character and the remaining lines indent with an arrow character. After typing the first line in the bullet list and pressing the Enter key, the next text line (*Ruler*) does not indent. To indent it, position the cursor at the beginning of the line and press the Tab key. After typing *Ruler,* press Enter and subsequent lines indent.

5. Type the remaining items:
   - *Thermometer*
   - *Barometer*
   - *Anemometer*
   - *Pencil, paper, computer, and software*

6. By indenting these lines, the bullets become filled squares. To change the squares to arrows, select the five indented bullet items by positioning the cursor before the word *Ruler* and, while holding down the left mouse button, drag downward to after the word *software* and release the mouse. The text should appear highlighted (highlighting text in this manner is referred to as selecting). With the text selected, click the right mouse button in the highlighted area and select *Bullets and Numbering* from the menu.

7. The Bullets and Numbering dialogue box appears (see Figure 4.20), which presents various bullet types. Select the arrow bullet type by clicking the Bulleted tab and clicking the appropriate cell.

8. Click *OK*. The bullets change to arrows. To deselect the text, click anywhere outside the textbox.

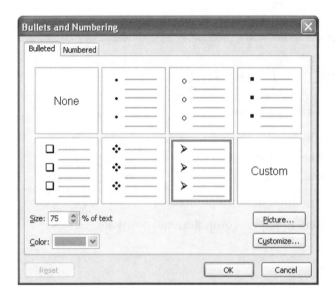

Figure 4.20
Bullets and Numbering

Adding Clip Art

1. We will insert a clip art image that represents or supports our topic about weather. Images are available from PowerPoint's clip art library. To insert clip art onto a slide, select *Picture* from the Insert menu and then click *Clip Art*. You can also click the Insert Clip Art button on the drawing toolbar. The task pane displays the Insert Clip Art options (see Figure 4.21). To search for clip art, type a keyword in the *Search for:* box and click *Go* or press the Enter key. Using the *Search in:* and *Results should be:* options, you can specify the location that you want to search and the file types that you are seeking (e.g., sounds, movies, photographs, and clip art).

Figure 4.21
Clip Art task pane

2. In the *Search for:* box, type *weather* and click *Go*. Small images (thumbnails) representing weather clip art will be displayed in the task pane (see Figure 4.21). If you do not want any of the images, you may also click the *Clip Art on Office Online* link at the bottom of the task pane. This option links to Microsoft's Clip Art and Media Web site containing numerous images that you can download.

3. For this presentation, select the rain clouds image located at the top left of the task pane. Insert it onto the slide by clicking on it. You can also insert the image

by selecting *Insert* from the drop-down menu that becomes available by positioning the mouse cursor over the image icon and clicking the downward arrow that appears on the right side of the thumbnail (see Figure 4.22).

Figure 4.22
Inserting clip art

Moving Clip Art and Resizing Text Objects

1. Now that we inserted the clip art, its size and placement need adjustment. There are eight small circles or sizing handles around the image (see Figure 4.23) that we can use to resize it. The handles also indicate that we selected the object. If you do not see the sizing handles around your clip art image, click on the image to select it and the handles appear.

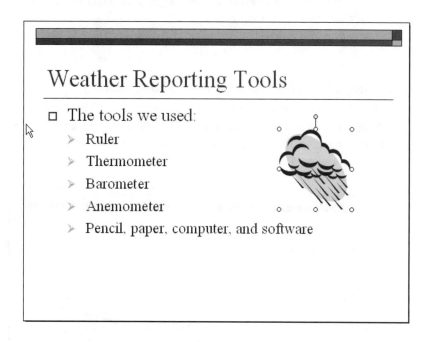

Figure 4.23
Sizing handles

2. To make the image larger, move the mouse cursor over one of the sizing handles and the cursor changes to an arrow. Click the upper-left sizing handle of the image and, while holding the left mouse button down, drag the sizing handle to the upper left. The image resizes. Pressing the CTRL key while dragging resizes the image proportionally. If you need to reposition the image, click the left mouse button in the center of the image and, while holding the left mouse button down, drag the image to the desired location. You may also notice a green dot attached to the sizing handle. Dragging this dot to the left or right rotates the image.

Let's get back to the school board presentation example and practice what we covered. We created a slide with a Title and Text layout, modified the bullets in the list, and added a clip art image to the slide. Here are the steps we followed:

1. Add a new slide by selecting *New slide* from the Insert menu.
2. Select *Title and Text* layout from the task pane.
3. Click in the *Click to add title* box and type the title: *Time-Based System*.
4. Click inside the *Click to add text* box and type: *Credits based on:* and press Enter.
5. Indent subbullets. With the cursor positioned at the beginning of the line, press the Tab key. Type the following bullet items and press Enter after each line:
   - *Time spent in class*
   - *Grade of D or better*
   - *Lack of consistency or uniform expectations for performance to earn diploma*
     Each item will indent under the *Credits based on:* text.
6. Select the three indented bullet items. Click the right mouse button in the selected area and select *Bullets and Numbering* from the menu. Click the checkmarks cell and then click *OK*.
7. Click anywhere outside the text box to deselect the text.
8. Select *Picture* from the Insert menu and then click *Clip Art*.
9. Enter a search term/keyword (e.g., "education") in the *Search for:* box of the task pane to search for an image.
10. When PowerPoint retrieves the images that relate to your search term, click one of them to insert it onto the slide.
11. Position and resize the image on the slide.

Adding a Title, Text, and Content Slide (Slide 4)

A fourth slide can now be added to the presentation. This slide has a Title, Text, and Content layout, which provides text areas for the slide title, a text list, and a placeholder for content (e.g., clip art, picture, graph, and so on). When we are finished, the slide will look similar to Figure 4.24.

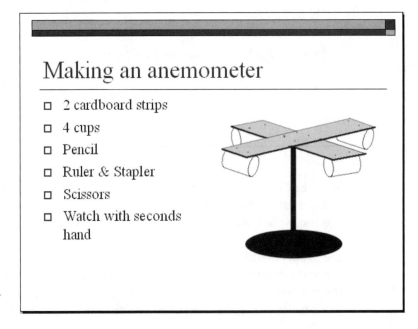

Figure 4.24
Title, Text, and Content slide

1. Add a new slide by selecting *New Slide* from the Insert menu.
2. Click *Title, Text, and Content* layout on the task pane (see Figure 4.25). After clicking the layout, the slide view looks like Figure 4.26.

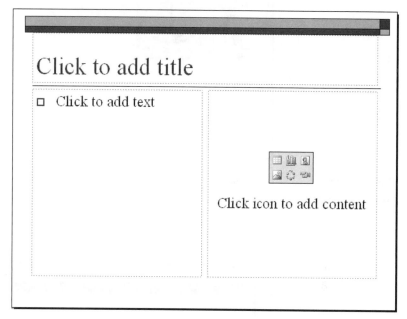

Text and Content Layouts

Figure 4.25
Title, Text, and Content layout

Figure 4.26
Slide view of Title, Text, and Content layout

3. Click inside the *Click to add title* box and type the following title: *Making an Anemometer.*
4. Click inside the *Click to add text* box and type the following text list:
   - *2 cardboard strips*   • *Ruler & Stapler*
   - *4 cups*   • *Scissors*
   - *Pencil*   • *Watch with seconds hand*
5. Add a picture to the slide. Suppose the project involves making an anemometer, which measures wind speed and direction. Let's also suppose that when making the anemometer we created a picture of it in a drawing program and saved it on the computer.

   Notice that the slide has a placeholder for content: *Click icon to add content* (see Figure 4.26). The six icons in the placeholder area represent different types of content that can be added to a slide, such as tables, graphs, clip art, pictures, diagrams, and media (audio and video).

6. Click the Insert Picture icon and the Insert Picture dialogue box appears (see Figure 4.27). *On the CD-ROM, locate the drawing of the anemometer, anemometer.tif. It is in the WeatherData folder within PowerPoint and Examples.* Click the image one time to select it; then click the Insert button.
7. Position the picture on the slide by clicking in its center and, while holding the left mouse button down, drag it to a desired location (see Figure 4.24).

Title Slide (Slide 5)

The first portion of the presentation covered the goals of the project, weather reporting tools, and making an anemometer. We now will change the presentation topic and discuss weather data collected in October. We need to convey to our audience that we are changing topics and a way to accomplish this is to insert a title slide. The complete slide will look similar to Figure 4.28.

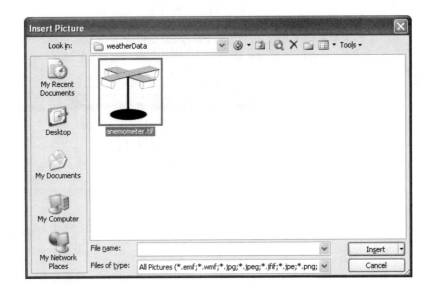

Figure 4.27
Insert Picture box

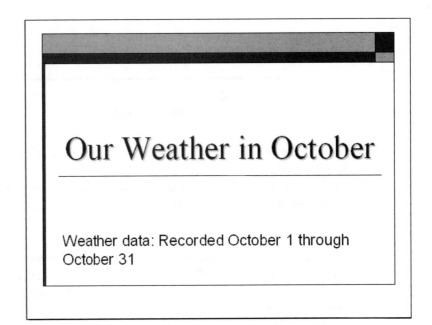

Figure 4.28
Title slide for new
topic

1. Add a new slide by selecting *New Slide* from the Insert menu.
2. Click *Title Slide* layout on the task pane.
3. Click in the *Click to add title* box and type: *Our Weather in October* (see Figure 4.29).
4. Click in the *Click to add subtitle* box and type: *Weather data: Recorded October 1 through October 31.*

Our Weather in October

Figure 4.29

Modifying Text

You can now adjust the font type, style, size, and positioning of the text.

1. To modify the title, click the title textbox to select it. The first time you click the box a line pattern border appears with sizing handles. Click the border again to change its appearance from a line to a dot pattern (see Figure 4.29). Notice that as you pass the mouse pointer over the border it changes to a four-pointed cross. When the border is a dot pattern, changes (e.g., font size or style) can be made to the contents of the textbox.
2. Click the small downward arrow in the Font box to display a list of fonts (see Figure 4.30). Select a font by clicking on the font name. For this slide, leave the font set to Times New Roman, because it is associated with the Quadrant.pot template. If you want to choose a different font, scroll through the font list and click a font name.
3. Click the small downward arrow in the Font Size box to display a list of font sizes. Select a size by clicking on the number. Choose a font size of 60 (see Figure 4.31).
4. Set the font style to bold, the text to shadowed, and the text alignment to centered by clicking the Bold **(B),** Shadow **(S),** and Center icons (see Figure 4.32). The Center icon centers the contents inside of the textbox. It does not center the textbox relative to the screen.

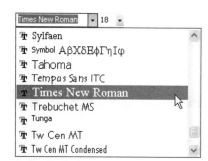

Figure 4.30
Font type

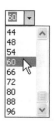

Figure 4.31
Font size

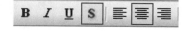

Figure 4.32
Font attributes

5. Click the subtitle textbox and set the font style to shadow **(S).**
6. The subtitle is directly under the title. We can move the subtitle to the lower portion of the slide by selecting it (clicking on it), clicking on its border, and then dragging the box. If the textbox is not selected or the border is not a dot pattern, the textbox will not move. A more accurate way to align the textbox in the lower portion of the slide is to use *Align or Distribute* on the drawing toolbar. The steps are as follows:
   - Select the subtitle and ensure that a dot pattern border displays around it.
   - Click *Draw* on the drawing toolbar. Pass the mouse pointer over *Align or Distribute* and from the drop-down menu click *Relative to Slide*. A check appears next to the *Relative to Slide* menu item. The menu disappears.
   - Click *Draw* on the drawing toolbar. Pass the mouse pointer over *Align or Distribute* and from the drop-down menu click *Align Bottom* (see Figure 4.33). The textbox appears toward the bottom of the slide.

Figure 4.33
Object alignment

Adding a Title, Text, and Content Slide (Slide 6)

For this slide, choose *Title, Text, and Content* layout. The final slide will look similar to Figure 4.34.

1. Add a new slide by selecting *New Slide* from the Insert menu.
2. Choose *Title, Text, and Content* layout from the task pane.
3. Click in the *Click to add title* box and type the following title: *October Assignments*.
4. Enter the following three items in the bullet list:
   - *Recorded daily rainfall and snowfall amounts*
   - *Recorded daily high and low temperatures*
   - *Recorded daily wind direction and speed at specific times of day*

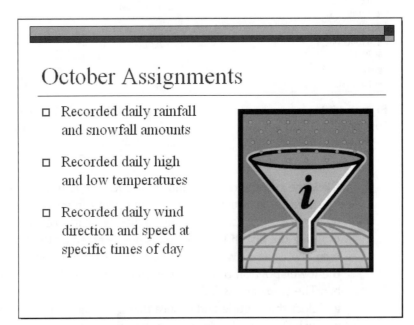

Figure 4.34
Title, Text, and Content slide

5. Set the line spacing. The list items are close together and readers may have difficulty discerning one item from another. Select the list textbox and click on its border so a dot pattern displays. Select *Line Spacing* from the Format menu and the Line Spacing box appears (see Figure 4.35).

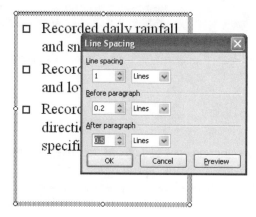

Figure 4.35
Line spacing

6. Set the *After paragraph* to 0.5 with the Lines option selected. There should now be more space between list items.
7. Add a clip art image to the slide that represents the topic. Adjust its size and position as needed.

Adding a Title and Text Slide (Slide 7)

For this slide, choose a Title and Text layout. The final slide will look similar to Figure 4.36.

1. Add a new slide by selecting *New Slide* from the Insert menu.
2. Choose *Title and Text* layout from the task pane.
3. Click in the *Click to add title* box to enter the following title: *Our Weather Research Team.*
4. Type the following bullet list items:
   - *The class was divided into Weather Research Teams (WRT) each being responsible for recording precipitation amounts, temperatures, and wind speed and direction.*
   - *Our team consisted of Lauren, Liam, Ben, Dennis, and Bruce.*

> ## Our Weather Research Team
>
> ☐ The class was divided into Weather Research Teams (WRT) each being responsible for recording precipitation amounts, temperatures, and wind speed and direction.
>
> ☐ Our WRT consisted of Lauren, Liam, Ben, Dennis, and Bruce.

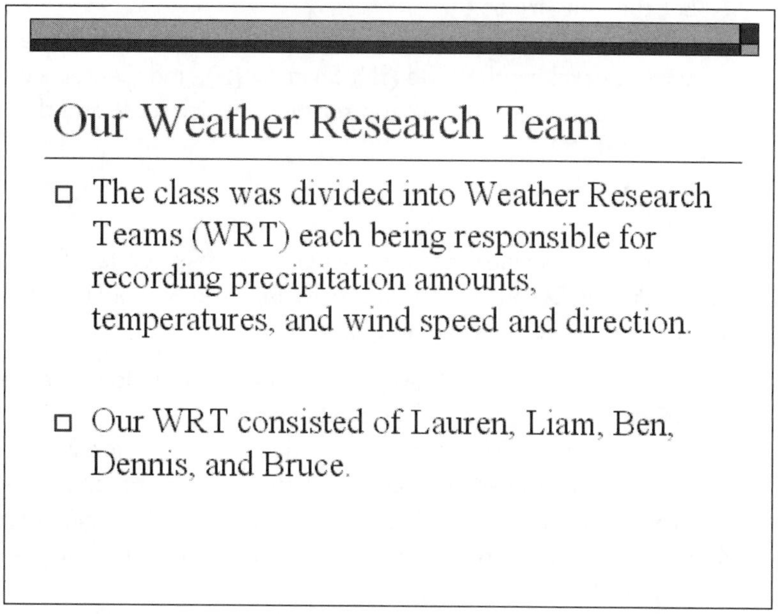

Figure 4.36
Title and Text layout

Returning to our school board presentation example, let's create three slides based on what we covered so far.

Title, Text, and Content Slide

1. Add a new slide by selecting *New Slide* from the Insert menu.
2. Click *Title, Text, and Content* layout on the task pane.
3. Click inside the *Click to add title* box and type the following title: *Performance-based System*.
4. Click inside the *Click to add text* box and type the following text list:
   - *Students demonstrate proficiency in all graduation requirements.*
   - *Seat time and passing grade no longer earns a degree.*
5. Add a picture or clip art to the slide. Click the placeholder for content: *Click icon to add content* and then select one of the six icons in the placeholder area that represents the type of content you want to insert.
6. Position the picture or clip art on the slide by clicking in its center and, while holding the left mouse button down, drag it to a desired location.

Title Slide

At this point in the presentation, the topic focus changes and we will indicate this shift in focus using a title slide.

1. Add a new slide by selecting *New Slide* from the Insert menu.
2. Click *Title Slide* layout on the task pane.
3. Click in the *Click to add title* box and type: *Why Change?*
4. Click in the *Click to add subtitle* box and type: *some important reasons.*
5. Click the title textbox to select it. Click the border again so that a dot pattern appears. With the border as a dot pattern, choose a font.
6. Set the font size to 66.
7. Set the font style to bold, the text to shadowed, and the text alignment to centered by clicking the Bold **(B)**, Shadow **(S)**, and Center icons.
8. Click the subtitle textbox and set the font size to 36 and the style to shadow **(S)** and bold **(B)**.

Title and Text Slide

The next slide will state reasons for why change is needed. This slide will have a Title and Text layout. Because there is an existing slide with a Title and Text layout, we will use the Slide Sorter to copy and paste it.

1. Click the Slide Sorter View button located in the lower-left portion of the PowerPoint workspace to enter the Slide Sorter.
2. Click one of the Title and Text layout slides (e.g., slide 2) to select it.
3. With the slide selected, choose *Copy* from the Edit menu. Click the last slide in the presentation (slide 5) and select *Paste* from the Edit menu. There are now six slides.
4. Change the text on the sixth slide. Double-click it to exit the Slide Sorter and return to the Normal view.
5. Click on the Title box to select it. A line pattern border appears around the box. Click on the border again and it changes to a dot pattern. Press the Delete key and the text changes to *Click to add title*. Type the new title: *America Is Unprepared.*

6. Click the bullet list textbox to select it. A line pattern border appears around the box. Click on the border again and it changes to a dot pattern. Press the Delete key and the text changes to *Click to add text.* Type a new list by entering the following items:
   - *"Literacy and the ability to think are the underpinnings of a free society." Thomas Jefferson.*
   - *Provide students with a proper background in history, economics, government, language, literature, science, technology, philosophy and the arts.*
7. Add clip art.

Adding a Title Only Slide with an Object (Slide 8)

For this slide, choose a Title Only layout. We will insert an Excel worksheet onto the slide to represent the data recorded for the first 15 days in October. The final slide will look similar to the screen shown in Figure 4.37.

Storing Weather Data in Excel

Day	Low	High	Speed	Direction	Rain fall (inches)	Snow fall (inches)
10/1/06	65	76	2	NW	0	
10/2/06	64	75	1	NW	0	
10/3/06	66	77	3	SE	0	
10/4/06	62	74	15	E	0	
10/5/06	65	80	22	E	0	
10/6/06	64	81	32	NE	0	
10/7/06	66	82	18	NE	0	
10/8/06	62	80	12	E	0	
10/9/06	65	84	15	SW	0	
10/10/06	67	83	22	NE	0	
10/11/06	68	83	32	NE	0	
10/12/06	66	80	7	E	1.5	
10/13/06	55	70	12	NW	0.25	
10/14/06	56	72	2	NW	0.15	
10/15/06	50	69	11	SW	0	

(Weather Data for Charleston, IL — Temperature columns Low/High; Wind columns Speed/Direction)

Figure 4.37
Completed slide with worksheet

1. Add a new slide by selecting *New Slide* from the Insert menu.
2. Choose *Title Only* layout from the task pane.
3. Click in the *Click to add title* box and type the following title: *Storing Weather Data in Excel.*
4. Place an Excel worksheet on the slide. Select *Object* from the Insert menu (see Figure 4.38). The Insert Object dialogue box appears (see Figure 4.39).

Figure 4.38
Insert Object menu item

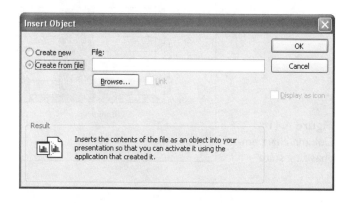

Figure 4.39
Insert Object box

5. Click the *Create from file* option. Click *Browse* and the Browse dialogue box appears (see Figure 4.40).

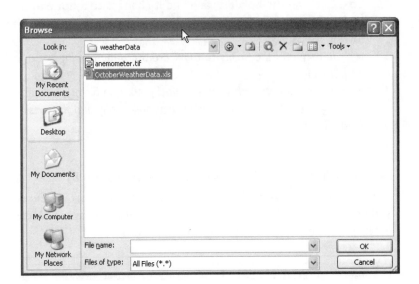

Figure 4.40
Browse box

6. *Locate the worksheet named OctoberWeatherData.xls on the CD-ROM. It is in the WeatherData folder (in PowerPoint and Examples) on the CD-ROM. Click the OctoberWeatherData.xls file one time to select it and then click OK and you will return to the Insert dialogue box.*

7. Click *OK* and the worksheet should appear on the slide.

Adding a Chart Slide (Slide 9)

Add the ninth slide to the presentation. This slide has a chart layout, which provides text areas for the slide title and a placeholder for a chart.

Suppose a weather research team located in Charleston, Illinois, and another team in Philadelphia, Pennsylvania, want to compare precipitation amounts for the month of October over a 3-year period. One way to present the data is shown in Figure 4.41.

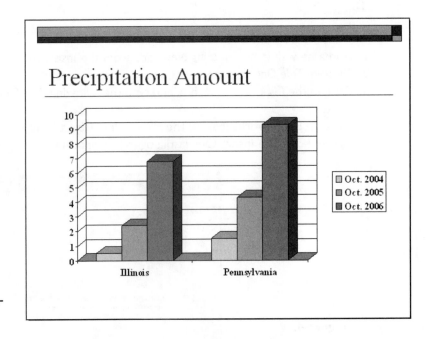

Figure 4.41
Column chart emphasizing state

1. Add a new slide by selecting *New Slide* from the Insert menu.
2. Choose *Title and Content* layout from the task pane.
3. Click in the *Click to add title* box and enter the following title: *Precipitation Amount.*
4. Click the Insert Chart icon (see Figure 4.42). Microsoft Graph opens and presents a datasheet with sample data. Click the uppermost left cell in the column header to select the contents of the datasheet (see Figure 4.43). Press the Delete key to delete the sample data.

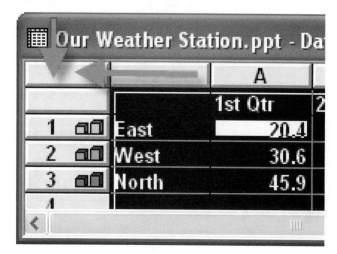

Figure 4.42
Insert chart option

Figure 4.43
Chart datasheet

Ordering Data

Before continuing, review quickly how to order data in the datasheet. The ordering of data in Microsoft Graph determines how data are plotted. For instance, if there are two categories labeled *Illinois* and *Pennsylvania* and you enter the Illinois data in Column A, then PowerPoint plots those data first on the left side of the chart. Data entered in column B appear next, and so on. Notice in Figure 4.44 that there is a column to the left of column A and a row between the column headers (A, B, C, and so on) and the row numbers. The first column (to the left of column A) is the data series column. Data entered there appear in the chart legend. The legend in Figure 4.41 appears on the right side of the chart. The row under the column headers is for the category titles.

Various aspects of data can be emphasized or grouped depending on their ordering. For example, data can be ordered to show how precipitation varied for each state by time (see Figure 4.44). The ordering of data illustrated in Figure 4.44 produces the chart shown in Figure 4.41. Notice in the datasheet of Figure 4.44 that the time periods are in the data series column and the category titles (states) and data are in columns A and B.

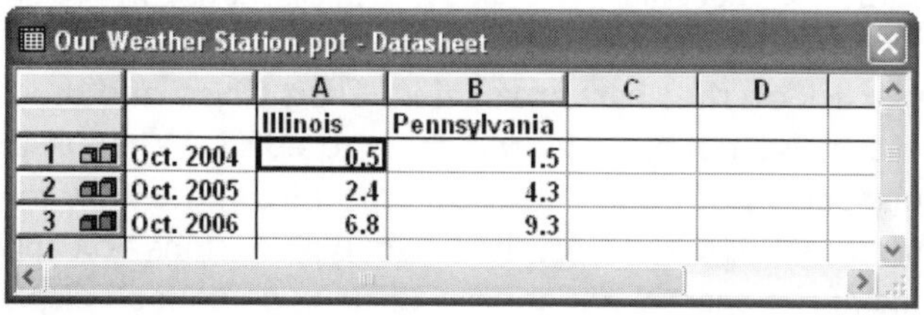

		A	B	C	D	
		Illinois	Pennsylvania			
1	Oct. 2004	0.5	1.5			
2	Oct. 2005	2.4	4.3			
3	Oct. 2006	6.8	9.3			
4						

Our Weather Station.ppt - Datasheet

Figure 4.44
Datasheet focusing on state

Alternatively, placing the states in the data series column and time periods in columns A, B, and C groups the data by time (see Figure 4.45). The ordering of data illustrated in Figure 4.45 produces the chart shown in Figure 4.46. In this example, the chart emphasizes time period and plots the states categories as the data series.

		A	B	C	D
		Oct. 2004	Oct. 2005	Oct. 2006	
1	Illinois	0.5	2.4	6.8	
2	Pennsylvania	1.5	4.3	9.3	
3					
4					

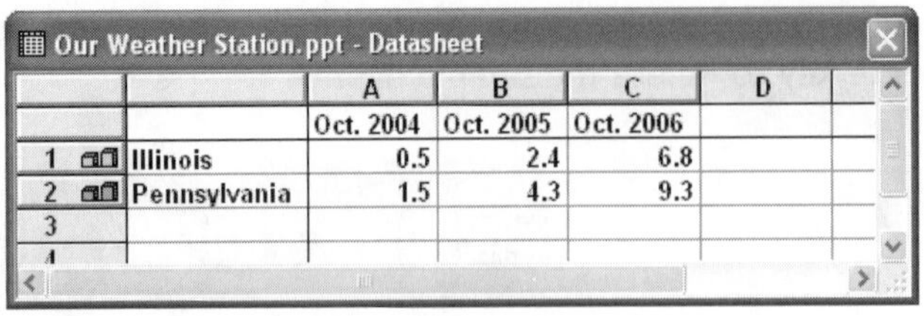

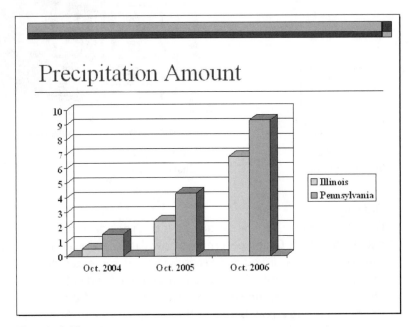

Figure 4.45
Datasheet focusing on time period

Figure 4.46
Chart emphasizing time

Setting the Chart Type

5. Prior to the discussion about ordering data, we removed the contents of the datasheet. Continuing with the chart example, we will now specify a chart type. Microsoft Graph offers numerous chart types, such as pie, column, bar, line, and area. To set a chart type, select *Chart type* from the Chart menu. Note that the Chart type menu is only available in the Chart mode. If you inadvertently click outside the chart area, you exit the chart-editing mode and you may not see the Chart menu. To enter the editing mode and make the Chart menu available, right-click on the chart area, select *Chart Object* and then *Edit* (see Figure 4.47). You can also double-click the chart to edit it. When in the editing mode, if the datasheet is not open, select *Datasheet* from the View menu.
6. After selecting *Chart Type,* the Chart Type options box appears (see Figure 4.48). Icons of the chart types appear. Clicking on an icon displays several formats for that particular chart type. A column chart is appropriate to compare precipitation amounts of two categories, for example, Illinois and Pennsylvania. Click

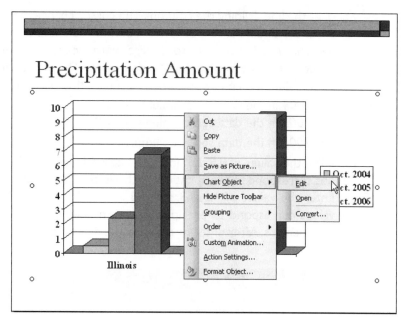

Figure 4.47
Editing chart

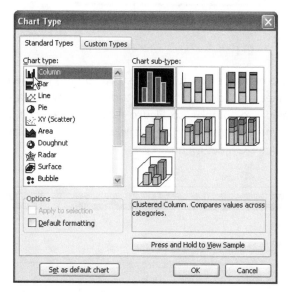

Figure 4.48
Chart Type options

Column under *Chart type* and then under *Chart sub-type* select the *clustered column* format by clicking in the appropriate box. The *clustered column* format box is the first box on the left under *Chart sub-type*. Notice that as you click on the chart subtype boxes, a description of each subtype appears at the lower-right portion of the Chart Type box.

7. Click *OK* to set the chart options. Selecting the *Custom Type* tab on the Chart Type option box allows you to create a customized chart.

8. There are two categories, Illinois and Pennsylvania. Type *Illinois* in the header cell of column A and *Pennsylvania* in the header cell of Column B. Some text may be hidden in the columns. The column width can be adjusted. Position the cursor

over the line dividing the columns. The cursor changes to a double-arrow cross. With the double-arrow on the column border, hold down the left mouse button, and drag left or right to enlarge or reduce the size of the column.

9. Enter three time periods for the data series. The data series column is the leftmost column. Each row is numbered. Enter the following:

   Oct. 2004 in the data series column, row 1

   Oct. 2005 in the data series column, row 2

   Oct. 2006 in the data series column, row 3

10. Enter the values of 0.5, 2.4, and 6.8 in cells A1, A2, and A3, respectively. These values correspond to precipitation in Charleston, Illinois, for the three time periods.

11. Enter the values of 1.5, 4.3, and 9.3 in cells B1, B2, and B3, respectively. These values correspond to precipitation in Philadelphia, Pennsylvania, for the three time periods. After entering the data, the datasheet should look like Figure 4.49.

		A	B	C	D	
		Illinois	Pennsylvania			
1	Oct. 2004	0.5	1.5			
2	Oct. 2005	2.4	4.3			
3	Oct. 2006	6.8	9.3			

Our Weather Station.ppt - Datasheet

Figure 4.49
Completed datasheet

12. To close the datasheet, click the Close button (X) on the upper-right corner of the datasheet or click anywhere outside the chart area in the slide pane. The chart should look similar to Figure 4.50. You can edit the chart by double-clicking in the chart area or right-clicking in the chart area and selecting *Edit* from the Chart Object menu.

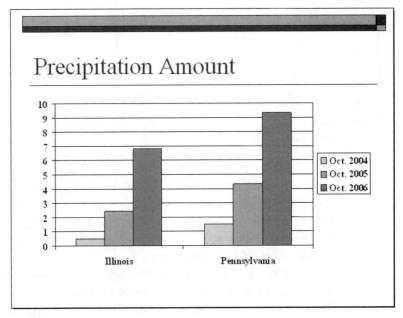

Figure 4.50
Completed slide

LET ME TRY

Returning to the school board presentation example, let's practice what we have covered so far. We created a slide with a Chart layout, entered data into a Microsoft Graph datasheet, and modified the chart layout. Here are the steps we followed:

1. Add a new slide by selecting *New Slide* from the Insert menu.
2. Choose *Title and Chart* layout from the task pane.
3. Click in the *Click to add title* box, and enter the following title: *Skills Needed: Critical Thinking and Problem Solving*.
4. Double-click the chart placeholder designated by *Double click to add chart*.
5. Click the uppermost left cell in the column header of the datasheet to select all the data. Press the Delete key to delete the sample data.
6. Select *Chart Type* from the Chart menu.
7. Click *Bar* under *Chart type*; then under *Chart sub-type* select the *Cluster Bar* format by clicking in the appropriate box.
8. Click *OK* to set the chart options.
9. In the datasheet, type *(%) of Jobs Requiring Skills* in the header cell of column A and *(%) of Today's Workforce with Skills* in the header cell of column B. Adjust the column widths as needed.
10. Enter three time periods for the data series: *1900* in the data series column, row 1; *1950* in the data series column, row 2; and *2000* in the data series column, row 3.
11. Enter the values of 10 and 4 in cells A1 and B1, respectively.
12. Enter the values of 30 and 15 in cells A2 and B2, respectively.
13. Enter the values of 60 and 20 in cells A3 and B2, respectively.
14. Close the datasheet by clicking the Close button on the upper-right corner or by clicking anywhere outside the chart area in the slide pane.

Adding a Title and Text Slide Using the Slide Sorter (Slide 10)

Now add another slide with a Title and Text layout. For this slide, use the Slide Sorter to make a copy of an existing slide, paste it, and alter its text to create the 10th slide. Copying and pasting slides in the Slide Sorter is one of the many approaches you can use to work efficiently. When you are finished, the slide will look similar to Figure 4.51.

1. Click the Slide Sorter View button located in the lower-left portion of the PowerPoint workspace to enter the Slide Sorter (see Figure 4.52). The Slide Sorter presents images of each slide in the slide show (see Figure 4.53). In this view, slides can be easily copied, pasted, reordered, and deleted. To reorder a slide, click on it and drag it to a new location in the slide show sequence. To delete a slide, click on it and press the Delete key.

    You can also accomplish many of the aforementioned tasks in the *Slide pane* of the Normal view.

2. To copy and paste a slide, click one of the Title and Text layout slides (e.g., slide 7) to select it. A black border appears around it. With the slide selected, choose *Copy* from the Edit menu. Click the last slide in the presentation (slide 9) and select *Paste* from the Edit menu. The 10th slide appears. Note that the pasted slide appears after the slide (i.e., slide 9) you selected.

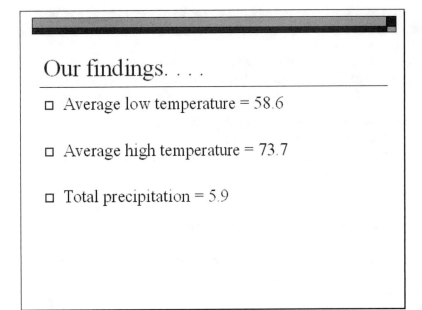

Our findings. . . .

□ Average low temperature = 58.6

□ Average high temperature = 73.7

□ Total precipitation = 5.9

Figure 4.51
Complete slide

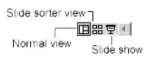

Figure 4.52
View options

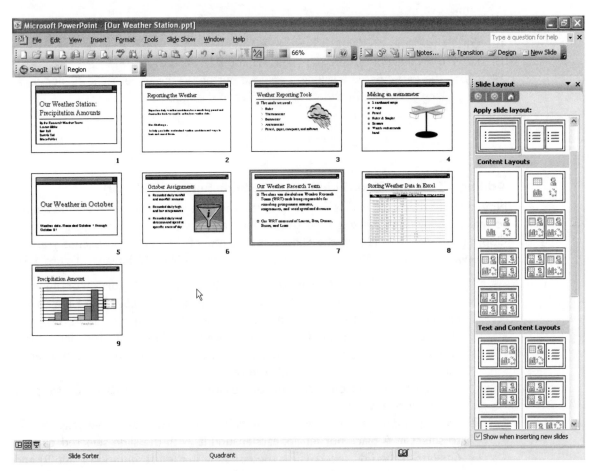

Figure 4.53
Slide Sorter view

3. There are now 10 slides, 2 of which are duplicates, slides 7 and 10. Change the text on the 10th slide. Double-click it to exit the Slide Sorter and return to the Normal view.

4. Slide 10's title box has text in it that can be replaced with *Our findings . . . .* To replace the text, click on the Title box to select it. A line pattern border appears around the box. Click on the border again and it changes to a dot pattern. Press the Delete key and the text changes to *Click to add title.* Type the new title, *Our findings . . . .*

5. To enter bullet items, click the bullet list textbox to select it. A line pattern border appears around the box. Click on the border again and it changes to a dot pattern. Press the Delete key and the text changes to *Click to add text.* Type a new list by entering the following items:
   - *Average low temperature = 58.6*
   - *Average high temperature = 73.7*
   - *Total precipitation = 5.9*

6. Select the bullet list textbox. Choose *Line Spacing* from the Format menu. In the Line Spacing box, enter *1* in the *After paragraph* box and select *Lines.* Click *OK.*

Adding a Title, Text, and Content Slide (Slide 11)

To complete the presentation, add one more slide. Again, use the Slide Sorter to copy and paste a slide.

1. Click the Slide Sorter View button to enter the Slide Sorter.

2. Click a Title, Text, and Content slide (e.g., slide 4) to select it. A black border appears around it. With the slide selected, choose *Copy* from the Edit menu. Click the last slide in the presentation (slide 10) and select *Paste* from the Edit menu. The 11th slide appears.

3. To change the text on the slide, double-click slide 11 to exit the Slide Sorter and return to the Normal view. The slide you create will look like the screen shown in Figure 4.54.

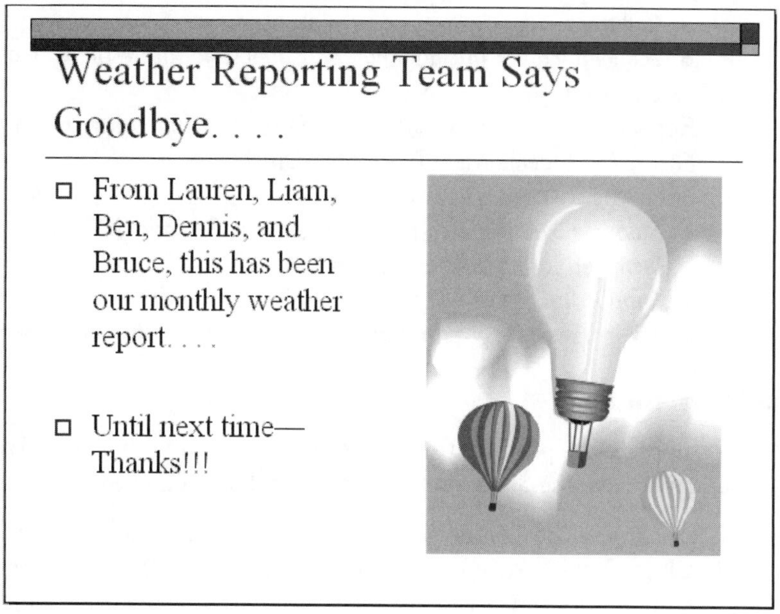

Figure 4.54
Completed slide

4. Replace the text in title textbox with *Weather Reporting Team Says Goodbye . . . .*
5. Enter the bullet items. Click the bullet list textbox to select it. A line pattern border appears around the box. Click on the border again and it changes to a dot pattern. Press the Delete key and the text changes to *Click to add text.* Type the new list. Enter the following items:
   - *From Lauren, Liam, Ben, Dennis and Bruce, this has been our monthly weather report . . . .*
   - *Until next time—Thanks!!!*
6. Delete the existing clip art image. Click it to select it and then press the Delete key. Add clip art representative of the topic and position it in a desired location.

LET ME TRY

Let's continue creating the school board presentation by adding two slides with a Title and Text layout and one slide with a Title, Text, and Content layout.

Title and Text Slides

1. Because we already have a slide (slide 6) with a Title and Text layout, use the Slide Sorter to copy it and paste it. Because we need two slides with this layout, paste the copied slide twice. Paste the slides after the last slide (slide 7). The presentation now has nine slides.
2. In the Slide Sorter, double-click slide 8 to return to the Normal view. Click on slide 8's Title box to select it. Delete the existing text and type: *The Five New Performance Standards Are:.*
3. Click the bullet list textbox to select it. Delete the existing text and enter the following items:
   - *Quantitative and scientific reasoning*
   - *Communication (including a culminating project)*
   - *Citizenship (including a service learning component)*
   - *Culture*
   - *School-to-career (including an education and future plans and a field experience)*
4. Add clip art.
5. Repeat these steps for slide nine. Enter the following title: *What Will Be Done to Ensure All Students Meet These Standards?*
6. Enter the following list items:
   - *Students who perform poorly on the 4th, 7th, and 10th grade WASL exams will be identified for additional support.*
   - *Support programs will exist in K–12.*
   - *Students will be given multiple chances to show they can meet the standards.*

Title, Text, and Content Slide

To complete the presentation, add one more slide with a Title, Text, and Content layout. Again, use the Slide Sorter to copy and paste a slide.

7. Click the Slide Sorter View button to enter the Slide Sorter.
8. Click a Title, Text, and Content slide (e.g., slide 4) to select it. Copy the slide and paste it after the last slide.
9. Replace the text in title textbox with *Gradual Phases.*
10. Enter the following bullet items:

- *2005 Communication Requirements*
- *2006 Quantitative and Scientific Reasoning Requirements + Requirements for 2005*
- *2007 Citizenship and Culture Requirements + Requirements for 2006*
- *2008 School-to-Career and Life Skills Requirements + Requirements for 2007*
- *Certificate of Mastery required for Graduation*

Previewing the PowerPoint Presentation in the Slide Show

You can now view the presentation in the Slide Show. Click the Slide Show button located in the lower left portion of the PowerPoint workspace to enter the Slide Show (see Figure 4.52). Advance the slides by clicking the left mouse button. To exit the Slide Show press the Escape (Esc) key or click the right mouse button on the slide and select *End Show* from the menu. Remember that at any point when you are developing the presentation you can view it in the Slide Show.

Saving the Presentation

It is a good idea to save your work frequently. Keep in mind that even though you see your presentation on-screen, it may not be saved. The more often you save your work, the less chance there is of losing a presentation or a portion of it. Any portion of your presentation that you do not save disappears when the computer is turned off.

There are two Save options, *Save* and *Save As,* located in the File menu.

Save

When you create a new presentation and select *Save,* the Save As dialogue box appears (see Figure 4.55), prompting you to determine a location in which to save the file, give the file a name, and specify a file format. When saving a new presentation, you will likely:

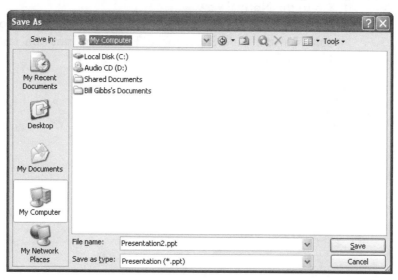

Figure 4.55
Save As box

- Click in the *Save in* box to specify the location to save the presentation.
- Type a name in the *File name* field.
- Assign a file format by clicking in the *Save as type* box.

If you do not provide a name, PowerPoint gives the presentation the name of *Presentation1.ppt.* By default, PowerPoint appends the .ppt extension to the file name and saves the file in a presentation (*.ppt) format. Several other file format options are available, such as .html, .mht, PowerPoint 97, and PowerPoint 95.

Once you have designated a location, name, and format for your presentation, PowerPoint saves all future changes accordingly. If you created a new presentation, added five slides, and saved it in the Office folder with the name *WeatherData.ppt,* a file named *WeatherData.ppt* would appear in the Office folder on your computer's hard drive. If you reopened the presentation, added two additional slides, and clicked *Save,* the two new slides would be automatically saved with the original five and the Save As dialogue box would not appear. The presentation would have seven slides.

1. Because the presentation in this chapter has not yet been saved, select *Save* from the File menu.
2. Click in the *Save in* box on the Save As dialogue box to locate the Office folder or another folder of your choice.
3. Type a name for the presentation in the *File name* box. Use *WeatherStation* for the name. Remember, PowerPoint appends the .ppt extension to the file name, resulting in *WeatherStation.ppt.*
4. Save the file as a PowerPoint show. Click *Save as* on the File menu. Select *PowerPoint show* (.PPS) from the *Save as type* option on the *Save as* box. *View the WeatherStation.pps on the CD-ROM (WeatherData folder) to see an example of the PowerPoint show.*

Save As

The Save As option allows you to save an existing presentation in a different location, under a different file name, or in a different file format.

Adding Slide Transitions

You can add slide transitions, such as wipes, dissolves, and fades, between slides. The effects display when viewing the presentation in the Slide Show.

1. Go to the Normal view.
2. To add a dissolve transition to each slide in the slide show, select *Slide Transition* from the Slide Show menu. The Slide Transition task pane appears (see Figure 4.56).

Figure 4.56
Slide Transition task pane

3. Click a transition (e.g., blinds horizontal, blinds vertical wipe, dissolve, etc.) and then click *Apply to All Slides* at the bottom of the task pane.

4. Set the speed of the transition and a sound by selecting an option under *Modify transition.*

5. Under *Advance slide,* check *On mouse click* so the slide advances and the transition occurs when the mouse button is clicked.

You can also select *Automatically after* to advance slides after a designated number of seconds. Checking this option and specifying a number of seconds sets the transition to occur and the slide to advance automatically after the specified time. This option is useful for creating self-running slide shows. *See the Schoolboard_SelRun.ppt and Schoolboard_SelfRun.pps files on the CD-ROM for examples.* Checking both the *On mouse click* and *Automatically after* (and specifying a time) sets the transition to occur automatically after the preset number of seconds. To advance the slide before the designated time, click the mouse.

6. Set the transition to apply to all of the slides by clicking *Apply to All Slides.* To preview the transitions, click *Play* or *Slide Show* on the Slide Transition task pane.

Saving as a Web Page

Suppose the weather research team wants to share the presentation with parents, teachers, and other students. One way to disseminate the presentation to a large audience is to make it available on the Web. In PowerPoint, you can save a presentation as a Web page (.htm; .html) or as a single file Web page (.mht; .mhtml), both of which can be viewed in a Web browser. *See WeatherStation.htm and WeatherStation.mht on the CD-ROM in the WeatherData folder for examples.*

As a Web Page

The Web Page (.htm; .html) option converts the presentation to HTML and stores all associated files on your computer or on removal disks. PowerPoint appends the .htm extension to the file name. For example, when saving *WeatherStation.ppt* as a Web page, PowerPoint assigns it the name *WeatherStation.htm.* In addition, PowerPoint creates a folder named *WeatherStation_files* that contains the HTML and graphic files associated with the presentation. You will need both the *WeatherStation.htm* and the *WeatherStation_files* folder or the presentation will not display properly on the Web. Thus, when uploading the presentation to the Web, you must upload the .htm file and the folder.

As a Single File Web Page

The Single File Web Page (.mht; .mhtml) option creates a single file with the .mht extension. For example, when saving *WeatherStation.ppt* as a Single File Web Page, PowerPoint assigns it the name *WeatherStation.mht* and it creates one file containing the presentation. The Single File Web Page format is convenient because the presentation is contained in a single file, unlike the Web Page format that creates several files and a folder. However, the Single File Web Page format typically produces a larger file size than the Web Page format.

It is important to note that even though you save a presentation as a Web page or a single file Web page and can view it, the Web-formatted presentation files need to be placed on a computer server for them to be available worldwide. A server is a computer (with server software) set up to perform many different functions. One of its primary uses is to serve applications and files. With respect to the Web, a server permits people from around the world to view Web documents using a browser (e.g., Internet Explorer, Netscape, Mozilla FireFox, and so on). Thus, after saving your presentation as HTML, you need the following to make it available on the Web:

- Access to a Web server that stores and serves your HTML files and graphics. Internet service providers (ISP) provide this service.
- File transfer software, such as Ws_FTP, that transfers the HTML files and graphics from your computer to a server.

Saving the Presentation as a Web Page

1. Select *Save as Web Page* from the File menu.
2. The Save As dialogue box appears (see Figure 4.57). Notice that PowerPoint selects the .mht format by default. Locate the folder in which you want to save the files by clicking in the *Save in* box. In this example, we will save it in a folder titled *WeatherData* located in the Office folder on our computer's C: drive. If you do not have a folder with this name and want to create one, click the Create New Folder button on the top right (third option from right) of the Save As dialogue box. When the *New Folder* box appears, enter a folder name and click *OK*.

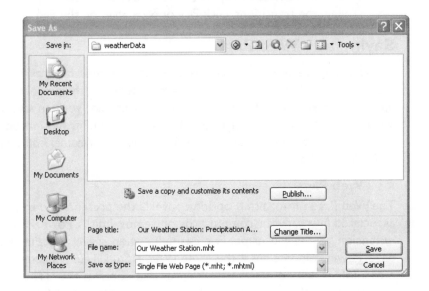

Figure 4.57
Save As box

3. Click the Publish button, which provides several options for saving the presentation, including the following:
   - *Publish what?* Specify the range of slides to be saved and whether to display speaker notes. For this presentation, select *Complete presentation* to save all slides.
   - *Browser support:* HTML files display differently depending on the browser and version. Specify the browser version that is most compatible with users' systems. Click *All browsers listed above*. This option creates a larger file but gives users greater flexibility in terms of the browser they use to view the presentation.
   - *Publish a copy as:* Change the page title by clicking the Change button. Use the *File name* box to specify a location to save the Web-formatted file and assign it a name. The Browse button allows you to specify a location other than the one presented. For this presentation, there is no need to change anything.
4. Click the Publish button and PowerPoint converts the presentation to a Web format. Note that when selecting *Save As. . .* from the File menu, PowerPoint chooses the Single File Web Page (.mht) format by default. Because we clicked

the Publish button on the *Save As* box, PowerPoint saved the presentation as a Web page (.htm) and not as a Single File Web Page.

If you do not want to modify any of the Publish options, click *Save* on the *Save As* box and PowerPoint converts the entire presentation to a Single File Web Page. If you want to save the presentation in a Web Page format, choose *Web Page (*.htm; *.html)* from the *Save as type* section on the *Save As* box.

When saving a presentation as a Web page, it is preferable to remove blank spaces in the file name. The computer server may not recognize file names containing blank spaces. For example, when converting a presentation named *Weather Station.ppt* to a Web page, the file should be saved as *WeatherStation.htm*.

Opening the Presentation in a Web Browser

1. Open a Web browser (e.g., Netscape or Internet Explorer) to view the presentation. In this example, use Internet Explorer. From Explorer's File menu, select *Open* and the *Open* dialogue box appears. If you know the location or path of your presentation, type it into the location box. If not, click *Browse* and the *Microsoft Internet Explorer* dialogue box appears (see Figure 4.58).

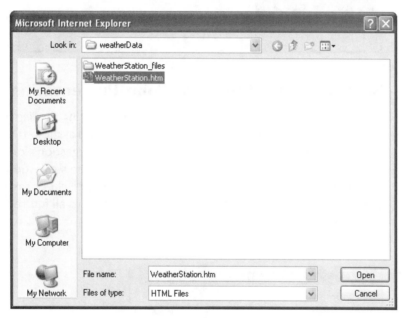

Figure 4.58
Microsoft Internet Explorer box

2. Locate the file on your computer. The file in this example is titled *WeatherStation.htm* and is located on the computer's C: drive within Office in a folder called *WeatherData*. After locating the file, click *Open*. Return to the *Open* dialogue box and click *OK*.

3. The presentation opens in the browser (see Figure 4.59). The left portion of the browser window contains the title of each slide. Clicking on a title displays the corresponding slide in the right portion of the browser window. Clicking Slide Show button at the bottom right of the window displays the presentation in full screen. Keep in mind that the presentation is not on the Web even though you can view it in a Web browser. At this point, you need to transfer the HTML-formatted files to a server to make them available worldwide.

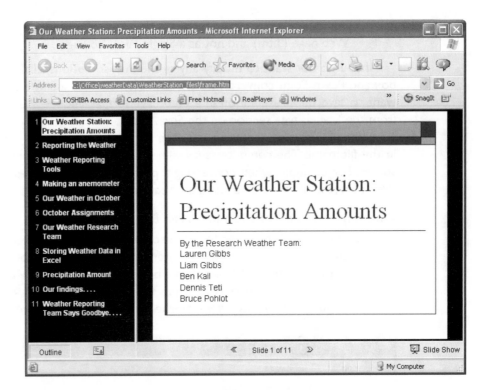

Figure 4.59
Presentation in
Browser window

Spell Checking the PowerPoint Presentation

Check the presentation for spelling errors by selecting *Spelling* from the Tools menu. When PowerPoint does not recognize a word, it displays it in the *Not in Dictionary* box (see Figure 4.60). In most cases, PowerPoint offers suggestions for correcting misspelled words. By clicking *Ignore,* the spell check disregards the suggestion. By clicking *Ignore All,* it disregards all future instances of the word in the spell check session. You can make the suggested change by clicking *Change. Change All* changes all future instances of the word in the spell check session.

Figure 4.60
Spelling box

If the word in the *Not in Dictionary* box is spelled correctly and PowerPoint does not recognize it, you can add it to PowerPoint's dictionary by clicking *Add.* Clicking *Suggest* causes PowerPoint to search the currently selected dictionary for possible suggestions of the correct word. AutoCorrect adds the spelling mistake to a list of errors and automatically corrects it on subsequent occurrences. The Ignore button changes to *Resume* when you exit the spell check session. Clicking *Resume* resumes the session. *Close* closes the Spelling dialogue box.

Printing the PowerPoint Presentation

PowerPoint provides several options for printing, such as slides, handouts, notes, or an outline. For this example, print handouts of the presentation. This is particularly useful if you want students or audience members to take notes while they listen to the presentation.

1. To print, select *Print* from the File menu and the *Print* dialogue box appears (see Figure 4.61).

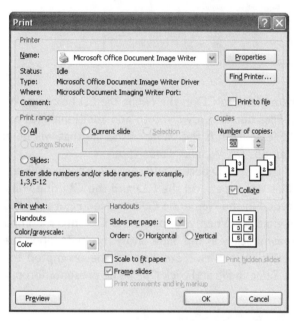

Figure 4.61
Print options

- **Printer Name box:** Selects the printer that will print the handouts.
- **Print range:** Specifies a range of slides to print. For our presentation, select *All*.
- **Copies:** Specifies the number of copies you want to print. If there will be 20 students in class, print 20 copies. Click the upward arrow under *Number of copies* until the number 20 appears. With each mouse click, depending on whether the upward or downward arrow is clicked, the number increases or decreases by increments of 1.
- **Print what:** Specifies whether to print slides, handouts, notes, or the outline. For this presentation, select *Handouts* by clicking the downward arrow. Click *Handouts* from the drop-down list. When the *Handouts* option is selected the *Handouts* area becomes active and you can specify how many slides to print on each page of the handout. Select six slides per page.

2. Check the *Color* and *Frame Slides* options and click *OK*.

Packaging a Presentation on CD

Make an autorun CD of your presentation and share it with colleagues and students. Those who view it do not need to install a Viewer or PowerPoint. PowerPoint 2003's viewer runs on Microsoft Windows 98 or later.

1. Open the presentation that you want to copy to a CD.
2. Select *Package for CD* from the File menu. The *Package for CD* box will be displayed (see Figure 4.62).

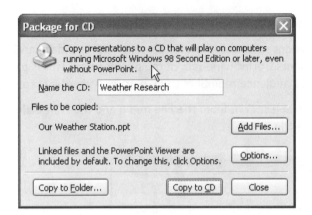

Figure 4.62
Package for CD box

3. Type a name for the CD in the *Name the CD* box (e.g., *Weather Research*).
4. The Add Files button allows you to add additional files to the CD. To the left of the Add Files button is the name of the file that will be copied. In Figure 4.62, the file name is *Our Weather Station.ppt*.
5. Click the Copy to CD button and recording begins. When recoding is complete, several files will appear on the CD and the CD title will correspond to the title you typed in the *Name the CD* box (see Figure 4.63). The *ppviewer.exe* runs the presentation. When you insert the CD into a computer, the presentation opens automatically in the Slide Show mode. To open the presentation manually, double-click *pptviewer.exe*. You will be prompted to select a PowerPoint (.ppt) file. Select a file and click *Open*. The presentation opens in the Slide Show.

Figure 4.63
Content of CD

LET ME TRY

The final Let Me Try activity builds on the other exercises in the chapter. In addition, it provides you with the steps needed to include photographs, video, and animation in your slide show. This Let Me Try is based on a genealogy assignment. It is abbreviated and we will only develop the first two slides of the genealogy assignment, which has a total of seven slides. You can work through an enhanced version of the Let Me Try by accessing *My family Tree.doc* in the Family Tree folder in Let Me Try on the accompanying CD-ROM. You can view a complete version of the slide show by opening *Family Tree.ppt* or *Family Tree.pps* in the Family Tree folder. The Family Tree folder is in PowerPoint inside the Examples folder on the CD-ROM.

Let's suppose that you give your students a genealogy exercise. Students must trace their family heritage back to at least two generations and create a visual presentation about their family. This activity creates the presentation and, in doing so, it integrates audio, video, and photographs into the slide show.

Slide 1: The Opening Slide

When complete, slide 1 will look like boxed Figure 4.1.

Figure 4.1
Complete slide

1. Open a new PowerPoint presentation.
2. Select *Blank slide* from Slide layout on the task pane. The first slide of this presentation has a slightly different appearance than all other slides.
3. We'll begin by placing a photograph in the background. Choose *Background* from the Format menu. The *Background* box appears (see boxed Figure 4.2). Select *Fill effects*

Figure 4.2
Background box

from the drop-down list (see boxed Figure 4.3). The *Fill Effects* box will be displayed. Click the Picture tab and then click the Select Picture button. Choose the *background.png* file located in the FamilyTree_images folder in PowerPoint within Examples. Click the *Lock picture aspect ratio* box and click *OK* (see boxed Figure 4.4). Click *Apply* on the Background box (do not click *Apply to All*). A photograph should appear on the slide.

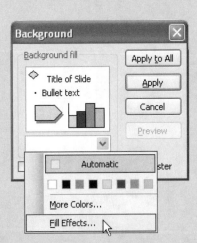

Figure 4.3
Background box

Figure 4.4
Fill effects

4. Insert an image title. Select *Picture* (*From File*) from the Insert menu. Locate *title.png* in the FamilyTree_Images folder and insert it. Position the image at the top left of the screen.

5. We have not named this slide yet. Click the Outline tab in the Outline pane. We will use the slide title to place our name. Type *By Calia Walters*. Set the font type to Verdana, the size to 32, and make the text bold (see boxed Figure 4.5). Click on the textbox to select it. Select *More Colors* from the Font Color button on the drawing toolbar. Click the Custom tab and set the colors to following values: Red—111, Green—105, and Blue—61. Click *OK*.

6. Now we will add two objects. Click the Rectangle tool on the Draw menu. With the rectangle tool selected, create a rectangle about 1.5 inches by 1.5 inches.

7. Right-click the rectangle and select *Format Autoshape* from the drop-down menu. Click the Colors and Lines tab.

In the drop-down menu to the right of *Color:* choose *Fill Effects. . . .* In the *Fill Effects* box, click the Picture tab and then *Select Picture*. Locate the *background.png* image again and insert it. Check the *Lock picture aspect ratio* and the *Rotate fill effect with shape*. Click *OK*.

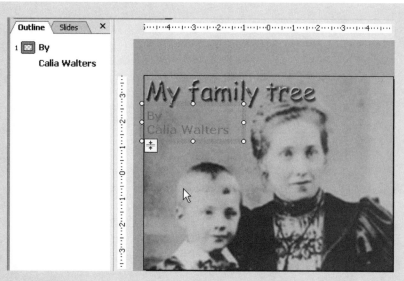

Figure 4.5
Title

8. Set the Transparency to 60%.
9. Under the Line section of the *Format Autoshape* box, select black for the color and select the thinnest line style (see boxed Figure 4.6). Click *OK*.

Figure 4.6
Colors

10. The rectangle should be selected and a green dot should appear at the top. Move the cursor over the green dot and rotate the rectangle to the left.
11. Repeat this procedure two more times. First, create a rectangle and insert the *letter.jpg* file. Set its transparency to 60%. Next, create another rectangle and insert the *girl.png* file. Set its transparency to 84%. After you have inserted the *girl.png* file, rotate it slightly to the left.
12. Finally, select *Curved Right Arrow* from *Block Arrows* in *Authoshapes* on the drawing toolbar (see boxed Figure 4.7).

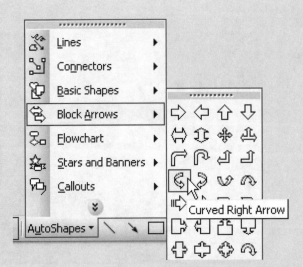

Figure 4.7
Curved Block
Arrow

Drag the arrow across the screen and then rotate it to the left. Refer to boxed Figure 4.1 to see how to position the arrow. In boxed Figure 4.1, the curve arrow extends across the slide. Right-click on the arrow and click the Color and Lines tab from *Format Authoshape*. Click *More Color* from the drop-down menu to the right of *Color:*. Click the Custom tab on the *Colors* box (see boxed Figure 4.8). Select *RGB* for color mode and enter the following values: Red—111, Green—105, and Blue—61. Click *OK*.

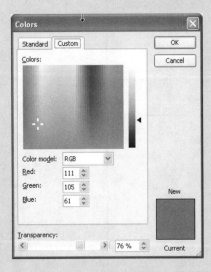

Figure 4.8
Custom color

13. Set the Transparency to 76% and set Line Color to *No Line*. Click *OK*.

Slide 2: Images and Video

14. Create a new slide. Select a blank slide from the Slide layout on the task pane.
15. Select *Slide design* and locate the *Texture.pot* design template.
16. Click *Color Schemes* on the task pane. At the bottom of the task pane, click *Edit Color Scheme* and the *Edit Color Scheme* box appears. Click the *Background* box and then click *Change color*.

17. On the *Background Color* box, click the Custom tab. Select *RGB* for color mode and enter the following values: Red—111, Green—105, and Blue—61. Click *OK* and then click *Apply*. The Texture background should now appear tan.

18. Insert an image title. Select *Picture* (*From File*) from the Insert menu. Locate *title.png* in the FamilyTree_Images folder and insert it. Position the image at the top left of the screen. Alternatively, you can go to slide 1 and copy it and then paste it on slide 2.

19. Because this slide show is about a student's family tree, we'll insert a drawing of a tree. Select *Picture* (*From File*) from the Insert menu. Locate *tree.png* in the FamilyTree_Images folder and insert it. The image extends beyond the dimensions of the screen. Position the cursor over the bottom right or left sizing handle and while pressing the Control key down, drag the sizing handle up and it resizes proportionally. Position the drawing in the middle of the screen.

20. With the drawing selected, choose *Send to Back* from the *Order* item on the drawing toolbar.

21. Go to slide 1 and copy the *Curved Right Arrow* and paste it on slide 2.

22. Next we will insert seven images to place on the family tree. Select *Picture* (*From File*) from the Insert menu. Locate the following image files in the FamilyTree_Images folder and insert them. Place the images around the tree.

   - *grandParentD.png*
   - *grndParentM.png*
   - *ggparentD.png*
   - *ggparentM1.png*
   - *ggparentM2.png*
   - *Mom.png*
   - *Parents.png*

23. Resize each image by selecting it and pressing the Control key while dragging the sizing handle.

Video

24. Next we'll insert a video. Select *Movie* (*From File*) from the *Movie and Sounds* item on the Insert menu. Locate the *Family.avi* file in the FamilyTree_Images folder. When inserting the movie, a prompt appears. Click *Automatically*. Position the video on the right side of the tree. To see where to position the video, open *Family Tree.ppt* or *Family Tree.pps* on the CD-ROM.

25. We have not named this slide yet. Click the Outline tab in the Outline pane. We will use the slide title to place our name. Type *My Family*. Set the font type to Verdana, the size to 48, and make the text bold. Click on the textbox to select it. Select *More Colors* from the Font Color button on the drawing toolbar. Click the Custom tab and set the colors to following values: Red—111, Green—105, and Blue—61. Click *OK*.

26. Rotate the text. With the textbox selected, select *Free Rotate* from the *Rotate or Flip* item on the Draw menu. Green dots will appear around the textbox. Position the cursor over the box and then drag and the text will rotate.

27. The first two slides of the My Family Tree activity are complete. You may continue to work on this activity by opening the *My family Tree.doc* on the CD-ROM.

A CHALLEGNE USING POWERPOINT 2003

For those who would like a challenge beyond the Let Me Try activities presented in this chapter, try the following exercises:

1. Have students create a genealogy presentation that includes various font types and styles, design templates, and clip art that complement the older-style photographs that students scan and include in the presentation. The presentations should depict at least one generation beginning with the most recent generation.

2. Have students present a book report on *Charlotte's Web*. The presentation should include photographs or clip art of all the animals depicted in the book.

3. For a science project, have students make an anemometer. While making this device, students should document the process with a camera and notes. Compile the notes and photographs in a PowerPoint presentation and present it to the class. The presentation may also include video of the anemometer rotating.

4. Create a class or school presentation portfolio. Have students collect photographs, write stories and poems, and create drawings representative of their positive feelings and attitudes about the class or school. Incorporate the photographs, stories, drawings, and so forth into a self-running presentation displayed in public areas (e.g., school lounge). The presentation may also include audio and video segments of school activities, students, and teachers.

5. Create an art exhibit presentation. Scan students' drawings and artwork into a PowerPoint presentation. Save the presentation as a Web page and distribute it on the Web for parents, teachers, and classmates to view.

6. Assign a design template and give a background color to only one slide in the presentation.

7. Assign a design template to a presentation and assign a different template to one slide.

8. Create a five-slide presentation that includes linked action buttons.

9. Create a slide that imports a chart created in Excel.

TYING IT ALL TOGETHER

This chapter presents many fundamentals to help you get started with PowerPoint. We created a presentation consisting of 11 slides with varying layouts. The slides contained text, clip art, and a chart. We saved the presentation in presentation (.ppt) and Web (.htm; .mht) formats and printed handouts. In addition, we copied the presentation to a CD-ROM.

5 EXCEL 2003

CHAPTER OUTLINE

LEARNING OBJECTIVES

At the completion of this chapter you will be able to:

- Start Excel and create a new workbook suitable for use in a variety of student learning activities
- Navigate the Excel workspace
- Add, modify, and manipulate data in a worksheet
- Chart worksheet data
- Add worksheets to a workbook
- Add formulas and functions in a worksheet
- Save a workbook
- Save workbooks as HyperText Markup Language (HTML) documents and add interactivity
- Print a workbook

TECHNICAL TERMS

The following are terms that you will encounter in the chapter and with which you will become familiar:

Workbook	**Formula**
Worksheet	**Function**
Cell	**Relative cell reference**

CHAPTER OVERVIEW

This chapter provides an introduction to Excel 2003. It focuses on Excel fundamentals and how to apply them to a variety of learning activities. The chapter's Show Me section presents instructions on how to use many of Excel's tools to create workbooks and edit and manipulate data in worksheets. Several Let Me Try student-oriented exercises give specific examples and step-by-step instructions for using Excel to accomplish a variety of learning tasks. Studying the chapter contents and working through the Let Me Try exercises will enable you to create workbooks suitable for many classroom learning activities.

How Teachers and Students Might Use Excel 2003

Teacher Production of Materials

Instruction/Learning	Classroom Management
Create an electronic grade book	Create inventory sheet for classroom equipment and materials
Create record keeping logs for students	Create budget sheets for classroom purchases
Create project work logs for students	Create worksheet to perform comparative analyses of student performance from year to year

Student Production of Materials

Instruction/Learning
Create worksheets that calculate travel costs to a country or state being studied
Create Web pages for a school weather station with which students from other schools can submit weather data.
Create a data collection and analysis worksheet with which students collect data on a particular topic (e.g., the television viewing habits of classmates) and perform comparative analyses

About Excel

Excel is a tool that you and your students can use to record, organize, and analyze information. With Excel you can perform mathematical calculations, sort data, and produce charts and graphs to visually represent information, among other things.

As you become familiar with Excel, you will come to realize the use of this application for many student learning and classroom management activities. Teachers can create Excel workbooks that contain information about student learning progress or they can create electronic grade books for entering and calculating student performance scores. In addition, they can create worksheets to record and maintain information about classroom equipment and supply costs.

Students can use Excel as an electronic data recorder to help them collect, record, and analyze information and data sets. They can manage projects with it. When given an assignment that requires a team effort, students can log project details and progress to ensure that the team is on task and on schedule. Suppose your students set up a school weather station to record local weather data throughout the school year. They use Excel worksheets to make daily entries of temperatures, wind speeds, precipitation, and barometric pressures for specific time periods. At the end of each month, students graph their data to visually depict the weather patterns that occurred during the month and present their findings to the class. Their worksheets include statistical charts and graphs, and photographs or videos of weather conditions to help enrich the presentations.

Using Excel, students can save their weather data in a HyperText Markup Language (HTML) format and place it on the Web to share with other students locally and around the world. They can set up an interactive Web-based worksheet, enabling students at other schools to enter local weather data. For example, several school weather stations could be set up across the county and, using a Web browser, students at each school could enter local weather data. The worksheet would calculate average wind speeds, temperature and precipitation levels, and so forth for each station, enabling all the schools to monitor and compare local weather conditions with those of remote stations.

These are only a few applications of Excel. As you become familiar with it, you are likely to find innovative ways to incorporate it into your classroom management and student learning activities.

Working with Excel

The primary purpose of this chapter is to introduce fundamental components and features of Excel so that you may use them in productive ways. To accomplish this objective, we present several examples throughout the chapter. Although the examples are specific, the steps and procedures they present for developing workbooks and worksheets are generic and applicable to a variety of classroom management tasks and learning activities. As you work through the chapter's content, substitute our examples with your own. *In addition, you can locate files that correspond to the chapter activities on the CD-ROM in the Excel folder under* Examples. *Additional Let Me Try activities can be found on the CD-ROM in the Let Me Try Exercises folder.*

A Word About the Excel Workspace

Before we create a workbook and corresponding worksheets, it is important to examine the Excel workspace, including the screen layout, functions, and tools. When you open Excel, it presents a new blank document, referred to as a workbook. Figure 5.1 depicts a new workbook. The main menu bar and the standard and formatting toolbars, which contain functions and tools to assist you with entering, modifying, and analyzing data, are located in the top portion of the workbook. Although the toolbars are often positioned at the top of the screen, they can be moved. With a few exceptions, the options on the main menu bar and standard and formatting toolbars are the same as those in other Office applications. You may notice, for example, that except for the *Data* item, the main menu bar is almost identical to the menu bar in Word and PowerPoint. On the standard toolbar, the Format Numerical Data buttons are unique to Excel. These five options include AutoSum, Insert Hyperlink, Sort Ascending, Sort Descending, and Chart Wizard. AutoSum automatically sums columns or rows; Insert Hyperlink inserts a hyperlink within a workbook; Sort Ascending and Descending sort data accordingly; and the Chart Wizard is designed to assist you with making charts and graphs.

The formatting toolbar has six unique options: Merge and Center, Currency Style, Percent Style, Comma Style, Increase Decimal, and Decrease Decimal (see Figure 5.1). The Merge and Center option combines multiple cells into a single cell and aligns the cell's contents. The Currency Style option sets the cell format to a dollar value. Percent Style sets the cell value to a percentage. The Comma Style option sets the cell value to a number with a decimal point. Finally, Increase and Decrease Decimal specify the number of decimal points in a cell value.

Below the menu and toolbars is the worksheet area where you will perform most of your data entry, modification, and analysis. This is also referred to as the Normal view.

A new workbook is made up of three blank worksheets or sheets. When the workbook opens, Sheet 1 appears foremost on the screen with Sheets 2 and 3 layered behind

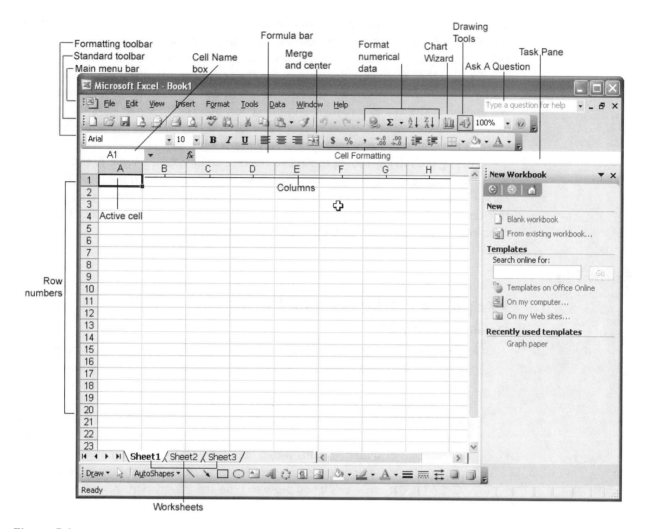

Figure 5.1
The Excel workspace

it. Each worksheet contains column and row headings, cells, gridlines, worksheet tabs, and scroll bars. Excel labels columns with letters (e.g., A, B, C) and rows with numbers. Columns extend vertically down the worksheet and rows extend horizontally. Excel designates cell names by the intersection of the column and row. For example, cell A1 is located in the first row (row 1) in column A. When you click inside a cell, its name or cell reference appears in the cell name box. Gridlines separate cells, columns, and rows.

Worksheet tabs and scroll bars are located at the bottom right of the worksheet. The tabs provide easy movement between worksheets. Clicking on a tab moves the selected worksheet to the foreground.

As data sets become large, columns and rows extend beyond the viewing areas of the computer monitor. To see them, scroll using the scroll bars and arrows located to the right of the worksheet. Click or hold the mouse button down on the scroll arrows and the screen moves in the corresponding direction. You may also drag the scroll bar in the desired direction while holding the mouse button down.

Moving About in a Worksheet

There are several ways to move across cells, columns, and rows. When you open a new workbook, cell A1 is active and ready for input. Begin to type and the information appears in the cell, as well as in the formula bar. After typing the information, pressing the

Enter key moves the active cell down one row. Pressing the keyboard arrow keys moves the active cell in the direction corresponding to the arrow key. For instance, if the active cell is A1 and you press the down arrow key, the active cell moves down from A1 to A2.

Pressing the arrow keys does not move the active cell when you are editing a cell's contents. If cell B2 contains a misspelled word, double-click in the cell and the cursor will appear in the cell as a flashing line (insertion point). The arrow keys allow you to move the cursor within the cell so that you may edit the word. To move the active cell when in the Edit mode, you must press the Enter or Tab key.

Pressing the Tab key moves the active cell one column to the right. Pressing the Tab key while holding the Shift key moves the active cell one column to the left. Clicking the cursor in any cell on the worksheet makes that cell active. Clicking and typing in a cell that contains information replaces the cell's contents. Double-clicking in a cell that contains information enables you to edit the cell's contents.

Show Me

Creating a Workbook and Worksheets

Opening Excel 2003

1. To create a workbook and corresponding worksheets, you need to open Excel. Click the Start button on the Windows taskbar. On the Start menu, move the mouse pointer over *All Programs* and the Programs submenu appears. Move the mouse over *Microsoft Office* and the Microsoft Office submenu appears. Click *Microsoft Office Excel 2003* and Excel opens. *Note:* Depending on how you installed Excel, it may be located in a different location on the Start menu. In most cases, it can be found under *All Programs* or under *Programs* within the Microsoft Office folder.

2. An Excel workbook opens, which contains three blank worksheets (see Figure 5.2). Cell A1 is the active cell. If you begin to type, the information appears in cell A1.

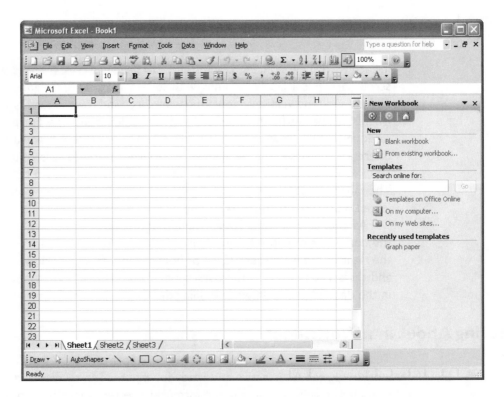

Figure 5.2
Blank worksheet

Entering Data in a Worksheet

Suppose you and your students form a school weather station. Using Excel, you record the daily low and high temperatures and precipitation. You are interested in collecting these data to observe weather patterns. Each month you ask students to analyze the data and present their findings (monthly high and low temperatures and precipitation) to the class. *To view an example of the final workbook, open the weather.xls file on the CD-ROM inside the Excel folder under* Examples.

1. For this example, we will create a simple monthly weather reporting sheet. Check that cell A1 is the active cell, indicated by a black frame around its border. Enter the following, *Weather Data for Charleston, IL: October 2005* into A1 and then press the Enter key. As you type, the text appears in the formula bar. *Weather Data for Charleston, IL: October 2005* appears in cell A1, and A2 becomes the active cell after you press the Enter key. Note that although *Weather Data for Charleston, IL: October 2005* may appear to extend beyond cell A1 to B1, C1, and D1, it is contained only in cell A1 (see Figure 5.3).

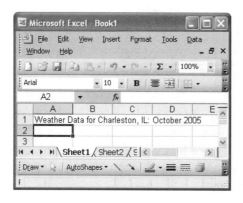

Figure 5.3
Data title

2. Create titles to describe the weather data collected by students. With cell A2 active, type *Day* and then press the Tab key (B2 becomes active). Type *Temperature* in B2 and press the Tab key two times, leaving cell C2 empty. Continue to enter the following data titles beginning in cell D2 and ending in cell G2: *Rain fall (inches), Avg. Low, Avg. High,* and *Total Precipitation.* When complete, your screen should look like Figure 5.4.

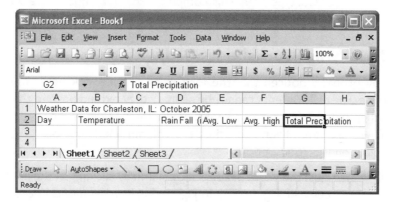

Figure 5.4
Weather data titles

Merge and Center

Before continuing, format the data titles. Formatting helps with entering the data correctly. Adjust the columns and cells so that all the data titles are readable. The main title for this data set is *Weather Data for Charleston, IL: October 2005,* which should extend across columns A through G. To extend this title, use the Merge command.

3. Select cells A1 through G1. Click in cell A1 and, while holding the mouse button down, drag across to cell G1 (see Figure 5.5).

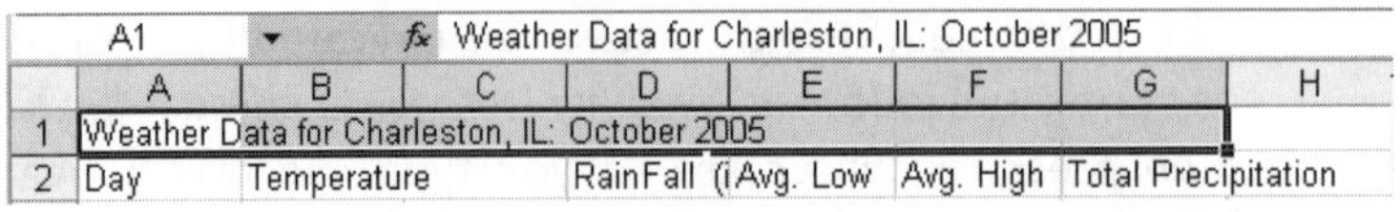

Figure 5.5
Multiple cell selection

	A	B	C	D	E	F	G	H
1	Weather Data for Charleston, IL: October 2005							
2	Day	Temperature		RainFall (i	Avg. Low	Avg. High	Total Precipitation	

A1   *fx* Weather Data for Charleston, IL: October 2005

4. Click the Merge and Center button (see Figure 5.6). The seven cells merge into one and the text becomes centered.

Figure 5.6
Merge and Center
sheet title

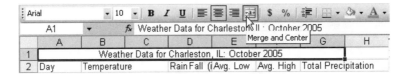

Arial   10   **B** *I* U $ %   A

A1   *fx* Weather Data for Charlestoñ II · October 2005

	A	B	C	D	E	Merge and Center G	H
1	Weather Data for Charleston, IL: October 2005						
2	Day	Temperature		RainFall (i	Avg. Low	Avg. High	Total Precipitation

5. You can merge cells B2 and C2 so that the *Temperature* title appears as a header for the daily low and high temperatures (see Figure 5.7). Select cells B2 and C2. Click in cell B2 and, while holding the mouse button down, drag across to cell C2. Click the Merge and Center button. The two cells merge into one and the text becomes centered.

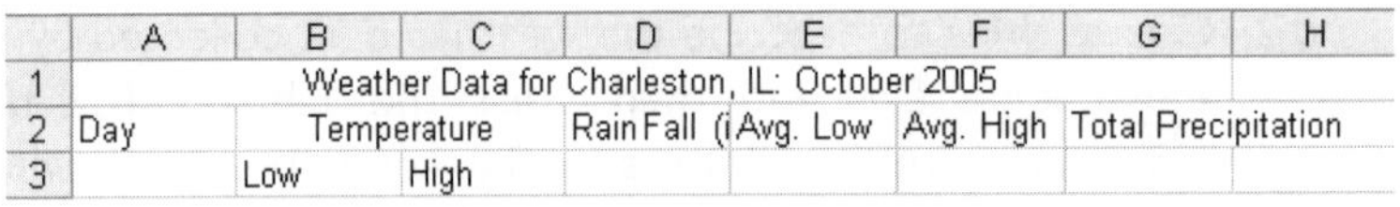

Figure 5.7
Merger and Center
subtitle

	A	B	C	D	E	F	G	H
1		Weather Data for Charleston, IL: October 2005						
2	Day	Temperature		RainFall (i	Avg. Low	Avg. High	Total Precipitation	
3		Low	High					

6. Create titles to indicate the low and high temperatures for each day of the month. Make cell B3 active by clicking in it. Type *Low,* then press the Tab key. In cell C3, type *High.* This completes the titles, but before you can enter the data, you need to do more formatting.

Modifying Worksheets: Adjusting Columns and Rows

You probably noticed that the formatting of the worksheet contents appears incomplete. The cell contents cannot be seen or they extend beyond the cell borders and into other cells. In this section, we will adjust the column widths and format the data titles. There are several ways to adjust the column width. For our purposes, Excel's AutoFit Selection is a good option.

1. Adjust the width of a specific column by clicking on the column header or within a cell (see Figure 5.8). In Figure 5.8, *Rain fall (inches)* does not fit in the cell D2 and needs adjusting. Click in cell D2.

Figure 5.8
Adjust column
width

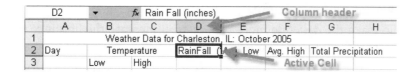

	A	B	C	D	E	F	G	H
1			Weather Data for Charleston, IL: October 2005					
2	Day		Temperature	RainFall (A	Low	Avg. High	Total Precipitation	
3		Low	High					

2. Choose *Column* from the Format menu and select *AutoFit Selection* (see Figure 5.9). The column width adjusts to fit the cell content.

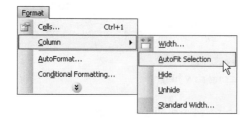

Figure 5.9
AutoFit Selection

3. Alternatively, you could format all the column titles simultaneously by clicking cell A2 and, while holding the mouse button down, dragging across to the G2 header. The columns are highlighted, or selected, as you drag across them (see Figure 5.10). With the column titles selected, choose *Column* from the Format menu; then select *AutoFit Selection*. The columns adjust to the data. If the columns are still selected, deselect them by clicking anywhere on the worksheet.

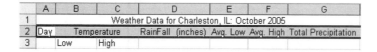

Figure 5.10
Column selection

	A	B	C	D	E	F	G
1			Weather Data for Charleston, IL: October 2005				
2	Day		Temperature	RainFall (inches)	Avg. Low	Avg. High	Total Precipitation
3		Low	High				

Notice on the Column submenu (see Figure 5.9) that there are four items in addition to AutoFit Selection: *Width, Hide, Unhide,* and *Standard Width.* Each of the items is described briefly as follows:

Width: Displays a box in which you can enter a dimension for the column width.

Hide: Hides a column, row, or selected set of columns or rows from view. This option may be useful when you want to view only specific segments of your data set.

Unhide: Reveals columns or rows that have been hidden using the Hide option. To reveal a hidden column or row, select the columns to the left and right of the hidden column and choose *Unhide*. For example, if you hide column B from view, you need to select columns A and C, then choose *Unhide* to reveal column B. To reveal rows, select the rows above and below the hidden row and choose *Unhide*.

Standard Width: Allows you to define a standard width for all columns in a worksheet. However, the standard width will not apply to columns that have been adjusted previously. To set a standard width, choose *Columns* from the Format menu and select the *Standard Width* submenu item. The Standard Width box appears in which you can specify a width value and then click *OK*. All previously unadjusted columns are set to the designated width.

Adjusting Row Height

To make the data title more pronounced, increase the height of the second row to set it apart from the main title and weather data.

4. Click in any cell of row 2. Select *Row* from the Format menu and then choose *Height*. The *Row Height* box appears (see Figure 5.11). Enter a row height of 24 and click *OK*. The row height increases across all columns (see Figure 5.12).

	A	B	C	D	E	F	G	
1				Weather Data for Charleston, IL: October 2005				
2	Day	Temperature		RainFall (inches)	Avg. Low	Avg. High	Total Precipitation	
3		Low	High					

Figure 5.11
Set row height

Figure 5.12
Increasing row height

Notice that the titles are aligned at the bottom of row 2. To align the text in the center of row 2, click the row number to select row 2. Select *Cells* from the Format menu and the *Format Cells* box appears (see Figure 5.13). Click the *Alignment* tab. Under *Vertical* select *Center,* then click *OK*. The text appears in the center of row 2 (see Figure 5.14).

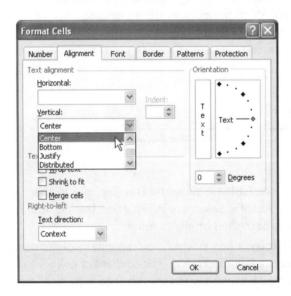

Figure 5.13
Format Cells box

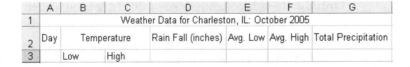

	A	B	C	D	E	F	G
1				Weather Data for Charleston, IL: October 2005			
2	Day	Temperature		Rain Fall (inches)	Avg. Low	Avg. High	Total Precipitation
3		Low	High				

Figure 5.14
Center aligned

You can now continue to enter data. For this example, enter the day of the month, temperatures (low and high), and rainfall in inches for each day, even though your students will likely record this information daily. The average temperature and total precipitation will be handled later.

5. Column A will contain dates corresponding to each day of the month. Format the column for this data type. Select column A by clicking on the column header. Choose *Cells* from the Format menu and the *Format Cells* box appears (see Figure 5.15). Click the Number tab, select *Date* from the *Category* area, choose a date type or the way you want the date to appear, and then click *OK*.

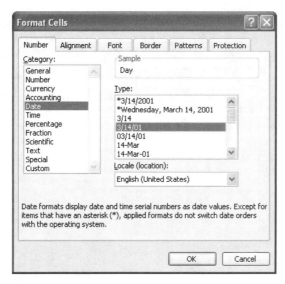

Figure 5.15
Format Cells box

6. Click in cell A4 and type the first date, *10/01/05*. You may notice an #### error after typing the date, which indicates that the column width is too narrow. If this occurs, select column A by clicking on the column header, then choose *Column* from the Format menu, and select *AutoFit Selection*. Your screen should look like Figure 5.16.

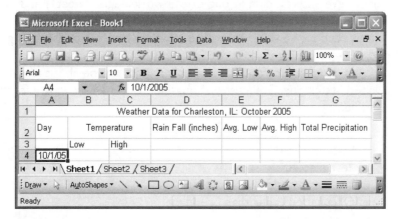

Figure 5.16
Enter data

7. Press the Tab key to accept the data, then cell B4 becomes active. Type the low temperature for the day and press the Tab key to make cell C4 active. Type the high temperature for the day. Press the Tab key again to make cell D4 active and type the amount of rainfall (in inches) for that day. Press the Enter key to move down to the next row. *Note:* Format cells containing temperatures and precipitation amount as *General*. Select the range of cells or columns to be formatted. From the Format menu, click the Number tab and under *Category* select *General*.

Enter a date, low and high temperatures, and rainfall amounts for each day of the month. Remember, press the Tab key to move to a cell in the adjacent column on the right. When you are finished, the worksheet should look similar to Figure 5.17.

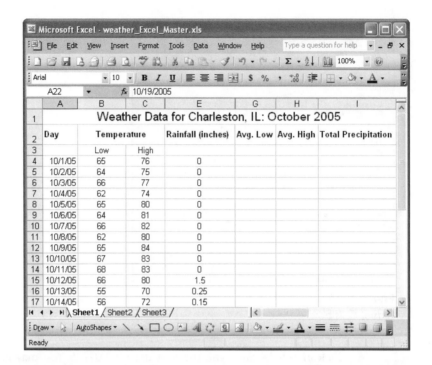

Figure 5.17
Completed worksheet

LET ME TRY

So far, we have opened Excel and created a new workbook that contains three worksheets. We entered data in one of the worksheets (Sheet1) and navigated around it using the Enter, Tab, and arrow keys. Finally, we modified worksheet columns and rows. In this section, we will incorporate what we have learned by using a new workbook example pertaining to the presidents of the United States.

Ask students to research and collect information about all the presidents of the United States. Specifically, they should find out the following information about each president:

- Month and year of birth
- State of birth
- Year elected
- Year term ended as president
- Occupation other than president
- Year of death

Once students collect this information, they can enter it into an Excel workbook for analysis. From the information, students can, among other things, calculate the age of the president when elected, his age at death, the states in which the majority of elected presidents were born, and the most common occupation of presidents other than the presidency. To view an example of a final workbook, open "presidents_Master.XLS" on the CD.

Creating a Presidential Information Workbook

1. Open Excell 2003.
2. When you open Excel, cell A1 is the active cell. Type *Presidential Information* in cell A1.

3. After typing *Presidential Information,* click anywhere outside cell A1 to deselect it and to exit the cell's text-editing mode. Now, select cells A1 through H1 and then click the Merge and Center button to center the title.

4. If cell A1 is not active, click it. From the *Format* menu, select *Row* and then *Height.* Type *24* in the *Row Height* box and click *OK.*

5. With cell A1 active, select *Cells* from the Format menu. Click the Alignment tab. Set the Horizontal and Vertical text alignment to *Center* and then click *OK.*

6. Click in cell A2 to make it active. Type the word *Name* for the column title. Press the Tab key to accept the data and move the active cell to B2 and type *Birth Month.*

7. Type the following six titles: *Birth, Death, Year Elected, Term Ended, Occupation,* and *State of Birth* in cells C2, D2, E2, F2, G2, and H2, respectively.

8. Click cell A3 to make it active and type *George Washington.* Press the Tab key to move to cell B3 and type *February* for his birth month. Enter the following information for George Washington in each of the corresponding cells:

   - Cell C3, *Birth:*   *1732*
   - Cell D3, *Death:*   *1799*
   - Cell E3, *Year Elected:*   *1789*
   - Cell F3, *Term Ended:*   *1797*
   - Cell G3, *Occupation:*   *Planter, Soldier*
   - Cell H3, *State of Birth:*   *Virginia* (Grolier, 1994)

9. After entering Washington's state of birth, Virginia, in cell H3, click in cell A4 to make it active. Alternatively, you can press the Enter key, which should make cell H4 active, and then press the left arrow key seven times until you reach cell A4.

10. Begin entering information about the next president, John Adams, and continue for as many presidents as you'd like.

11. Select *Save* from the File menu. Assign the workbook a name and designate a location to save it. Click the Save button. Saving workbooks is discussed in more detail in the "Saving and Naming a Workbook" section of this chapter.

Modifying Worksheets: Formatting Text

In this section, we return to our weather data and adjust the text of the worksheet by modifying the font type, size, style, and color of cell contents.

1. Click in cell A1. Set the font type to Arial by clicking the *Font* box (see Figure 5.18) on the formatting toolbar and selecting *Arial.*

Figure 5.18
Font type

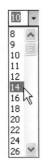

Figure 5.19
Font sizes

2. Set the font size 14 by clicking the *Font Size* box (see Figure 5.19) on the formatting toolbar and selecting *14*. The result of the font type and size changes can be seen in Figure 5.20.

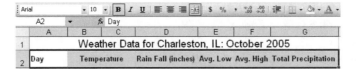

Figure 5.20
Adjusted font type and size

3. Adjust the font style of the titles. Select cells A2 through G2 by clicking in cell A2 and, while holding the mouse button down, dragging to cell G2 (see Figure 5.21).

Figure 5.21
Set font styles to
multiple cells

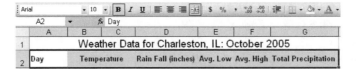

4. Click the Bold button on the formatting toolbar. The Bold button appears as a **B** on the formatting toolbar.
5. After setting the style to Bold, you may notice that portions of the titles in columns D through G do not display. To adjust this, select cells D2 through G2 and then select *Columns* and *AutoFit Selection* from the Format menu (see Figure 5.22).

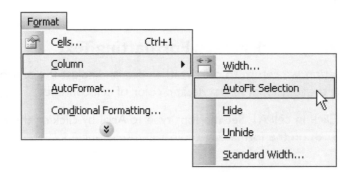

Figure 5.22
AutoFit Selection

6. You can now assign a Fill Color of black to row 2 and set the font color to white. On the left side of the worksheet, click the row heading number 2, which represents the second row. Clicking 2 selects the entire row. Alternatively, you can select cells A2 through G2 by dragging across them.
7. On the formatting toolbar, click the down arrow located on the right side of the Fill Color tool. A palette of color choices displays (see Figure 5.23). Click on the black square and the row fill color changes to black.

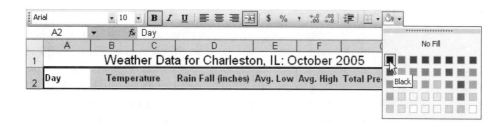

Figure 5.23
Row fill color

8. Because the fill color and font color of row 2 are both set to black, you cannot see the text titles (*Day, Temperature, Rainfall (inches), Avg. Low, Avg. High, Total Precipitation*). With row 2 selected, click the down arrow located on the right side of the font color tool. The color choices palette will display (see Figure 5.24). Click on the white square and the font color changes to white. Row 2 should now have a black background with white text (see Figure 5.25).

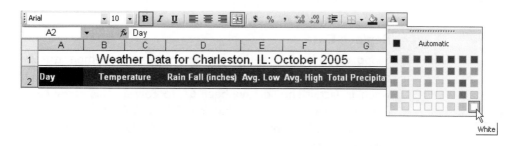

Figure 5.24
Text color

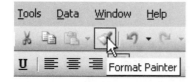

Figure 5.25
Row text and background color

If you prefer, you can apply the same attributes (font type, color, and so on) to the *Low* and *High* titles under *Temperature*. One way to set these attributes is to select cells B3 and C3 and repeat the steps previously presented. Alternatively, using the Format Painter icon (see Figure 5.26), you can apply the attributes of one cell or a group of cells to another cell or range of cells.

Figure 5.26
Format Painter

For example, select cells E2 and F2 and then click the Format Painter icon. Click cell B3 and the attributes of cells E2 and F2 are applied to B3 and C3. Notice that Excel applies the attributes to the same number of cells that you selected prior to clicking the Format Painter icon.

Modifying Worksheets: Editing Data

In this section, you will alter the data entered into the school weather station workbook. Specifically, you will edit the contents of a cell, replace the contents of a cell, and delete data.

Edit Data

1. Suppose one of the titles is misspelled in the school weather station worksheet. Assume that the last column title is spelled *Total Percipitation* instead of *Total Precipitation*. Double-click cell G2, which contains the misspelled title. After double-clicking in the cell, the cursor appears inside the cell as a flashing line, referred to as the *insertion point*. You are now able to edit the text (e.g., select, add, delete, etc.).
2. Select the second and third letters of *Percipitation* (see Figure 5.27) and, with the letters selected, type *re*. Press the Enter or Tab key to accept the changes and move the active cell. You can also edit *Percipitation* on the formula bar.

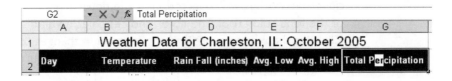

Figure 5.27
Edit cell data

Replace Data

Suppose you inadvertently assigned a wrong low temperature amount for a particular day in the worksheet. You may have entered 23 for the low temperature on October 2 when, in fact, it should have been 64. To correct this error, click on the cell containing the value that needs to be changed. Click cell B5. Type the new temperature of 64. The old value of 23 is replaced with 64. Press the Enter or Tab key to accept the change and move the active cell.

Delete Data

Suppose you mistakenly entered data in the *Avg. Low* and *Avg. High* columns for October 2 and now need to remove it. Click on the cell(s) containing the data you want to delete. Select cells E4 and F4 and press the Delete key. The contents of the cell are removed.

Saving and Naming a Workbook

Before continuing, you need to save your workbook. It is important to save your Excel documents frequently because any unsaved portion of a workbook disappears when you turn the computer off. In this section, we describe naming and saving a workbook. There are three save options on the File menu: *Save, Save As,* and *Save as Web Page*.

Save

When you create a new workbook and then select Save, the *Save As* dialogue box (see Figure 5.28) appears, requesting that you assign the file a location in which to be saved, give the file a name, and specify a file format. When saving a new workbook, you will most likely:

- Click in the *Save in* box to specify the location to save the workbook.
- Type a name in the *File name* field.
- Assign a file format by clicking in the *Save as type* box.

If you do not provide a name, Excel gives the workbook the name of *Book1.xls*. By default, Excel appends the *.xls* extension to the file name and saves the file in a Microsoft Excel workbook (∗.xls) format. A number of formats are available for saving documents, including *Web Page, Microsoft Excel 97–2003, XML,* and *text* (.txt).

Once you have designated a location, name, and format for your workbook, Excel saves all future changes accordingly. For example, if you created a new workbook, added

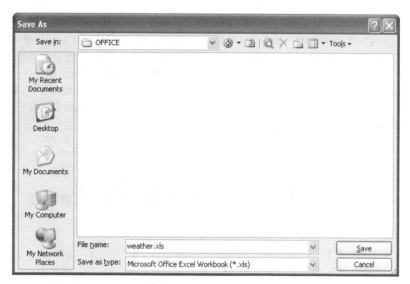

Figure 5.28
Save As box

10 rows and 5 columns of data, and then saved it in the Office folder with the name *weather.xls,* a file named *weather.xls* appears in the Office folder on your computer's hard drive. If you reopened the workbook, added five additional rows of data, and clicked *Save,* the 5 new rows are automatically saved with the original 10 and the *Save As* dialogue box does not appear. The workbook now has a total of 15 rows and 5 columns.

1. Because you have not yet saved the workbook, select *Save* from the File menu.
2. Click in the *Save in* box on the *Save As* dialogue box to locate the Office folder (or select another folder of your choice).
3. Type a name for the workbook in the *File name* box. Use *weather* for the name. Remember, Excel appends the .xls extension to the file name, resulting in *weather .xls.* The document should be saved as a *Microsoft Office Excel Workbook*∗ .xls) file, so be sure that this format type appears in the *Save as type* box. Click *Save.*

Save As

The Save As option allows you to save an existing Excel workbook in a different location, under a different file name, or in a different file format.

Save as Web Page

The *Save as Web Page* option allows you to save an Excel workbook as a Web Page (.htm; .html) or as a Single File Web Page (.mht; .mhtml), both of which can be viewed in a Web browser.

Modifying Worksheets: Inserting Rows and Columns

So far you have created a worksheet to record daily weather data and formatted its appearance. In the following sections, we will expand on this example by adding data to the worksheet and performing calculations.

Suppose that after creating the weather station worksheet, you found that you overlooked a date (October 4) and a column for snowfall. To add the *October 4* data and a *snowfall* column, first insert a row below rows 6 and 7 and then insert a column after *Rainfall (inches).* These actions provide the space to place the previously unrecorded data.

Inserting a Row

When inserting rows, Excel places the newly inserted row above the cursor position or active cell. For example, if the active cell is row 23, the contents of row 23 are pushed down into row 24 and the inserted row becomes row 23.

To insert the *October 4* data, position the cursor within row 7. Select *Rows* from the Insert menu and a new empty row appears (see Figure 5.29). Enter the following data in row 7: *10/4/05, 62, 74, 0*.

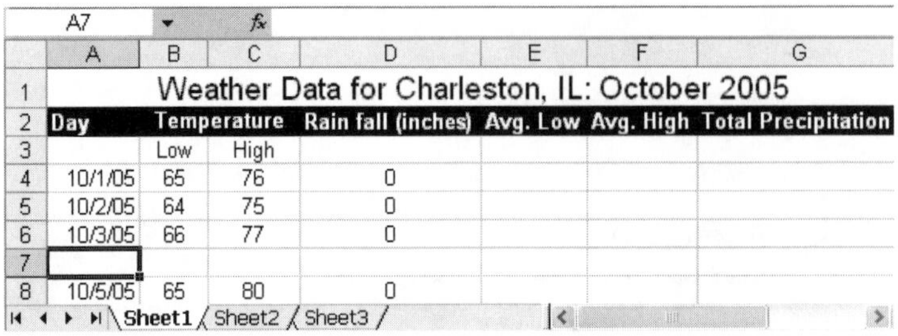

Figure 5.29
Inserting a row

	A	B	C	D	E	F	G
1			Weather Data for Charleston, IL: October 2005				
2	Day	Temperature		Rain fall (inches)	Avg. Low	Avg. High	Total Precipitation
3		Low	High				
4	10/1/05	65	76	0			
5	10/2/05	64	75	0			
6	10/3/05	66	77	0			
7							
8	10/5/05	65	80	0			

Inserting a Column

Insert a column after *Rainfall (inches)* to place the snowfall amounts. When inserting a column, Excel places the newly inserted column to the left of the cursor position or active cell. For example, if the active cell is in column E, the contents of column E are pushed to the right into column F and the inserted column becomes column E.

Click anywhere in column E (Avg. Low). Select *Columns* from the Insert menu and a new empty column appears, in which we can enter snowfall amounts (see Figure 5.30). Add the title *Snowfall (inches)* to cell E2.

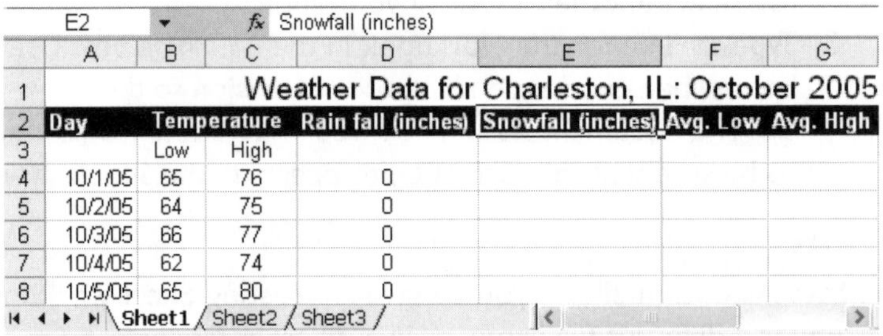

Figure 5.30
Inserting a column

	A	B	C	D	E	F	G
1				Weather Data for Charleston, IL: October 2005			
2	Day	Temperature		Rain fall (inches)	Snowfall (inches)	Avg. Low	Avg. High
3		Low	High				
4	10/1/05	65	76	0			
5	10/2/05	64	75	0			
6	10/3/05	66	77	0			
7	10/4/05	62	74	0			
8	10/5/05	65	80	0			

After inserting a column or row, the Format Painter icon appears and presents cell formatting options. Clicking the down arrow next to the Format Painter icon displays a list of formatting choices (see Figure 5.31). You can format the inserted row or column like the row or column adjacent to it, or you can clear the formatting. For our purposes, select the default option. *Format Same as Above* for a row and *format same as left* for a column.

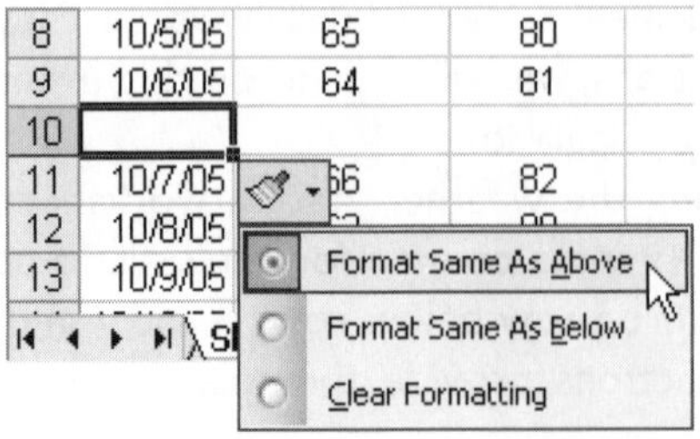

Figure 5.31
Format Painter

8	10/5/05	65	80
9	10/6/05	64	81
10			
11	10/7/05	66	82
12	10/8/05		
13	10/9/05		

- ○ Format Same As Above
- ○ Format Same As Below
- ○ Clear Formatting

Formulas

Excel allows you to write formulas to make calculations. A formula can be a series of numbers, cell references, or names that, when placed in a specific sequence or combination, produce a new value. All formulas start with an equal sign (=). Suppose you want to place the sum of three cells (A1, A2, A3) of data into a new cell, A4. Double-click in cell A4, which activates the formula bar. On the formula bar, type an equal sign (=) and then type the formula *A1+A2+A3* to add the values in the three cells (see Figure 5.32).

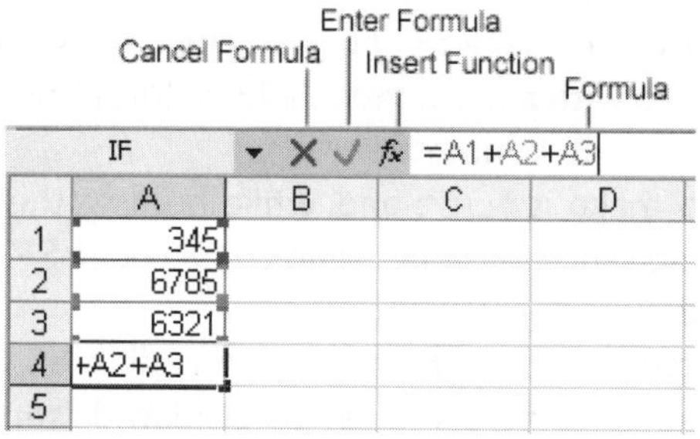

Figure 5.32
Formula bar

This formula adds the contents of cells A1, A2, and A3, and the sum of the cells appears in cell A4. After typing the formula, click the *Enter Formula* option or press the Enter key. You can cancel the formula by clicking the *Cancel Formula* option.

For the weather station example, suppose you want to determine the differences between the low and high temperatures for a particular number of days. To get a cursory look at how many degrees the temperature increased, calculate the differences between the low and high temperatures for the first five days in October.

1. Insert a column to calculate the temperature difference. In the weather station workbook (*weather.xls*), click anywhere in column D. Select *Columns* from the Insert menu and a new empty column appears to calculate the temperature differences (see Figure 5.33). Click in cell D2 and give the column the title of *Degree Change*. Notice that a portion of the title in D2 does not display. To adjust the title, select cell D2, then select *Columns* and *AutoFit Selection* from the Format menu.

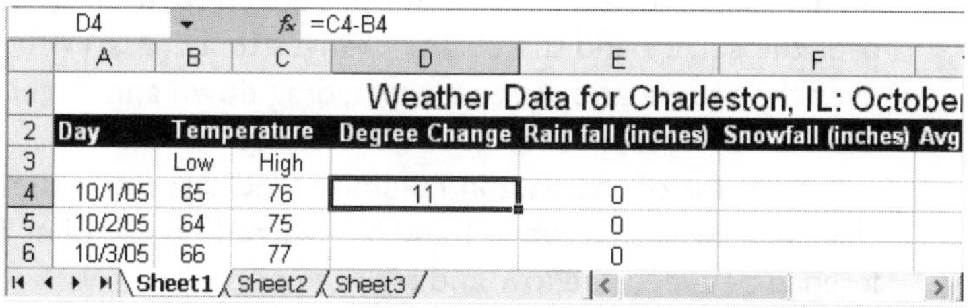

Figure 5.33
Cell formula

2. For this example, we will calculate temperature differences for the first five days of October. Begin by subtracting the low temperature in cell B4 from the high temperature in C4 to get the degree difference.

    Click in the cell that corresponds to *October 1,* which is D4. Type an equal sign (=) followed by C4-B4. Once you type the equal sign, Excel displays the *Formula Cancel* and *Enter* options. Double-clicking in cell D4 makes the Formula options appear automatically. The complete formula should look like the following: *=C4-B4*

3. Click the Enter Formula option or press the Enter key to accept the formula. If the temperatures in cells C4 and B4 in your workbook were 76 and 65 respectively, 11 should appear in cell D4.

Copy and Paste Formulas

You could calculate the temperature differences for October 2 through October 5 by entering a formula for each day. However, a more expedient approach is to copy the formula in cell D4 and paste it for each of the other days.

4. Click in cell D4 to make it active.
5. Click the Copy button or select *Copy* from the Edit menu. Notice that the cell becomes surrounded with a marquee (blinking dots) border to indicate that the computer copied the cell contents.
6. Click in cell D5 to make it active and, while holding the mouse button down, drag to cell D8, which should correspond to October 5. All cells from D5 to D8 should be selected.
7. Click the paste button or select *Paste* from the Edit menu. The formula is pasted in each cell and the calculated values are displayed (see Figure 5.34). Click in each cell of column D and look closely at the formulas. Excel automatically adjusted each cell reference to the appropriate row. So, for example, cell D5 contains the formula =C5-B5, cell D6 contains the formula =C6-B6, and so on. The automatic referencing of cells is referred to as relative addressing.

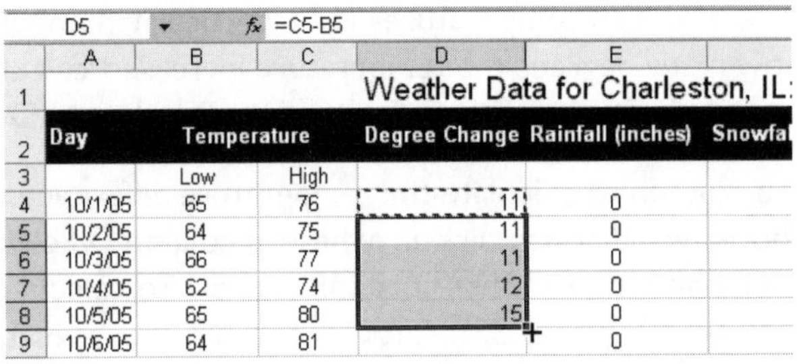

Figure 5.34
Copy and Paste formulas

8. In addition to copying and pasting the formula, you can use the Auto Fill option. Notice in Figure 5.34 that cells D5 through D8 have a black border around them. A small square appears at the bottom right of the border. Pass the mouse over the square and the cursor changes to a cross. With the cursor positioned over the square and set to a cross, drag down and Excel copies the formula of the previous cell, with relative addressing.

A review of the data in column D indicates that the greatest temperature change between October 1 and 5 occurred on October 5, with 15 degrees difference between the low and high temperatures.

Functions

In the previous example, you created a formula (=C4−B4) to calculate the differences between daily low and high temperatures. Excel provides built-in formulas called *functions* that perform calculations. For instance, to find the average temperature difference for October 1 through October 5, you could use the AVERAGE function.

For this example, insert a new row after row 8. You will place the average temperature difference in cell D9. With the new row inserted, click in cell D9 to make it active.

On the Formula bar, click the Insert Function option and the *Insert Function* box appears (see Figure 5.35). This box presents a number of functions that you can use. You can also search for function. Click *AVERAGE* under *Select a function,* then click *OK.*

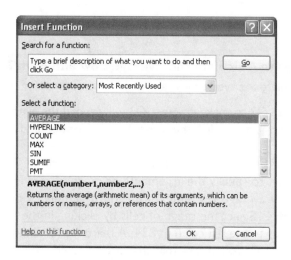

Figure 5.35
Insert Function box

The *Function Arguments* box appears (see Figure 5.36) and requests a defined range of cells for the average. Our cell range is D4 through D8. To define the cell range for the function arguments, click in the beginning cell (D4) and, while holding the mouse down, drag to cell D8. D4:D8 displays in the *Number 1* field of the *Function Arguments* box, indicating that the average of these cells will be calculated. Click *OK.* These steps average the values in cells D4 through D8 by placing the following function in cell D9:

$$=\text{AVERAGE (D4:D8)}$$

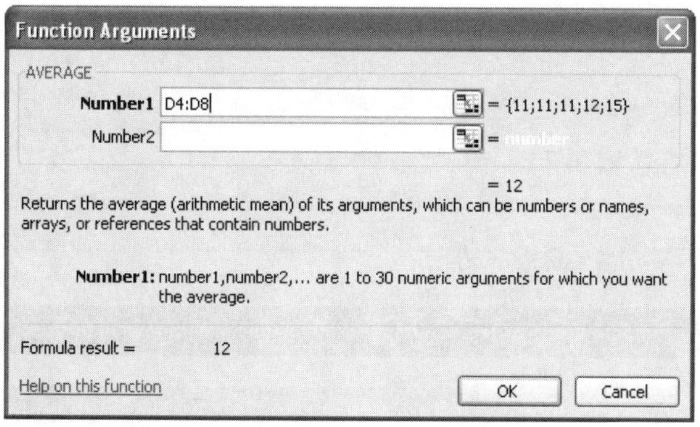

Figure 5.36
Function Arguments
box

The result is 12. The AVERAGE formula is built into Excel and thus we refer to it as a function. Alternatively, you could write your own formula to average the column D values but it would be less efficient to do so. Entering the function = *AVERAGE (D4:D8)* into cell D9 produces the same result as entering the following formula: = *(D4+D5+D6+D7+D8)/5*

Structure of Functions

In Figure 5.37, notice that the structure of the function begins with an equal sign followed by the function name. The function arguments (I4:I18), or the range of cells on which the SUM function is performed, are enclosed in parentheses.

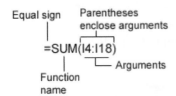

Equal sign   Parentheses
              enclose arguments

=SUM(I4:I18)

              └── Arguments

Function
name

Figure 5.37
Function structure

Using Functions to Calculate the Average Low and High Temperature

You can now calculate the average low and high temperatures for the month of October.

1. Click in cell G3 to make it active. G3 will record the average low temperature.
2. On the Formula bar, click the Insert Formula option and the *Insert Function* box appears.
3. Click *AVERAGE* under *Select a function* and then click *OK*. The *Function Arguments* box appears to specify the arguments or range of cells for the AVERAGE function. For the average low temperature, the argument or cell range is B4 through B34 (B4:B34). Select the range of cells by clicking in the beginning cell (i.e., B4) and dragging to the last cell (i.e., B34). A marquee (blinking dots) border appears around the cells to indicate that they are selected. After selecting the cells, the cell range appears in the *Number 1* field of the *Function Arguments* box (see Figure 5.38). Click *OK* on the *Function Arguments* box.
4. The average low temperature appears in cell G3.
5. To calculate the average high temperature, click in cell H3. Repeat the preceding steps for the high temperature in cells C4 through C34.
6. The average low and high temperatures for October are **58.64516** and **73.741935**, respectively. These cells can be formatted to display only one decimal point. Select cells G3 and H3. Choose *Cell* from the Format menu. Click the Number tab and under *Category* select *Number*. In the *Decimal Places* box type 1 or use the down arrow to decrease the decimal places.

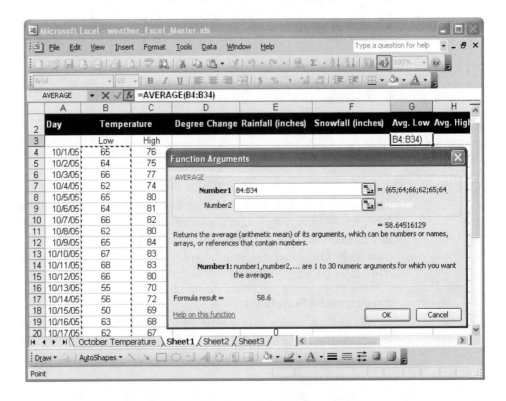

Figure 5.38
Specify arguments

Using Functions to Calculate the Total Precipitation for the Month

You can use the SUM function to calculate the total precipitation for October. Before performing the calculations, suppose that on October 29 the amount of snowfall was 1 inch and on October 31 it was 0.5 inch. In cell F32 enter the value of 1 and in cell F34 enter the value of 0.5.

1. Click in cell I3 to make it active. I3 will record the total precipitation.
2. On the formula bar, click the Insert Formula option and the *Insert Function* box appears.
3. Click *SUM* under *Select a function* and then click *OK*. The *Function Arguments* box appears to specify the arguments or range of cells for the SUM function. For the total precipitation, the cell range includes both columns E and F (remember, snowfall amounts are in column F for October 29 and 31).
4. Select the range of cells to perform the SUM function by clicking in the beginning cell (i.e., E4) and dragging to the last cell (i.e., F34). A blinking dotted border appears around the cells to indicate that they are selected. After selecting the cells, the cell range appears in the *Number 1* field of the *Function Arguments* box (see Figure 5.39).

Click *OK* on the *Function Arguments* box. The total precipitation for October is 5.9 inches.

Figure 5.39
SUM function—
selecting multiple
columns

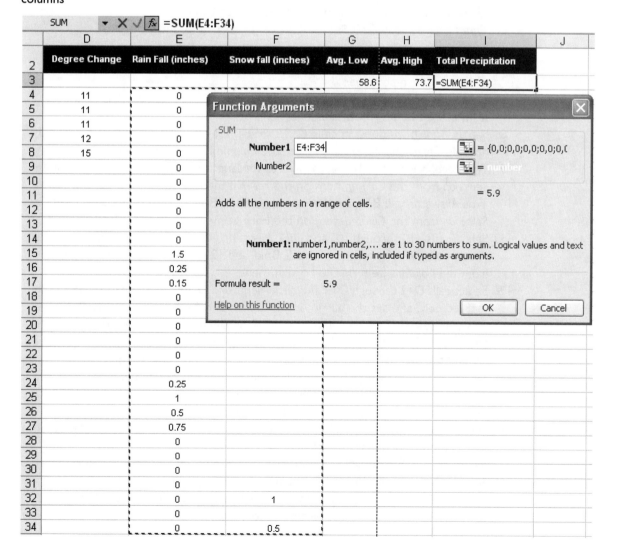

To practice using Excel functions, let's work on another Let Me Try that creates a short quiz. In this activity, we will create a matching question that requires the student to match photographs to a text label. For a completed version of this activity, go to the CD-ROM and open the *FamilyTree_Quiz.xls* file in the Family Tree folder. *Family Tree* is inside the Excel folder under *Examples*.

1. Open Excel and create a new worksheet.
2. Save the worksheet as *familyTree_Quiz.xls*.
3. Select cells A1 down through H4. With the cells selected, choose *Merge and Center*.
4. Type *My Family Tree Quiz* in the merged cells. Set the font to Verdana at a size of 28 points and Bold.

    Set the alignment of the merged cells to *Top*. Set the alignment by clicking in the cell and select *Cells . . .* from the Format menu. Click the Alignment tab and select *General* under *Horizontal*, and *Top* under *Vertical* on the *Format Cells* box.
5. Select cells A5 through H8 and choose *Merge and Center*. Type the following: *Match the item in the Relative column with the Photograph in the Photograph column. Type the letter of photograph in the Answer column next to the label the photo matches.* To ensure that the text fits in the merged cell, select *Wrap text* under *Text Control* in the *Format Cell* box (select *Cells . . .* from the Format menu and click the Alignment tab). Set the alignment of the text to *Center*.
6. Type *Relative* in cell C10. Set the font to Verdana, Bold, and 12 point.
7. Enter the labels:
    - In cell C11 type *Mother*.
    - In cell C12 type *Father*.
    - In cell C13 type *Mother's Parents*.
    - In cell C14 type *Father's Parents*.
8. Set the font of the text in cells C11 through C14 to Verdana and 12 point with no bold. Select *AutoFit Selection* from the *Column* item on the Format menu.
9. Type *Feedback* in cell A10. Set the font to Verdana, Bold, and 12 point. Select *AutoFit Selection* from the *Column* item on the Format menu.
10. Type *Answer* in cell B10. Set the font to Verdana, Bold, and 12 point. Select *AutoFit Selection* from the *Column* item on the Format menu.
11. Select cells E10 through I10 and click *Merge and Center*. Type the following label, *Photographs*. Set the font to Verdana, Bold, and 12 point. Choose *AutoFit Selection* from the *Columns* item on the Format menu.
12. Select cells D12 through D14 and click *Merge and Center*. Type the letter **A.** in the merged cells and set the alignment to *Center*. Set the font to Verdana, Bold, and 12 point. Set this font type and size for all remaining photo letters (B, C, and D).
13. Select cells E11 through F16 and click *Merge and Center*. Place a solid border around the merged cells and fill them with a light gray background color.
14. Select cells G12 through G14 and click *Merge and Center*. Type the letter **B.** in the merged cells and set the alignment to *Center*.
15. Select cells H11 through I16 and click *Merge and Center*.
16. Select Cells D19 through D21 and click *Merge and Center*. Type the letter **C.** in the merged cells and set the alignment to *Center*.
17. Select cells E18 through F23 and click *Merge and Center*. Place a solid border around the merged cells and fill them with a light gray background color.
18. Select cells G19 through G21 and click *Merge and Center*. Type the letter **D.** in the merged cells and set the alignment to *Center*.

19. Select cells H18 through I23 and click *Merge and Center.* Place a solid border around the merged cells and fill them with a light gray background color.

20. Insert the following images located on the CD-ROM in the Family Tree folder—Family Tree is inside the Excel folder under Examples:
    - Dad.png
    - Mom.png
    - grandparentD.png
    - grandparentM.png

21. Insert the images by selecting *Picture (From File)* from the Insert menu. Place each image over one of merged cell blocks. See boxed Figure 5.1 for an example.

Answer	Relative	Photographs		
	Mother	A.		B.
	Father			
	Mother's Parents			
	Father's Parents			
		C.		D.

Figure 5.1
Image placement

Defining the Correct and Incorrect Answers

We need to determine the correct and incorrect answers. For instance, the *Relative* column lists *Mother* in cell C11 (see boxed Figure 5.1). The photograph of the mother is labeled as **C.** in boxed Figure 5.1. Therefore, to respond correctly to this item the student must type a **C** in the *Answer* column in the cell to the left of the label *Mother.* Here is how the answer looks if we follow the layout in boxed Figure 5.1:

C: Mother
A: Father
D: Mother's Parents
B: Father's Parents

22. With this information, type the following in cells K11 through K14:
    - In cell K11 type C
    - In cell K12 type A
    - In cell K13 type D
    - In cell K14 type B

The Formula

23. Click in cell A11, which should be in the same row as the *Mother* label. Type the following formula:
    =IF (B11=K11, "Correct", "Try again")
    This formula checks to see if what the student types in cell B11 matches what we defined as the correct answer in cell K11. If it does match, then it displays "Correct." If it does not match, then it displays "Try again."

24. Click in cell A11 and copy the formula and paste it into cells A12, A13, and A14. You should notice that the cell references change to match the row numbers. When you enter the correct letter, the content of the A11–A14 cells should change.

25. To hide the correct answers, select column K and then choose *Hide* from the *Column* item on the Format menu.

To practice using the IF function, open the Jellybeans.xls file on the CD-ROM in the Excel folder under Examples. *The Jelly beans worksheet uses the IF function along with the OR logical function.*

Moving and Copying Data

This section describes how to copy and move data within a worksheet; you will often need to perform these tasks when working with data sets.

Moving Data

Suppose you entered the October snowfall amounts incorrectly. Instead of snowfall events occurring on October 29 and 31, they actually took place on October 26 and 28, so these values need to be moved to the appropriate cells.

1. Select cells F32 and F34. Click cell F32 to make it the active cell and, while holding the mouse button down, drag downward to cell F34.
2. Position the cursor over the selected area's border and the cursor changes to a four-point arrow. Click on the border and drag the selection to the appropriate cells, F29 and F31. As you drag the selection, its border becomes shaded and it snaps to the cell's border.
3. Release the mouse button when the values are over cells F29 and F31 and the values move.
4. Another way to move data is to select the data that you want to move and click the Cut button or select *Cut* from the Edit menu. Click in the location where you want to move the data. Click the Paste button or select *Paste* from the Edit menu.

Copying Data

Data can be copied from one group of cells to another or from one column to another. Suppose you want to make a copy of column A (the days of the month) on the right side of our worksheet to more easily view the precipitation amounts with their corresponding dates.

1. Select cells A4 through A34.
2. Position the cursor over the selected area's border and the cursor changes to a four-point arrow. Press the Control (Ctrl) key while clicking on the border and drag the selection to the desired column, J. As you drag the selection, its border becomes shaded and it snaps to the column's border. Note that pressing the Control (Ctrl) key while moving the selection copies it to the destination. If you do not press the Ctrl key, Excel moves the selection instead of copying it.
3. Release the mouse when the values are over column J and the selection is copied.

Another method of copying data is to select the data that you want to copy and click the Copy button or select *Copy* from the Edit menu. Click in the location where you want to copy the data. Click the Paste button or select *Paste* from the Edit menu.

LET ME TRY

In the previous sections, we learned how to edit, replace, and delete worksheet data; insert columns and rows; and to use formulas and functions. Let's practice some of these concepts using our president example. Suppose that we ask our students to make the following calculations:

- Calculate presidents' ages at death
- Calculate presidents' ages in first year of office
- Use an Excel function to calculate the average age of each president in his first year of office

Calculate Presidents' Ages at Death

1. Open the *presidency.xls* workbook. To view an example workbook open "presidents.xls" or president_master.xls" on the CD.
2. Insert a new column before the current column E (*Year Elected*). Click the column E header to select the column. Choose *Columns* from the Insert menu. Excel inserts a new column.
3. Label the new column *Age at Death*. Click in cell E2 and type *Age at Death*. If the title exceeds the cell borders, click outside the cell to deselect it and to exit the cell's text-editing mode. Click in cell E2 again and select *AutoFit Selection* from *Column* on the Format menu.
4. Click in cell E3 and type the following formula: $= (D3-C3)$. Press the Enter key. This formula subtracts the value in cell C3 (*year of birth*) from the value in D3 (*year of death*) to give us the president's age at death.
5. To copy this formula for the remaining presidents, click in cell E3. Select *Copy* from the Edit menu. Select cells E4 through E39 and then choose *Paste* from the Edit menu. Note that only cells up to cell E39 (Richard Nixon) were selected because there is no date of death for the remaining presidents, except Ronald Reagan. Since we already copied the formula, we can paste it into cell E42 (Ronald Reagan). Click in cell E42 and then click the Paste button or select *Paste* from the Edit menu. Regan's age at death should be 93.

Calculate Presidents' Ages in First Year of Office

6. Insert a new column before the current column H (*Occupation*). Click the column H header to select the column. Choose *Columns* from the Insert menu. Excel inserts a new column.
7. Label the new column *First Term Age*. Click in cell H2 and type *First Term Age*. If the title exceeds the cell borders, click outside the cell to deselect it and to exit the cell's text-editing mode. Click in cell H2 again and select *AutoFit Selection* from the *Column* item on the Format menu.
8. Click in cell H3 and type the following formula: $= (F3-C3)$. Press the Enter key. This formula subtracts the value in cell C3 (*year of birth*) from the value in F3 (*year elected*) to give us the president's age during his first term in office.
9. To copy this formula for the remaining presidents, click in cell H3. Select *Copy* from the Edit menu. Select cells H4 through H45 and then choose *Paste* from the Edit menu. Alternatively, you can use the *Auto Fill* option. Click in cell H3 to make it active. With the cursor positioned over the small square at the bottom right of the active cell border, click and drag down and Excel will copy the formula of the previous cell, with relative addressing.

Use an Excel Function to Calculate the Average Age of Each President in His First Year of Office

10. Click cell H46 below all the *First Term Ages*.
11. Click the Insert Formula option on the Formula bar.
12. Select the AVERAGE function from the *Function* box. Specify the cell range from H3 to H45 and click *OK*. The average age appears in cell H46.

Charting Excel Data

In this section, we will use the weather data to chart daily temperatures. When you complete this section, you will have produced the line chart shown in Figure 5.40.

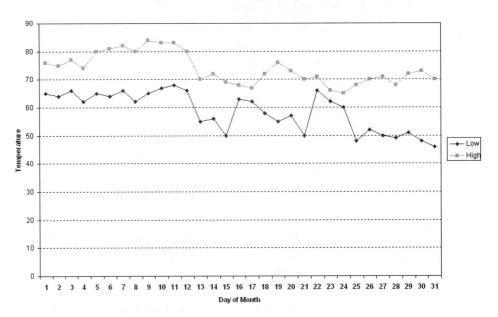

Figure 5.40
Line chart

The Excel Chart Wizard (Step 1)

1. Select the range of cells from B4 through C34, which are the low and high temperatures for the month of October.
2. Click the Chart Wizard button or select *Chart* from the Insert menu to open the Chart Wizard (Step 1). The Chart Wizard (see Figure 5.41) presents four steps to create a chart. In Step 1, there are numerous chart types from which to select, such as pie, column, bar, line, and area. They are presented under the *Standard types* tab. You can also customize your own charts by clicking the *Custom type* tab. Notice that under the *Chart type* portion of the box, icons of the chart types appear. Clicking on an icon displays several subtypes for that particular chart type.

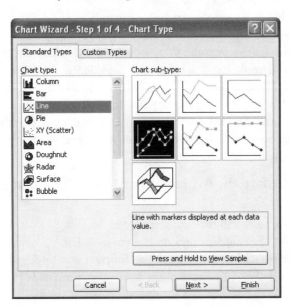

Figure 5.41
Chart Wizard
(Step 1)

3. A *Standard type* chart will be appropriate for your purposes. Click *Line* under *Chart type*. This displays the data as a line chart. Under the *Chart sub-type* area, select the first subtype in the second row (with markers to display each data value) and then click *Next* to go to the *Chart Wizard Step 2* dialogue box (see Figure 5.41).

The Excel Chart Wizard (Step 2)

4. Specify the range of cells and data labels of the chart in Step 2. We have already specified the temperatures in cells ranging from B4 through C34. If you did not already specify the range, click the Collapse Dialogue icon at the right side of the *Data range* box and then select the cells.

   The *Step 2* dialogue box (see Figure 5.42) displays a miniature version of the chart with lines representing the low and high temperatures. It presents the temperature range (0 to 90) on the Y-axis and the days of the month (1 to 31) on the X-axis.

5. The Series tab allows modification of data ranges and series labels.

6. Click on the Series tab to change the series labels. *Series1* represents the low temperatures in column B and *Series2* represents the high temperatures in column C.

7. In the *Series* box, highlight the *Series1* label and then click the Collapse Dialogue icon located on the right side of the *Name* box (see Figure 5.43). This action collapses the *Step 2* dialogue box so that you can select the cell to be used for the *Series1* label. Cell B3 contains the word *Low,* which will be the *Series1* label.

8. Click cell B3. Notice that when selecting the cell, the cell range (=Sheet1! B3) displays in the *Chart Source Data–Name* box (see Figure 5.44).

9. Click the Collapse Dialogue icon to return to the *Chart Wizard (Step 2)* box. The contents of cell B3 (*Low*) are now the *Series1* label.

10. Change the *Series2* label by highlighting *Series2* under the *Series* box. Click the Collapse Dialogue icon located on the right side of the *Name* box.

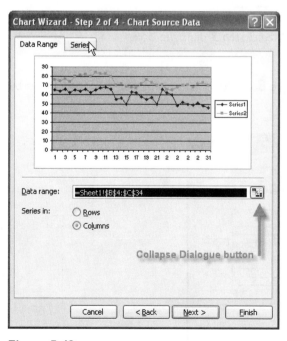

Figure 5.42
Chart Wizard (Step 2)

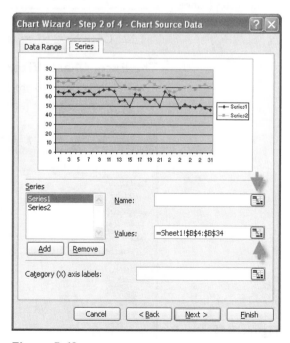

Figure 5.43
Cell range, X-axis category

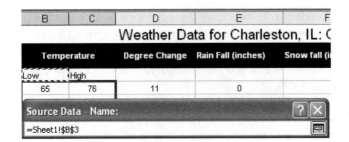

Figure 5.44
Select Series1 label

11. Click in the cell that will serve as the *Series2* label, C3 (*High*), then click the Collapse Dialogue icon to return to the *Chart Source Data–Name* box (see Figure 5.45).

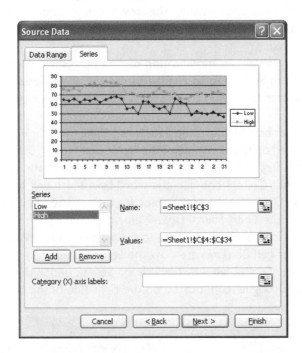

Figure 5.45
Select Series2 label

12. Click *Next* to go to the *Chart Wizard Step 3* dialogue box.

The Excel Chart Wizard (Step 3)

The *Chart Wizard Step 3* dialogue box allows you to format the chart. Begin by giving it a title (see Figure 5.46).

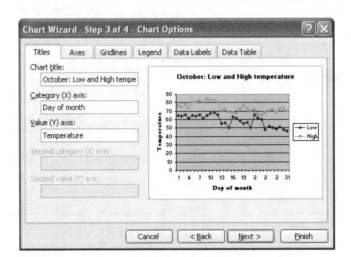

Figure 5.46
Chart Wizard
(Step 3)

13. Click the Titles tab. Enter *October: Low and High Temperature* in the *Chart title* box.
14. Enter *Day of Month* in the *Category (X) axis* box and *Temperature* in the *Value (Y) axis* box.
15. Click the Axes tab. If it is not already selected, check the *Category (X) axis* box and then click the button to the left of *Automatic*. Make sure the *Value (Y) axis* box is checked (see Figure 5.47).

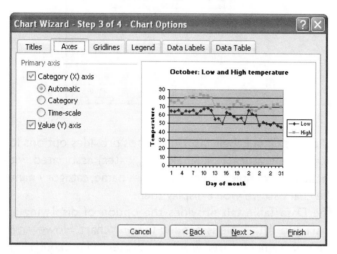

Figure 5.47
Chart Wizard (Step 3) axes

16. Click the Gridlines tab to set the style of the gridlines behind the chart columns. Only major gridlines should appear on the Y-axis, so deselect all options except *Major gridlines* under *Value (Y) axis* (see Figure 5.48).

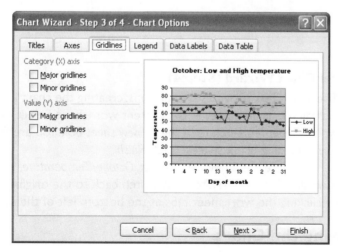

Figure 5.48
Chart Wizard (Step 3) gridlines

17. The Legend tab provides options to show or hide the chart legend and to specify its placement. Click the Legend tab and select the *Show Legend* box if it is not checked. The placement of the legend should be *Right* (see Figure 5.49).

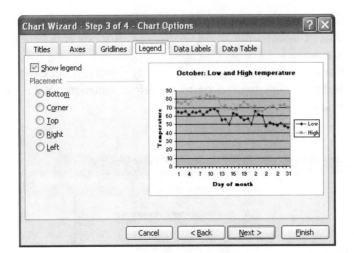

Figure 5.49
Chart Wizard
(Step 3) legend

18. Click the Data Labels tab. *Data Labels* provides options for displaying the values (e.g., temperatures) or labels (e.g., dates) associated with the columns. In this particular example, adding the series name, category name, or values will crowd the chart so we won't display them.
19. The Data Table tab provides the option of displaying a data table below the chart. No data table is needed for our chart. However, if a table was included, the daily temperatures would be presented in tabular format.
20. Click *Next* to continue on to *Chart Wizard (Step 4)* (see Figure 5.50).

Figure 5.50
Chart Wizard
(Step 4)

The Excel Chart Wizard (Step 4)

21. The *Step 4* box provides two options: creating the chart in a new worksheet or including it as an object in the current worksheet. Select *As new sheet* and then type *October Temperature* in the *As new sheet* box. You are limited to 31 characters, including blank spaces. Click *Finish*.

    Excel creates a new worksheet, *October Temperature,* in which the chart displays (see Figure 5.51). You can switch back to the original worksheet (Sheet1) by clicking the worksheet tabs at the bottom left of the screen.

Modifying the Chart

You can modify the X-axis labels, chart background color, and titles. Make sure you are in the *October Temperature* worksheet. If you are not, click on the appropriate worksheet tab at the bottom left of the screen.

Adjust X-Axis Labels: Orientation

Notice that as you click on various sections of the chart, they become selected. For example, clicking on the chart title *October: Low and High Temperature* selects it. A shaded

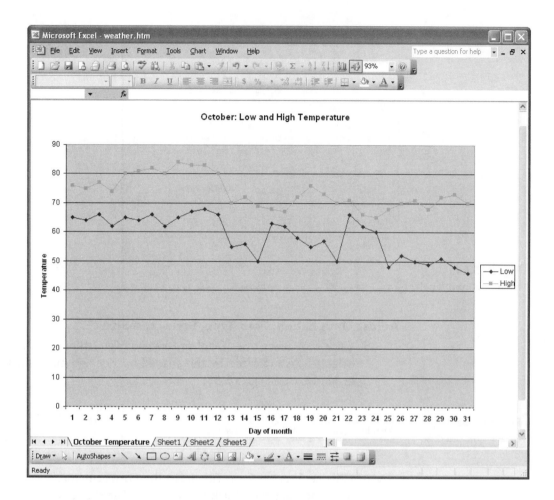

Figure 5.51
New worksheet
chart

border and eight small blocks appear around it, indicating that it is selected (see Figure 5.52).
Once selected, the title can be moved, edited, or deleted.

Figure 5.52
Chart title selected

Adjust X-Axis Labels: Font Type, Style, and Size

1. Click the X-axis labels section (*Day of Month*) of the chart located below the
   columns (see Figure 5.53). Two small blocks above the days of the month at each
   end of the X-axis labels indicate that the labels are selected.

Figure 5.53
X-axis labels

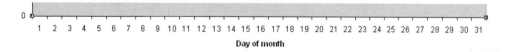

2. Choose *Selected Axis* from the Format menu to display the *Format Axis* dialogue
   box (see Figure 5.54).
3. Click the Font tab to adjust the font type and size. Set the font type to Arial, the
   style to Bold, and the size to 10 points.
4. Click *OK* to accept the changes to the X-axis labels.

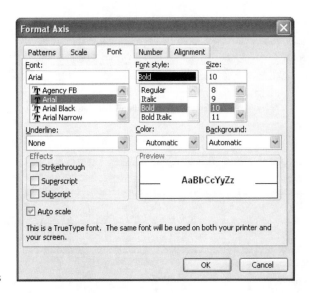

Figure 5.54
Format X-axis labels

Adjust Data Labels: Font Type, Style, and Size

5. Click the Chart title (*October: Low and High Temperature*). Clicking on the title selects it, as indicated by the shaded border and eight small blocks appearing around it (see Figure 5.55).

Figure 5.55
Chart title selected

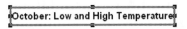

6. Choose *Selected Chart Title* from the Format menu. The *Format Chart Title* dialogue box appears. Click the Font tab. Set the font type to Arial, the style to Bold, and the size to 16 points (see Figure 5.56). Click *OK* to accept the changes to the chart title.

Figure 5.56
Format Chart Title

Adjust Chart Gridlines

Gridlines are horizontal lines running through the chart. They provide a visual referent for the data series lines and the Y-axis. However, the lines in your chart may interfere with the visual clarity of the data points, so they can be adjusted.

7. Single-click on a gridline. Clicking on any line selects all the lines.
8. Choose *Selected Gridlines* from the Format menu. The *Format Gridlines* dialogue box appears (see Figure 5.57).

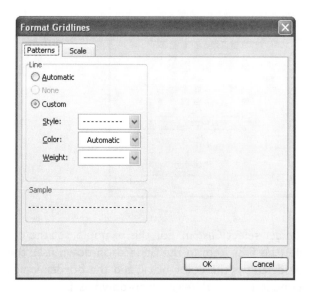

Figure 5.57
Format gridlines

9. Click the Patterns tab.
10. Click *Custom* in the *Line* section.
11. Click the down arrow to the right of the *Style* box to display a list of line styles. Choose a pattern option. In this example, the third item in the list is selected (see Figure 5.58).

Figure 5.58
Format gridlines
style

12. Set the color to *Automatic*.
13. Set the weight to the lightest (the dotted line).
14. Click *OK*.

Adjust Chart Background Color

To improve readability, change the solid gray background color of the chart to white.

15. Click in the chart background or plot area to select it. Be careful not to click on data series lines or mistakenly select the gridlines.
16. Click *Selected Plot Area* from the Format menu and the *Format Plot Area* dialogue box appears (see Figure 5.59).

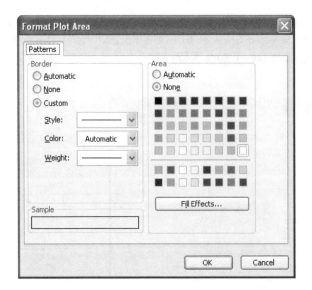

Figure 5.59
Format chart background color

17. Under *Border* select *Custom.* For this example, set the chart border to a solid line style (the first item in the Style drop-down list); the color to *Automatic,* which by default is the color black; and the border weight to a thin solid line (the second item in the Weight drop-down list).

18. Under *Area* choose *None,* which removes the chart's background color, then click *OK.*

19. An alternative way to set the chart background color is to first click the chart background or plot area to select it. Click the Fill Color tool on the Formatting menu and select *No Fill* (see Figure 5.60).

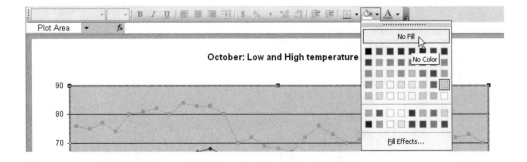

Figure 5.60
Set chart background color

LET ME TRY

In the *presidents.xls* file on the CD-ROM that accompanies the book, you will find a column labeled *States of Presidents* and another labeled *Number of Presidents from State.* These columns list the presidents' states of birth and the number of presidents from each state. Use this information to create the bar chart presented in this exercise.

Charting Presidents by State of Birth

1. In both the *States of Presidents* and *Number of Presidents from State* columns, select rows 2 through 21.
2. Choose *Chart* from the Insert menu or click the Chart Wizard icon.

3. Click the Standard tab on the *Chart Wizard (Step 1)* dialogue box and then click *Column* under *Chart type*. Choose a chart subtype and click *Next*.

4. Preview the chart in the *Chart Wizard (Step 2)* box and then click *Next*. Adjust the data series if necessary.

5. Type *Number of Presidents by State* in the *Chart title* box of the *Chart Wizard (Step 3)* dialogue box.

6. Click the Legend tab of the *Chart Wizard (Step 3)* dialogue box and deselect the *Show Legend* option. Click *Next*.

7. Select *As new sheet* in the *Chart Wizard (Step 4)* dialogue box and enter *Number of Presidents by State* in the *As new sheet* box. Click *Finish*.

Saving as a Web Page

This section uses the example of sharing weather data over the Web. Suppose you and your students form school weather stations as do five other schools throughout the country. You record the daily low and high temperatures and precipitation. You want to share the data with students at other schools to observe how weather patterns differ nationally. You can save a workbook as a Web Page (.htm; .html) or as a Single File Web Page (.mht; .mhtml), both of which can be viewed in a Web browser.

Saving a Workbook as a Web Page

The Web Page (.htm; .html) option converts the workbook to HTML and stores all associated files on your computer. Excel appends the .htm extension to the file name. For example, when saving *WeatherStation.xls* as a Web Page, Excel assigns it the name *WeatherStation.htm*. In addition, Excel creates a folder named *WeatherStation_files* that contains the HTML and graphic files associated with the workbook. You will need both the *WeatherStation.htm* and the *WeatherStation_files* folder for the workbook to display properly on the Web (see files on CD). When uploading the workbook to the Web, you must upload the .htm file and the folder.

Saving a Workbook as a Single File Web Page

The Single File Web Page (.mht; .mhtml) option creates a single file with the .mht extension. For example, when saving *WeatherStation.xls* as a Single File Web Page, Excel assigns it the name *WeatherStation.mht* and it creates one file containing the workbook (see files on CD). With the Single File Web Page, you only need to upload one file to the Web server. However, this format typically produces a larger file size than the Web Page format.

Even though you save a workbook as a Web Page or a Single Web Page and can view it, the Web-formatted workbook files need to be placed on a computer server for them to be available worldwide. After saving a workbook as HTML, you need the following to make it available on the Web:

- Access to a Web server that stores and serves your HTML files and graphics. Internet service providers (ISP) provide this service.
- File transfer software, such as Ws_FTP, that transfers the HTML files and graphics from your computer to a server.

1. Open the *weather.xls* workbook containing the weather station data.

2. To save the weather station workbook in an HTML format, select *Save As Web Page* from the File menu.

3. The *Save As* dialogue box appears (see Figure 5.61). Click in the *Save in* box to locate the folder where you want to save the files. In this example, we will save

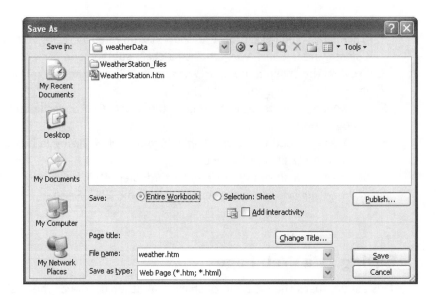

Figure 5.61
Save As Web Page

it to a folder titled *WeatherData* located in the Office folder on the computer's C: drive. If you do not have a folder with this name and want to create one, click the Create New Folder button on the top right (third option from right) of the *Save As* dialogue box. When the *New Folder* box appears, enter the folder name and click *OK*.

4. Click the Publish button (see Figure 5.61), which provides several options for saving the workbook, including the following:

- *Choose:* Specifies the worksheet (e.g., Sheet1, Sheet2, or Sheet3), a range of cells to be saved, or the entire workbook. Select *Items on Sheet1 and then Sheet; All contents on Sheet1*. If you created a line chart in a previous Show Me exercise, *Chart 1 (Line)* appears under the *Choose* box.

- *Viewing option:* Check *Add interactivity with: Spreadsheet functionality* to make the page interactive. For example, you may want students from other schools to enter weather data. Checking this option enables anyone using Internet Explorer 4.1 or greater to enter and analyze data. It is important to note that if this option is checked, users will be unable to view the page with a Web browser other than Internet Explorer 4.1 or greater. If you or your students do not use Internet Explorer 4.1 or greater, do not check this item.

- *Change:* Changes the page title. Click the Change button, then type *Weather Data* in the *Set Title* dialogue box (see Figure 5.62) and click *OK*.

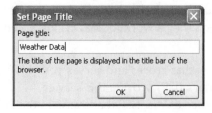

Figure 5.62
Set Page Title box

With a Web browser, users can bookmark Web pages to quickly return to them without having to type (sometimes long) addresses. Internet Explorer uses the term *Favorites* to refer to bookmarks. Once you have bookmarked a page, you can select it from a list of titles (see Figure 5.63) and go directly

Figure 5.63
Bookmarks/
Favorites

to it. The page title assigned to a Web page is used as the bookmark or favorite title. For example, if you visit an interesting Web site about weather data that has an excessively long address, you could bookmark it. On subsequent visits to the site, you select it from the bookmark list to avoid retyping the address. In such cases, the page title (e.g., *weather data*) is used as the bookmark and it displays in the bookmark list.

- *File name:* Specifies a file name and location to save the Web page. By default, Excel assigns a file name of *Page.mht.* Enter the file name of *weather.mht.* When saving a workbook in a Web format, it is preferable to remove blank spaces in the file name. The computer server may not recognize file names containing blank spaces. For example, if we are converting a workbook named *weather data.xls* to a Web format, the file should be saved as *weatherdata.mht* or *weatherdata.htm.*

- *Browse:* The Browse button allows you to specify a location to save the HTML file other than the one presented. Leave this option unchanged in your workbook.

5. Click the Publish button (see Figure 5.64) and Excel begins to convert the workbook to a Web page. Notice that by selecting *Items on Sheet1* on the *Publish as Web Page* box, Excel saves the file as a Single File Web Page (.mht).

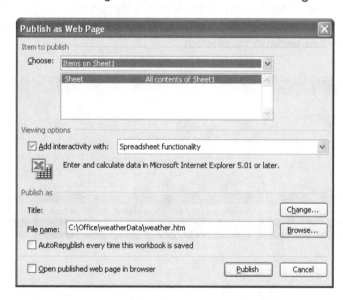

Figure 5.64
Publish as a Web
Page

Opening the Workbook in a Web Browser

1. Open a Web browser (e.g., Netscape or Internet Explorer) to view the workbook. For this example, use Internet Explorer. Remember, if you checked the *Add interactivity* option, you must use Internet Explore 4.1 or greater to view the workbook.

    From Internet Explorer's File menu, select *Open* and the *Open* dialogue box appears (see Figure 5.65). If you know the location or path of your workbook, type it into the location box. If not, click *Browse* and the *Microsoft Internet Explorer* dialogue box appears (see Figure 5.66).

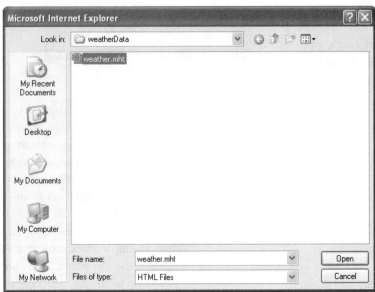

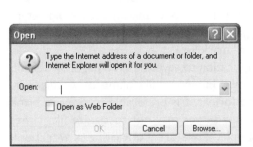

Figure 5.65
Open box

Figure 5.66
Microsoft Internet Explorer box

2. Locate the file on your computer. For this example, open the file called *weather.htm* located on the computer's C: drive within Office and in the folder called *WeatherData*. After locating the file, click *Open*. Return to the *Open* dialogue box and click *OK*.

3. The workbook opens in the browser. If you are using Internet Explorer, the Web page should look like Figure 5.67. You can enter values into the worksheet, as well as perform calculations.

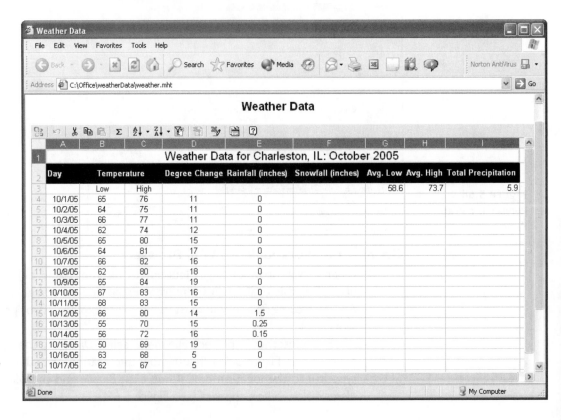

Figure 5.67
Internet Explorer
interactive Web
page

4. If you did not select the *Add interactivity* option, you will be unable to interact with the worksheet, but you will be able to view it with Web browsers other than Internet Explorer 4.1. Figure 5.68 presents the noninteractive worksheet.

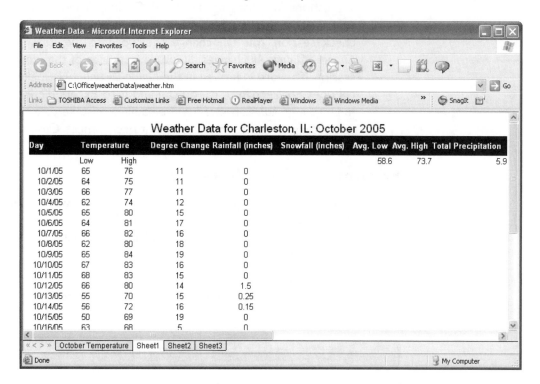

Figure 5.68
Internet Explorer noninteractive Web page

Keep in mind that the workbook is not on the Web even though you can view it in a Web browser. At this point, you need to transfer the HTML-formatted files to a server to make them available worldwide.

Spell Checking the Excel Workbook

1. Open the *weather.xls* workbook.
2. Check the workbook for spelling errors by selecting *Spelling* from the Tools menu or click the Spelling icon on the standard toolbar. If your workbook contains spelling errors or words Excel does not recognize, the *Spelling* dialogue box displays (see Figure 5.69).

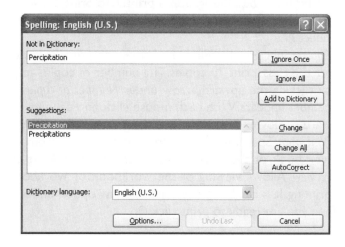

Figure 5.69
Spelling box

When Excel does not recognize a word, it identifies it in the *Not in Dictionary* section of the *Spelling* dialogue box. For example, in Figure 5.69, Excel encountered a misspelling of the word *Precipitation* (*Percipitation*). Excel offers suggestions for changing the word. Clicking *Ignore Once* ignores the suggestion. Clicking *Ignore All* ignores all future instances of the word in the spell check session. You can change the word to Excel's suggestion by clicking *Change*. *Change All* changes all future instances of the word in the spell check session. If a word identified in the *Not in Dictionary* is spelled correctly and Excel does not recognize it, you can add it to Excel's dictionary by clicking *Add to Dictionary*. *AutoCorrect* adds the spelling mistake to a list of errors and automatically corrects it on subsequent occurrences. *Close* closes the *Spelling* dialogue box.

Printing the Excel Workbook

Excel has several printing options. An entire workbook, worksheet, or selected cells within a worksheet can be printed. Printing worksheets or selections from a worksheet is particularly useful, for example, when students and teachers share and discuss their data analysis results.

1. Open the *weather.xls* workbook.
2. To print, select *Print* from the File menu and the *Print* dialogue box appears (see Figure 5.70).

Figure 5.70
Print box

- *Printer Name box:* Designates a printer to print the workbook.
- *Print range:* Specifies a range of pages to print. For this workbook example, select *All*.
- *Copies:* Specifies the number of copies to print. Because the weather data is for the class, print 20 copies. The number of copies to print can be changed by clicking the upward arrow under *Number of copies* until the appropriate number appears. With each mouse click, and depending on whether the upward or downward arrow is clicked, the number increases or decreases.
- *Print what:* Specifies whether to print a selection from a workbook, an entire workbook, or the currently active sheets. *Select Active Sheet(s)*.
- *Preview:* Allows viewing of the workbook or workbook selection prior to printing. It is similar to the Print Preview option under the File menu.
3. When you are ready to print click *OK*.

Page Break Preview

Excel also provides a Page Break Preview, which allows you to view and set page breaks within worksheets. Notice in Figure 5.71 that a dashed line, or page break indicator, separates column G from H; the page breaks after column G. In other words, page 1 ends with column G and page 2 begins with Column H. If you printed the worksheet, columns A through G would print on page 1 and column H would print on page 2. You can adjust page breaks by positioning the mouse over the page break and, while holding the mouse button down, dragging the page break to a desired location.

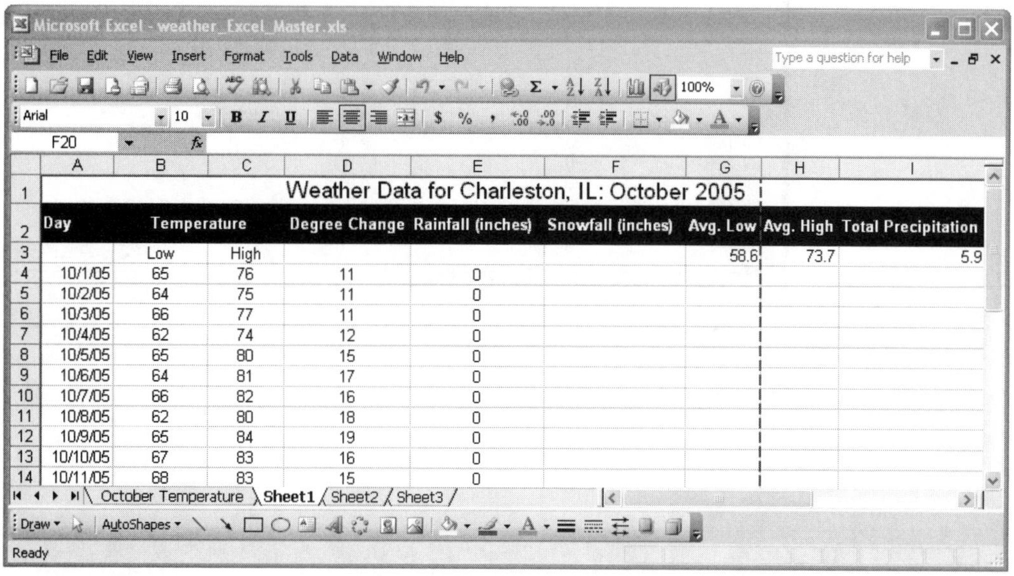

Figure 5.71
Page Break Preview

You can switch between the Normal view and Page Break Preview by selecting either option (Normal or Page Break Preview) under the View menu.

Print Preview

Prior to printing a worksheet, it is advisable to preview it in Print Preview. Often the data you enter into a worksheet extend beyond the viewing area of your computer monitor. Print Preview allows you to see what a printed copy of your worksheet will look like prior to it being printed. To preview a worksheet, select *Print Preview* under the File menu.

Web Page Preview

View your worksheet as a Web page by using the Web Page Preview option under the File menu. This option opens a Web browser, such as Internet Explorer, and displays the worksheet in the browser window (see Figure 5.72). Keep in mind that even though you can view the worksheet in a browser it does not reside on the Web and is therefore only accessible on your computer. The purpose of the Web Page Preview option is to see how your worksheet displays in a browser. Once you are satisfied with it, you can transfer the worksheet to a Web server in order for it to be available on the Web.

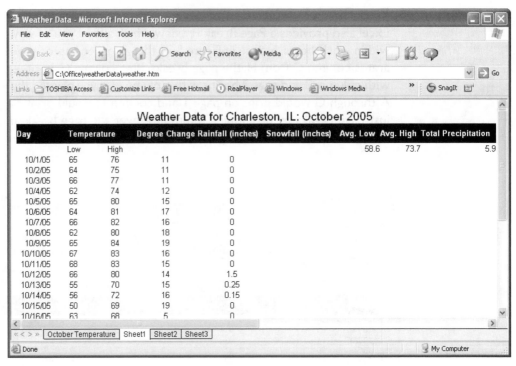

Figure 5.72
Web Page Preview

A CHALLENGE USING EXCEL 2003

For those who would like a challenge beyond the Let Me Try activities presented in this chapter, try the following exercises.

1. Using Excel, record the daily high and low temperatures and precipitation for one month. For each day, ask students to calculate the temperature change and to record the average change in temperature for the month. Ask students to calculate the average high and low temperatures and the total precipitation.

2. Create an Excel worksheet that lists all the presidents of the United States. Include the presidents' dates of birth, dates of death, states of birth, election years to office, years terms ended, and occupations. With this information, ask students to calculate the states with the most presidents, the age of each deceased president when he died, the most popular occupation other than president, and the number of presidents from each state. Finally, ask students to create a column chart that represents all states in which a president was born and the number of presidents from those states.

3. Create a worksheet of data pertaining to the nine planets in the solar system, including their distance from the sun. Calculate the distance each planet is from one another.

4. Create a study habits worksheet. For one month, ask students to record the number of hours they study, read, and watch television. Record this information by day of the week and date. At the end of the month, chart the data to observe trends in studying, reading, and television viewing.

TYING IT ALL TOGETHER

In this chapter, we created an Excel workbook containing several worksheets. Our workbook served as an electronic weather data recorder. We organized data according to Excel's row-and-column format and formatted the worksheet layout, including font type, size, and style. Excel's formula capability and built-in functions allowed us to calculate the differences between daily high and low temperatures and precipitation averages. We created a chart of our data results with Excel's Chart Wizard. We walked through the steps of saving the file in a workbook (.xls) and in HTML (.htm) format.

REFERENCES

Grolier. (1994). *The American presidents*. Danbury, CT: Grolier Incorporated.

Microsoft Corporation. (2004). *Excel specifications and limits*. Retrieved August 5, 2004 from http://office.microsoft.com/assistance/hFWS.ASPX? AssetID= HPO5199291103

6 ACCESS 2003

CHAPTER OUTLINE

LEARNING OBJECTIVES

At the completion of this chapter you will be able to:
- Start a new database
- Create tables for data display
- Create forms for input of data
- Create reports of the database
- Edit the data and fields that display the data
- Create queries of the information in the database
- Print reports
- Save the database

TECHNICAL TERMS

The following are terms that you will encounter in the chapter and with which you will become familiar:

Field

Record

Table

Form

Queries

Report

CHAPTER OVERVIEW

This chapter provides an introduction to Access 2003. The content focuses on Access fundamentals and how to apply them to a variety of learning activities. Using the example of creating a "planets" database for student use, the chapter's Show Me section presents instructions on how to use many of Access 2003's tools for creating databases and editing and manipulating the information in the database. Several Let Me Try student-oriented exercises give specific examples and step-by-step instructions for using Access 2003 to accomplish a variety of learning activities. Studying the chapter contents and working through the Let Me Try exercises will enable you to create databases suitable for many classroom learning activities.

Each one of the illustrations given in this chapter may be found on the CD accompanying the text. You may follow along with the document as you go through the text by pulling it up from the CD. Also, other examples using Access may be found on the CD.

About Access

Access is a database program that allows you to store and manage information. Some individuals think of a database program as an electronic stack of index cards that can be sorted and reported electronically. A database consists of objects, such as tables, forms, reports, and queries. Access allows you and your students to collect information, organize it, and report the information.

For teachers, databases have many applications that can be used in class. Databases allow you to "design and teach technology-enriched learning activities that connect content standards with student technology standards" (International Society for Technology in Education, 2004). Students can create their own databases to help them learn subject matter while using technology.

How Teachers and Students Might Use Access 2003

Teacher Production of Materials

Instruction/Learning	Classroom Management
Keep records of readings, related notes, and citations	Monitor classroom books
Create material database for thematic units support	Monitor classroom videotapes/DVDs
Store list of curriculum content objectives	Classroom inventory
Store teaching activities and strategies	Student and parent/guardian information
Create a database of Civil War battles from Fort Sumter to Lee surrendering at Appomattox	Student allergy information

Student Production of Materials

Instruction/Learning

Create state information database (e.g., capital, flower)

Create a database of addresses

Create U.S. presidents database (e.g. birth date, years in office, previous jobs)

Create a database of local political figures

Create a "books read" database

Create a database of rectangles, squares, or other basic geometric shapes

Create a famous persons database (e.g., scientists, mathematicians, Nobel Prize winners)

Create a database of resources for a report

Working with Access

The primary purpose of this chapter is to help you become familiar with the fundamental components and features of Access 2003 so that you may use them in productive ways in your classes and with your students. To accomplish this objective, we present several examples throughout the chapter that will help you learn Access and apply it to your teaching and learning activities. Although the examples here may be specific, the steps and procedures for developing databases, including tables, forms, queries, and reports, are generic and applicable to a variety of classroom management tasks and learning activities. As you work though the chapter's content, substitute our examples with your own. You can locate files that correspond to the chapter activities on the CD in the "Access" folder under "Examples".

A Word About the Access Workspace

Before starting the actual database program, it is imperative to plan for the type of information you will place in your database and how it will be organized. What kind of information will you query from the data, and how will it be stored in the database? What kind of reports will you generate from the data?

Unlike Word documents and Excel spreadsheets, Access requires that a database be created and saved prior to data entry. When you open the database program, you will find toolbars common to other Microsoft products; however, you are also presented with options (on the task pane) for what database you would like to open, rather than a blank document, as in Word or Excel (see Figure 6.1).

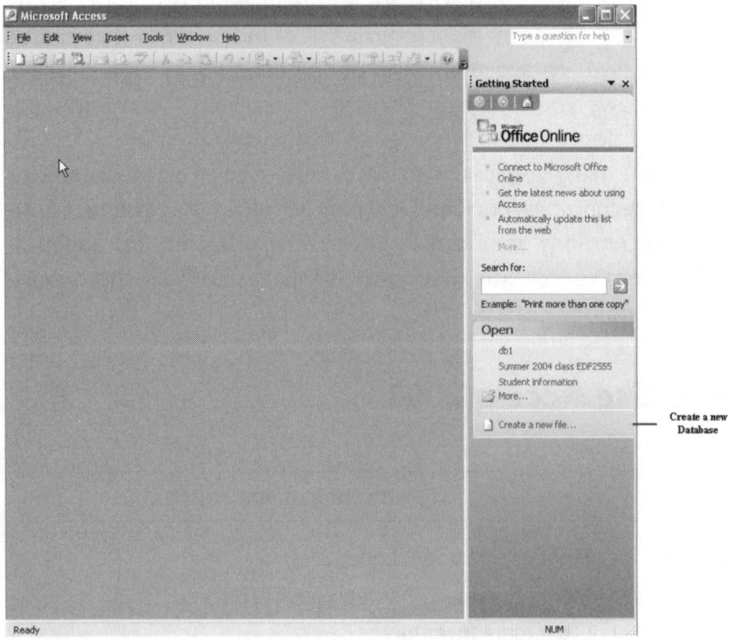

Menus and Toolbars

The Access menu options and toolbars are similar to other Microsoft Office 2003 applications. In this section, we present those items that are unique to Access 2003.

Figure 6.1
Access opening screen

The menu bar (see Figure 6.2) contains Access's main menu items. Clicking the left mouse button on any menu item displays a drop-down list of choices. There are several options not found in other programs in Office, including icons to work with data, such as filtering and sorting.

Figure 6.2
Main menu bar

The Standard Toolbar

Depending on what part of Access you are working with, various standard toolbars are available. Unlike other Microsoft Office products, Access offers options for the operations you want to perform. When a table is opened the toolbar shown is available for use. Its unique features include: view, sort by ascending, sort by descending, filter by section, filter by form, new record, delete record, database window, and new object. Note that view and view object have arrows next to them indicating pull-down menus for further selections. When opening a previously constructed database, the toolbar displays unique functions (see Figure 6.3).

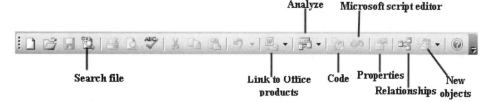

Figure 6.3
Standard toolbar for opening documents

Format in Table View

Also unique in table view of the database is the Format pull-down menu, which allows you to modify column widths, rename columns, hide and unhide columns, and freeze and unfreeze columns (see Figure 6.4). The Hide and Unhide Columns options allow you to reveal and hide columns in a database. The Freeze and Unfreeze Columns options prohibit or allow changes to columns in the database. Formatting allows for the modification of a datasheet's appearance on the screen and when printed.

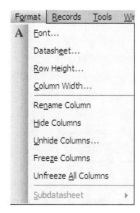

Figure 6.4
Format menu

Show Me

Creating a Database

Opening Access 2003

1. To create a database and corresponding tables, forms, and reports, you need to open Access 2003. Click on the Start button on the Windows taskbar. On the Start menu, move the mouse pointer over *Programs,* then to *Microsoft Office* and click on *Microsoft Access.* When Access opens, you are presented with options for creating a new database, opening an existing database, creating a new database from an existing file, or opening a new template.

2. For the first project, and to become acquainted with the database, click on *Blank database* under the New file section of the task pane (see Figure 6.5).

Figure 6.5
New Blank database

3. The File New Database window appears. As you create a database, you must decide where to save it (e.g., the computer's hard drive, a floppy disk, a Zip disk, and so on). In this example, save the database onto drive A: (a floppy disk), name it *my class,* and click *Create* (see Figure 6.6). You can save the database to other locations (e.g., the local disk, C: hard drive), but remember where you save it. Access appends the .mdb extension to the end of the file name so that the *my class* database is actually named *my class.mdb.* For an example of the completed database, see "my class.mdb" on the CD.

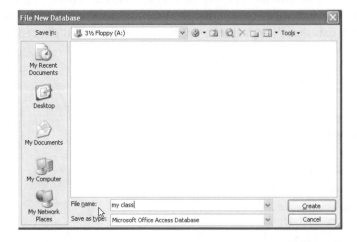

Figure 6.6
Naming the database

If the database is used on more than one computer, you may want it saved on a floppy disk, Zip disk, jump drive, or server. This will enable you to make backup copies of the database and to easily transport it to other computers. There are multiple ways to make backup copies and transport the database. You can, for example, save the database to the computer's hard drive and then copy it onto a floppy or Zip disk. If your computer is connected to the Internet or a local area network (LAN), you may be able to transfer backup copies of the database to other computers over the network or make it accessible to users through a server.

Creating a Table Using a Wizard

1. After saving the database the Database window appears. Click *Create table by using wizard,* then click *Open* (see Figure 6.7). There are other methods of creating a database, but the wizard offers a useful way to get started because it "walks" you through the process. Look at the sample tables and fields on the Table Wizard window for future reference. You may be able to identify some tables or topics that you or your students can use for class projects and assignments (see Figure 6.8).

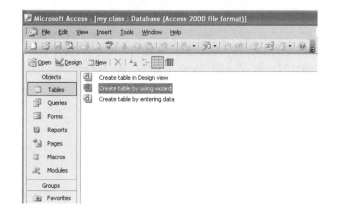

Figure 6.7
Create table by using wizard

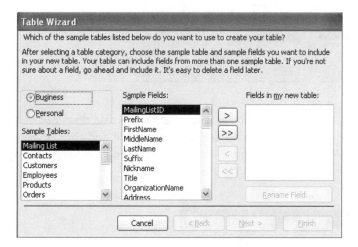

Figure 6.8
Table Wizard screen

2. On the Table Wizard screen, you will see the Business or Personal options and also the *Sample Tables* box.
3. Click on the Business option, then scroll down through the Sample Tables and click *Students* (see Figure 6.9).

Figure 6.9
Sample Tables

4. Scroll through the Sample Fields list. For this example, you will use only some of the possible fields. Note that there are four boxes with arrows next to the *Sample Fields* box. The top two arrows indicate selection of fields that will go into the new table. By selecting a field name in the *Sample Fields* box and clicking the single arrow, only that field is selected for the new table. You can select multiple fields individually by repeating this process numerous times. If you click in the double arrow, all fields are automatically selected for the table. The bottom two arrows deselect the field(s) for the new table. Select the following fields: *First Name, Middle Name, Last Name, Parents Name, Address, Phone Number,* and *Email Name* (see Figure 6.10).

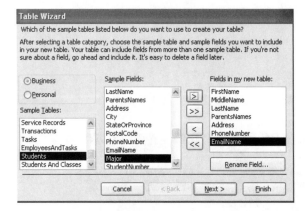

Figure 6.10
Selecting fields for a new table

5. You can choose to rename a field if the title does not fit the descriptor in Sample Fields. To rename the field, highlight it and click on the Rename Field button. A box will pop up allowing you to rename the field more appropriately. Rename the field and click *OK* (see Figure 6.11).

Figure 6.11
Renaming a field

6. Click *Next,* which brings up the screen that allows you to name the table. You may want to call it something other than the name of the database. This screen

also allows you to select a primary key; otherwise, the software package will set a primary key for you. A primary key is a field that uniquely identifies each record in a table. In this case we want the software to select the primary key. Title the table *My class* and click *Next* (see Figure 6.12).

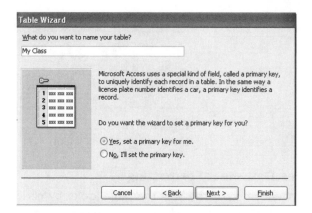

Figure 6.12
Naming the new table

7. After clicking *Next,* the wizard allows you to select how you would like to enter information in the database. You can choose to modify the table design, enter data directly into the table, or enter data into the table using a form the wizard creates for you. In this case, we select *Enter data directly into the table* and click *Finish* (see Figure 6.13).

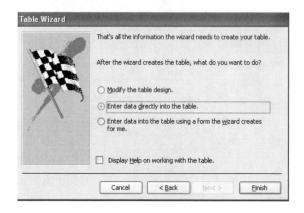

Figure 6.13
Form of entering data

8. You are now presented with the table you created. You can enter data into each of the columns (see Figure 6.14).

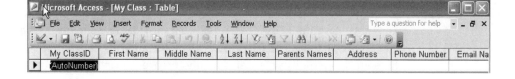

Figure 6.14
Table data entry

Modifying Tables: Adjusting Column Width

Notice that some of the field titles do not appear completely. To adjust the field width, select *Format* then *Column Width*. Type in a number for the column width, or drag the right border of the column selector to the appropriate size (see Figures 6.15 and 6.16).

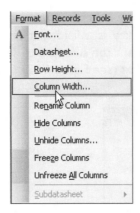

Figure 6.15
Column Width

Figure 6.16
Designating column width

Modifying Tables: Datasheet Formatting

You can change the format, or the way the table looks, by clicking on *Format* and selecting *Datasheet*. This allows you to change the appearance of the cells in the table, for example, to show gridlines, the background color, or gridline color, and the type of lines that separate the fields and records. A sample of what you select is shown on the screen (see Figures 6.17 and 6.18).

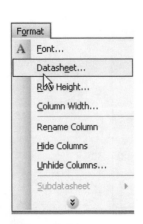

Figure 6.17
Datasheet format

Figure 6.18
Datasheet formatting window

LET ME TRY

So far, we have opened Access, created a new database by using the Database Wizard and created a table. The database is blank because no data have been entered. You now have an opportunity to enter data and create reports for the database.

Entering Data

1. In the table *My Class* enter information using the accompanying table as a guide. Once the data are entered into the table it should look like boxed Figure 6.1. See "my class.mdb" on the CD for an example.

First Name	Middle Name	Last Name	Parents Names	Address	Phone # Area code 218	Email
Helen	Marie	Aster	Ralph	301 Jefferson	531-6622	chma
Frank	John	Coster	Mike	222 Grant	531-4421	cfjc
Megan	Anne	Espinosa	Elaine	322 Van Buren	531-6211	cmae
Teresa	Mary	Teti	Annette	515 Lincoln	531-5656	ctmt
Freta	Monica	Pohlot	Joy	600 Lincoln	531-3823	cfmp
Phonix	Joy	Lario	Earl	212 Taft	531-6237	cpjl
Melissa	Rebecca	Bonzi	Alfred	578 Court	531-4651	cmrb
Kela	Francis	Jones	Keia	449 Green	531-6541	ckfj

Figure 6.1
Data in the table

First Name	Middle Name	Last Name	Parents Names	Address	Phone Number	Email Name
Kelly	Ann	Carter	Jim	301 Jefferson	531-6223	cukac
Freda	Campbell	Dewey	John	499 Greeen	531-4222	cufcd
Phoenix	Jackie	Deno	Emil	212 Taft	531-2111	cfpjd
Ariel	Monique	Cross	Lou Ann	631 Lincoln	531-9494	cuamc
Monica	Key	Wilis	Ralph	780 Court	531-8875	cfmkw
Ray	Alphonse	Testa	Elaine	214 Madison	531-7984	cfrat
Phillip	Michael	Murray	Joy	718 Lincoln	531-8927	cfpmm
Juan	Louis	Montalto	Annette	144 Ashby	531-3195	cfjlm
Antonio	Samuel	Celano	Marco	936 Oak	531-7389	csasc

Microsoft Access - [My Class : Table]
File   Edit   View   Insert   Format   Records   Tools   Window   Help   Type a question for help

2. After the data are entered, save the data by clicking on the Disk icon on the standard toolbar or by clicking *File* and then *Save*. This saves the data in the database.
3. Click on *File* and then *Close*, or click on the X in the upper-right corner of the screen to close the table.
4. The screen now appears in the Create Table menu that displayed when we originally created the table using the wizard. Notice that the table we just created, *My Class*, appears in the list of tables (see boxed Figure 6.2).

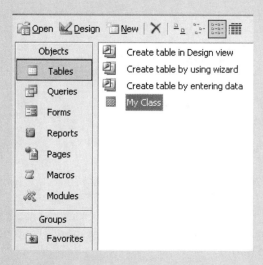

Open   Design   New   X

Objects
Tables
Queries
Forms
Reports
Pages
Macros
Modules
Groups
Favorites

Create table in Design view
Create table by using wizard
Create table by entering data
My Class

Figure 6.2
List of tables

Creating a Report

1. Notice the Objects list along the left side of the window. To print a report of the database created, highlight *Reports* on the Objects list and click on it.

2. A new screen appears listing *Create report in Design view* and *Create report by using wizard.* Highlight *Create report by using wizard* and click on it (see boxed Figure 6.3).

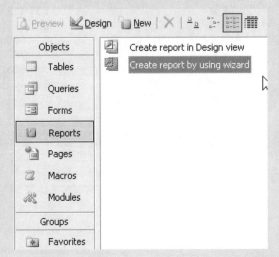

Figure 6.3
Creating a report

3. As you create a report, you can select the table or query on which to base your report. Because you only have one report there will be no selections in that window. The fields you created will appear and you will be able to select the fields that you want to appear in your report.

4. Select the following fields for the report: *First Name, Last Name, Phone Number,* and *Email Name.* Select the fields by clicking on the field to highlight it, then clicking the top arrow. Once you have selected all of the fields, click *Next* (see boxed Figure 6.4).

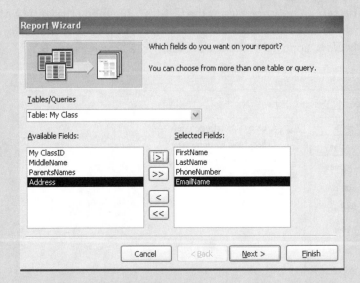

Figure 6.4
Selecting fields
for a report

5. It is possible to group the data in a particular order so that related data appear together in the report. In our case we do not want to group the data; click *Next* (see boxed Figure 6.5).

6. The next screen allows you to sort your records on your report by field. You can sort by ascending or descending order, and you can sort by up to four fields in this order. Select Last Name for the first field to be sorted in ascending order, then click *Next* (see boxed Figure 6.6).

7. There are several options available in laying out the report to be printed. The next screen again allows you to make choices. These choices include report layouts in

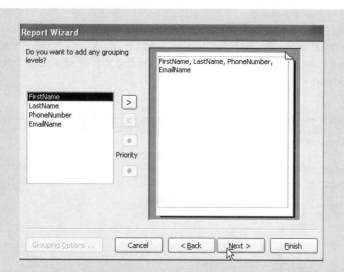

Figure 6.5
Grouping levels
in a report

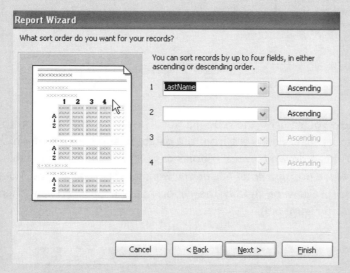

Figure 6.6
Sorting records

columns, tables, and justified. As you click on the different layouts, examples appear in the box at the left of the layout styles. You may choose the page orientation to be portrait or landscape. Select *Tabular* and *Portraits,* then click *Next* (see boxed Figure 6.7).

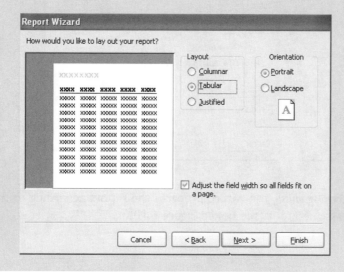

Figure 6.7
Layout of a
report

8. Several styles of typeface and graphic designs are available including Bold, Casual, Compact, Corporate, Formal, and Soft Gray. As you highlight each style an example appears in the box to the left of the list of styles. Select *Corporate,* then click *Next* (see boxed Figure 6.8).

Figure 6.8
Style of a report

9. Now you can give the report a title. The program allows you to give a title to the report that is different from the database and table from which the information has been drawn (several reports can be printed from one table). In the space below the prompt *What title do you want for your report?* type *Morning Class.* You can also preview or modify the report design. Click *Preview,* then click *Finish* (see boxed Figure 6.9).

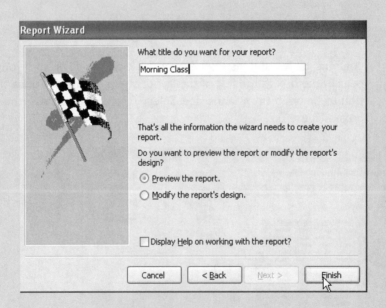

Figure 6.9
Report title

10. By clicking *Finish,* the wizard prepares the report according to the specifications you assigned to it (see boxed Figure 6.10).

Morning Class

Last Name	First Name	Phone Number	Email Name
Carter	Kelly	531-6223	cukac
Celano	Antonio	531-7389	csasc
Cross	Ariel	531-9494	cuamc
Deno	Phoenix	531-2111	ctpjd
Dewey	Freda	531-4222	cufcd
Montalto	Juan	531-3195	ctjlm
Murray	Phillip	531-8927	ctpmm
Testa	Ray	531-7984	ctrat
Wilis	Monica	531-8875	ctmkw

Figure 6.10
Finished report preview

Printing a Report

1. To print your report, select *File* from the menu bar and highlight *Print* (see boxed Figure 6.11). The document will print as shown on the screen to the printer specified in the program screen. You can also click on the Printer icon on the standard toolbar. The date of printing and the page number will be shown at the bottom of the document.

2. You can select *File* and then *Save*. Or you can click on the Disk icon to save the report to a disk. Once the database has been saved, press *Close* then *Exit* (see boxed Figure 6.12).

Figure 6.11
Printing the report

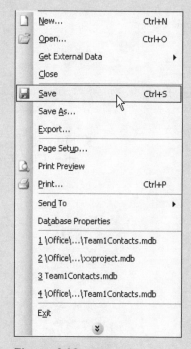

Figure 6.12
Saving the report

Creating a New Database Using Design View

1. Many times assignments require databases that are not found in the Database Wizard. We will now create a new database of information about the planets in the solar system. Students can work in groups; each group will collect information about a specific planet. The data can be compiled and shared with the entire class to work on some basic concepts about the planets.

2. Planning is imperative when it comes to creating a database. The fields in which information is gathered must be decided, and the information that is important to the project and the desired results must be considered.

3. The fields the class has decided on include name, diameter, mass, temperature range, atmosphere, moons, rotation, distance from the sun (orbit), and composition of the planet. See "Planets.mdb" on the CD for an example.

4. Open the Access program and click on *Create a new file,* then click *OK* (see Figure 6.19).

Figure 6.19
Blank Access database

5. Make sure you have a floppy disk in the drive. Name this database *Planets,* and then Click *Create* (see Figure 6.20).

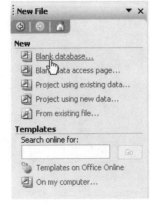

Figure 6.20
Creating a new database

6. You could create a table by entering data directly into the table, but the first group of students to enter data would have to set up all the fields for the rest of the class. Instead, we will use *Create table in Design view* to set up this database. Highlight *Create table in Design view* and click *Open* (see Figure 6.21).

Figure 6.21
Create table in Design view

7. The field names have already been decided on by the class. Field types also must be addressed; this is the type of data to be entered into the field. Field types include:
   ■ Text: Text, letters, numbers, and other characters
   ■ Memo: Holds an unlimited amount of text
   ■ Number: Formatted number
   ■ Date/Time: Dates, times or date/time combinations
   ■ Currency: Money values
   ■ AutoNumber: Automatically assigns a number when a record is added
   ■ Yes/No: Shows Values as yes/no, true/false
   ■ OLE Object: Object linking and embedding; for objects such as pictures and word documents
   ■ Hyperlink: Hyperlink addresses that jump to Web sites, database objects, or other files
   ■ Lookup Wizard: starts a wizard that places look-up constraints in a field.
8. Enter the field names and data types as appropriate (see Figure 6.22).

Field Name	Data Type
Name	Text
Mass	Text
Diameter	Text
Temperature Range	Text
Atmosphere	Text
Moons	Text
Rotation	Text
Distance from the sun	Text
Composition of the planet	Text

Figure 6.22
Field name and data type

9. As you enter the field names, data is presented in the bottom portion of the screen indicating the information you have selected about this field. The data type appears in a pull-down menu. After all fields have been entered and the data types selected, you will have an opportunity to enter descriptions with each field name. (Do not enter descriptors at this time.) Close this screen by clicking the X in the upper right corner (see Figure 6.23).

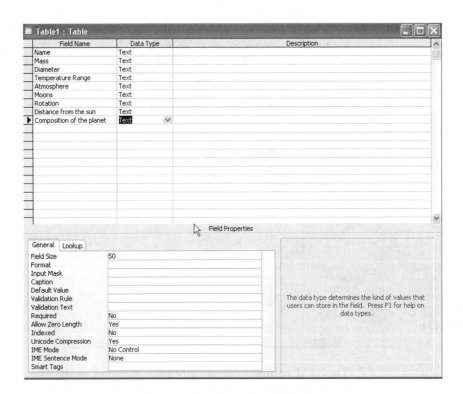

Figure 6.23
Field information

10. As you close the screen, you will be asked if you want to save this table. Save it as *Planets* and click *OK* (see Figure 6.24).

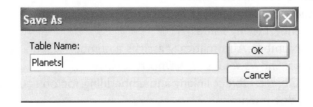

Figure 6.24
Save as *Planets*

11. The table will appear on the list of planet information. Click *Planets* to highlight it, then click *Open* (see Figure 6.25).

Figure 6.25
Opening *Planets*
table

12. You can now enter data into this table (see Figure 6.26).

Figure 6.26
Table data entry

ID	Name	Mass	Diameter	Temperature Ra	Atmosphere	Moons	Rotation
(AutoNumber)							

Rearranging Fields

13. After forming the table you may want to rearrange the fields in the database table format. Click on the field *Moons* to highlight it (see Figure 6.27). Position the mouse over the field and drag the field to a new location next to *Name*. A thick line appears where the field will relocate.

Figure 6.27
Rearranging fields

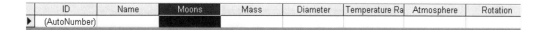

ID	Name	Mass	Diameter	Temperature Ra	Atmosphere	Moons	Rotation
(AutoNumber)							

14. The new field appears at the new location (see Figure 6.28).

Figure 6.28
New location

ID	Name	Moons	Mass	Diameter	Temperature Ra	Atmosphere	Rotation
(AutoNumber)							

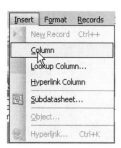

Figure 6.29
Inserting new fields

Adding Fields

15. To add fields to the table, click on the field name to the right of where you want the field to appear. Click *Insert,* then click *Column* (see Figure 6.29).

Deleting Fields

16. To delete a field click on the name of the field you want to delete. Click *Edit,* then click *Delete Column* (see Figure 6.30).

Figure 6.30
Delete column

17. Close this table by clicking on the X in the upper-right corner. This will bring you back to the Table listing. Note that the table *Planets* is now on the list (see Figure 6.31).

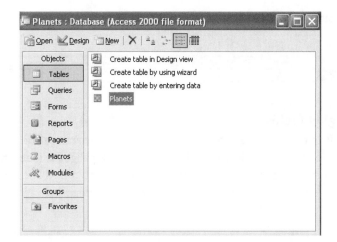

Figure 6.31
Table list

Creating a Form

1. From the Objects list, click on *Forms*. This gives you a list of options for creating forms. Because groups of students will enter data into this database at various times, a Forms format of data entry will probably be the easiest format for them to use (see Figure 6.32).

Figure 6.32
Forms list

2. Select *Create form by using wizard,* and then click *Open.* The wizard screen appears (see Figure 6.33).

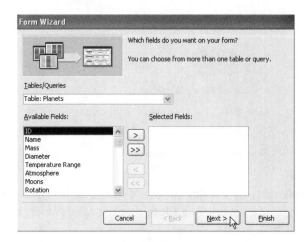

Figure 6.33
Form Wizard

3. The wizard allows you to select the fields to use in your form. It looks similar to previous wizard screens in the Access programs.
4. Select fields by using the arrows to add or remove items from the form. Select all fields, click *Next* and move to the next screen.
5. As you select different layouts, illustrations of the layouts appear in the shaded box to the left of the list. Select *Columnar* for this form, then click *Next* (see Figure 6.34).

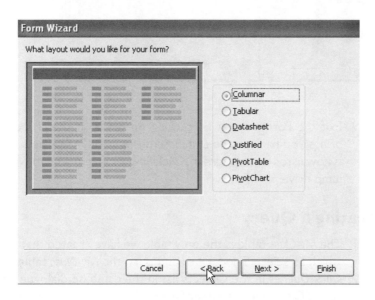

Figure 6.34
Form layout

6. Next you can select the styles you want to use for the form. Again, illustrations show the styles as you highlight each one. Select *International* for this database, then click *Next* (see Figure 6.35).
7. You will be asked to title this form (see Figure 6.36). Use *Planets* as the title, then click *Finish*. The form you created appears. Students can fill in missing data or review information that has been placed in the database thus far.
8. The form has now been set up and the students can enter information they find in texts or on the World Wide Web. Data can now be entered into the fields (see Figure 6.37).

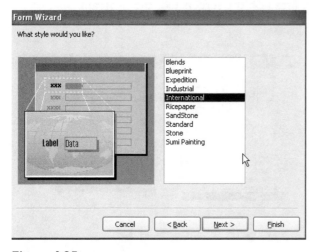

Figure 6.35
Style of the form

Figure 6.36
Title of the form

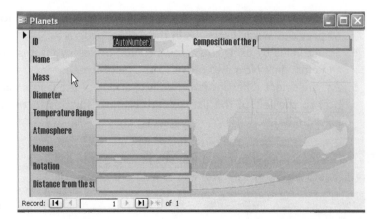

Figure 6.37
Form for data entry

9. Exit the Form format by clicking on the X at the top of the *Forms* box. This brings you back to the *Database* dialog box. The planets form you just created is now listed on this screen. Click *Save* to save the form we have created to your jump drive.

Creating a Query

1. The *My Class* table is the only table we have created that has any data in it from which to select. Select *Open* and open the *My Class* table from the floppy disk.
2. Click *Queries* in the Objects list in the database dialogue box.
3. Select *Create query by using wizard*. This will be a similar process to using other wizards in Access. Click *Open* (see Figure 6.38).
4. The query allows you to select portions of the database and show only those selected fields. Select *First Name*, *Last Name*, and *Address*. Click *Next* (see Figure 6.39).
5. The next screen allows you to name the query. Name the query *My Class Addresses*, then click *Finish* (see Figure 6.40).
6. The results of the query appear. Place the results in ascending or descending order by clicking on the A–Z or Z–A icon on the toolbar (see Figure 6.41).
7. Save the results of this query by clicking on *Save* or on the Disk icon on the toolbar. Close this screen by clicking on the X. This takes you to the Query list, and *My Class Address* is now listed on the screen. Exit the program.

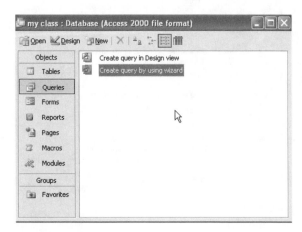

Figure 6.38
Query using wizard

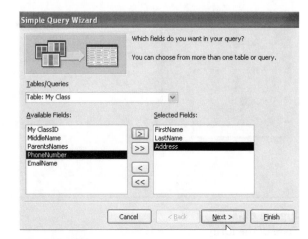

Figure 6.39
Selecting fields

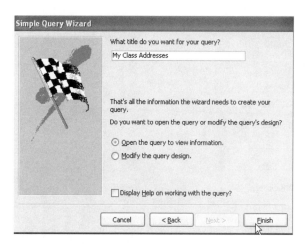

Figure 6.40
Query title

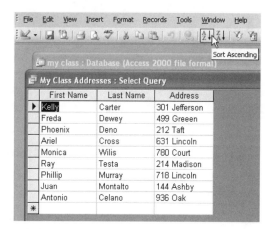

Figure 6.41
Query results

LET ME TRY

So far we have created a database for students entered in data, and selected addresses for the student in a query. Let's print a report of the query results.

Printing Query Results in a Report

1. Open *Microsoft Access*.
2. When the open an existing file screen appears, highlight *My Class* and click *OK*.
3. Click on *Report* in the Object list.
4. Highlight and click *Create a report using wizard*.
5. In the box or Table/Query, select *Query: My Class Addresses* (see boxed Figure 6.13).

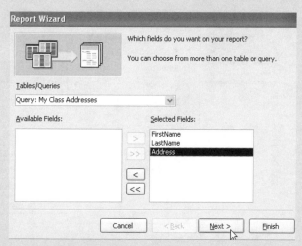

Figure 6.13
Report form query

6. Select all fields, then click *Next*.
7. No grouping is necessary; click *Next*.
8. Sort records by last name A–Z, then click *Next*.
9. Select a table layout and click *Next*.
10. Select the bold style and click *Next*
11. Use the title *My Class Addresses* and click *Finish*.
12. Select the Print icon from the toolbar and print the document to the appropriate printer.
13. The finished document will look like boxed Figure 6.14. See "my class.mdb" on the CD for an example.

My Class Addresses

Last Name	First Name	Address
Carter	Kelly	301 Jefferson
Celano	Antonio	936 Oak
Cross	Ariel	631 Lincoln
Deno	Phoenix	212 Taft
Dewey	Freda	499 Greeen
Montalto	Juan	144 Ashby
Murray	Phillip	718 Lincoln
Testa	Ray	214 Madison
Wilis	Monica	780 Court

Figure 6.14
Report address

Mail Merge

Databases can be used to insert information into letters that you write using Word, perhaps to personalize a letter. In order to perform the Mail Merge function in Word, a database must be created first. You will be using the data in the My Class database in this mail merge. You will be writing a short note to your class members confirming their e-mail addresses. See "Mail merge letter.doc" for an example on the CD.

1. Open *Microsoft Word* and a new blank document.
2. To begin a mail merge, choose the Tools listing from the standard toolbar and select *Letters and Mailings* and *Mail Merge Wizard* (see boxed Figure 6.15).

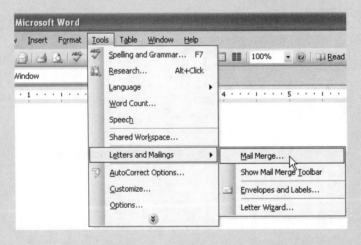

Figure 6.15
Mail Merge
selection

3. Select *Letters* for the type of document you are working on.
4. The options of a mail merge include letters; e-mail messages just like a letter but intended for electronic delivery; mailing labels that allow you to specify the size of label wanted; and a directory that provides a list of all data forming a list.
5. Click on *Starting a document* at the bottom of the Mail Merge panel. You will notice that this is step 1 of six steps set up by the wizard.
6. Select the option of *Current document* to start your letter. *Templates* and *Inserting mail merge information from previously existing documents* are also options (see boxed Figure 6.16).

7. Select *Current Documents* from the panel on the next step and select *Next: select recipients* (see boxed Figure 6.17).

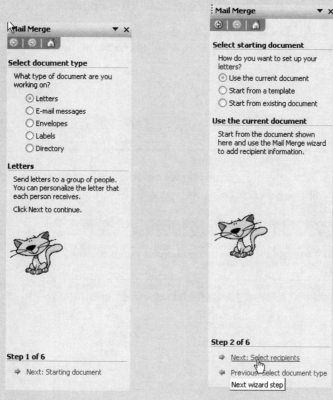

Figure 6.16
Select starting document

Figure 6.17
Use Current document

8. Click on *Select recipients* from the wizard list at the bottom of the Mail Merge panel (step 3 of six steps in the wizard).
9. Select *Use an existing list* from the choices provided.
10. Click on *Next: Write your letter* and the program will ask for the source of your database. In this case you would select the drive to which you saved the *My Class* database, and then click *Open* (see boxed Figure 6.18).

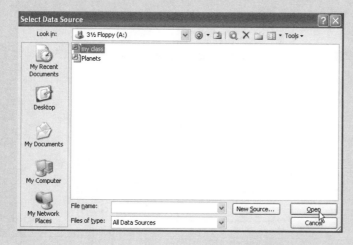

Figure 6.18
Selecting database for Mail Merge

11. You will need to select the table the data will be drawn from, in this case choose *My Class* (see boxed Figure 6.19).

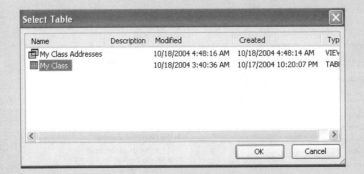

Figure 6.19
Selecting table

12. You will be given an opportunity to edit your address list. At this point in time you will not, so click *OK* (see Figure 6.20).

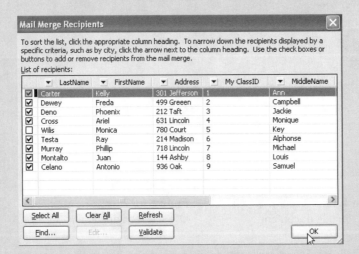

Figure 6.20
Database editing

13. Again click *Next: write your letter* and additional options will appear in the Mail Merge panel. Before selecting any of those options, type in today's date and press the Enter key twice. You will only be using the salutation in this letter because you do not have complete mailing address information in your database.
14. Click on *Greeting line* from the Mail Merge panel and select the information as presented. Do look at the various options, but select the automatic selection (see boxed Figure 6.21).

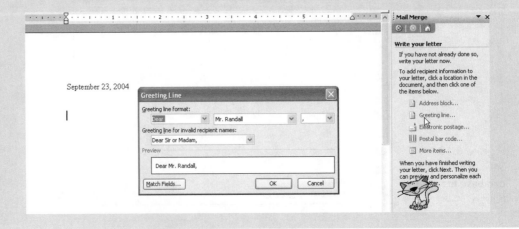

Figure 6.21
Greeting line

15. After selecting the greeting line, press Enter twice and type in the following information: *I am reviewing the e-mail addresses of my class and would like to confirm that the following is your e-mail address:*

16. Select *More items* from the Mail Merge panel and select *Email Name* from the listing (see boxed Figure 6.22) and click *Insert.*

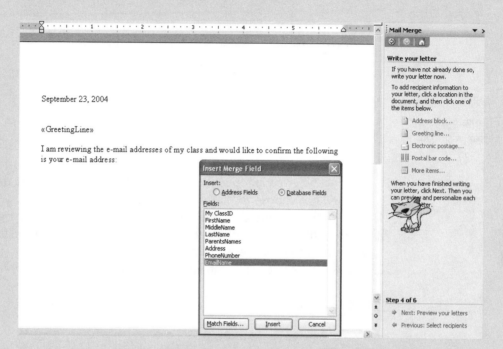

Figure 6.22
Inserting e-mail data

17. The placeholder for the e-mail will be inserted. Then click *Close* (see boxed Figure 6.23).

Figure 6.23
Insert Merge Field

> I am reviewing the e-mail addresses of my class and would like to confirm the following is your e-mail address: «EmailName».

18. Type a period after the placeholder and then finish the letter by typing the following: *If this address is not correct, or has changed, please provide a correct address the next time that class meets, or send the address to my e-mail account noted on the school Web site. Thank you.* Press Enter twice and type in *Sincerely,* press Enter three times and then type in your name. The completed short letter will look like boxed Figure 6.24.

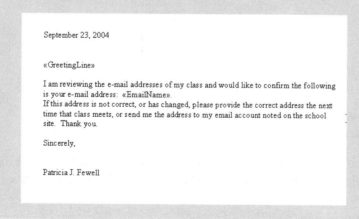

Figure 6.24
Letter with placeholders

19. Click on *Next: preview your letter* from the Mail Merge panel. This will allow you to see the first letter that has been completed (see boxed Figure 6.25).

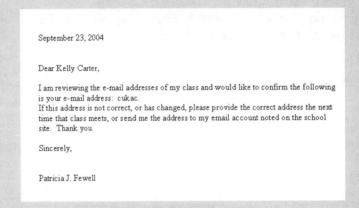

September 23, 2004

Dear Kelly Carter,

I am reviewing the e-mail addresses of my class and would like to confirm the following is your e-mail address: cukac.
If this address is not correct, or has changed, please provide the correct address the next time that class meets, or send me the address to my email account noted on the school site. Thank you.

Sincerely,

Patricia J. Fewell

Figure 6.25
Letter with data inserted

20. You will be given an opportunity to edit the recipient list. At this point in time you will not choose to do this.
21. Select *Next*, complete the merge from the wizard (see boxed Figure 6.26).
22. You will then be given the option of printing the letters or editing each individual letter to further personalize the letter.
23. You will choose to print the letter (see boxed Figure 6.27).

Figure 6.26
Complete the merge

Figure 6.27
Print the completed merge

24. You will be given the option to print all or part of the letters at this point in time. Select the current record by clicking on the Radial button, and then clicking on *OK* (see boxed Figure 6.28).

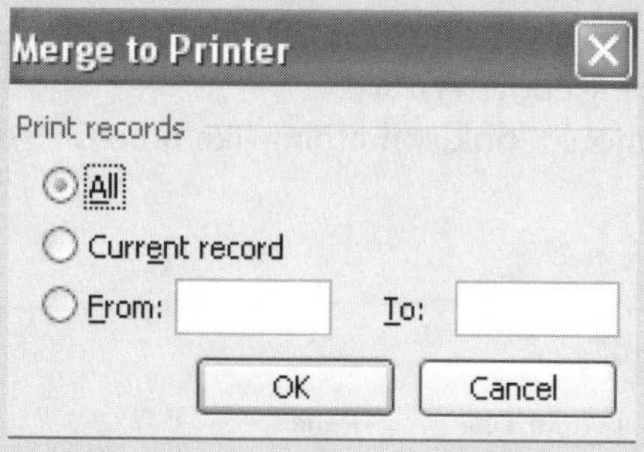

Figure 6.28
Merge to Printer

25. Print the document to the appropriate printer.
26. The finished document should look like boxed Figure 6.29.

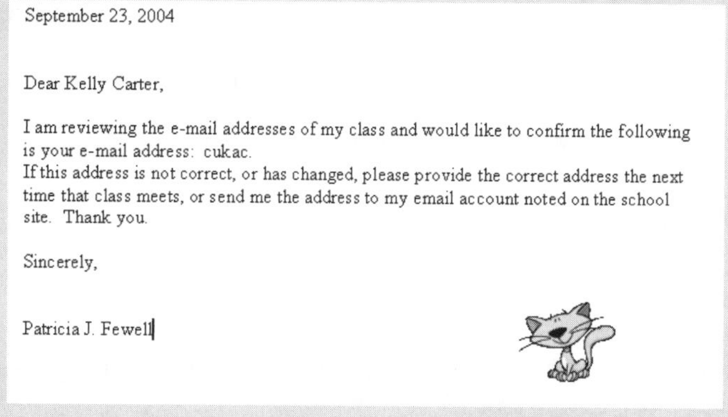

September 23, 2004

Dear Kelly Carter,

I am reviewing the e-mail addresses of my class and would like to confirm the following is your e-mail address: cukac.
If this address is not correct, or has changed, please provide the correct address the next time that class meets, or send me the address to my email account noted on the school site. Thank you.

Sincerely,

Patricia J. Fewell

Figure 6.29
Mail Merge letter

LET ME TRY... AGAIN

To practice creating a database, let's create a database of the Gary Paulsen books that students could read.

1. Open Access.
2. Select *Create a new file*.
3. Select *Create a new database*.
4. Create a database entitled *Gary Paulsen books* on your thumb drive (whatever drive it designates, i.e., drive F)
5. Create a table using the wizard.
6. Select *Personal* from the database choices.
7. Select *Books* from the database listing.
8. The fields that you should select are: *Title, Copyright year, Pages,* and *Notes*
9. Enter the following data (see boxed Figure 6.30).

Title	Copyright Year	Pages	Notes
Hatchet	1987	189	plane crash
Brian's Hunt	2003	112	
Brian's Return	2001	144	
The Island	1990	208	
guts	2002	160	
Escape from Fir	1995	80	

Figure 6.30
Gary Paulsen books

10. Once the data has been entered, close the window.
11. Create a report using the Report Wizard.
12. The completed report should look something like boxed Figure 6.31.

Books

Title	Copyright Year	Pages
Hatchet	1987	189
Brian's Hunt	2003	112
Brian's Return	2001	144
The Island	1990	208
guts	2002	160
Escape from Fire Mountain	1995	80
Sentries	1965	

Figure 6.31
Report of Gary
Paulsen books

A CHALLENGE USING ACCESS 2003

For those of you who would like a challenge beyond the Let Me Try activities presented in this chapter, try the following exercises.

1. Create a database about the characters of a book you have recently read. Fields could include character name, gender, characteristics, and role in the book.

2. Create a database of all of the plants that are in and around the school building, including the common name, scientific name, where these plants may be found, and a description of the plants.

TYING IT ALL TOGETHER

In this chapter, we created two Access databases. We produced tables, forms, reports, queries, and mail merges from these databases. All of these objects were saved to a data source. The reports of the databases, queries, and mail merge were printed.

REFERENCES

International Society for Technology in Education (ISTE). (October 14, 2004). Profiles for technology literate teachers. ISTE Web page. Available: http://cnets.iste.org/teachers/t_stands.html.

7 OUTLOOK 2003

CHAPTER OUTLINE

LEARNING OBJECTIVES

At the completion of this chapter you will be able to:
- Display a summary of the current day using Outlook Today
- Send an e-mail message
- Check incoming e-mail messages
- Construct a calendar
- Create an address book using Contacts
- Create several reminder notes
- Delete unwanted items in folders

TECHNICAL TERMS

The following are terms that you will encounter in the chapter and with which you will become familiar:

Outlook Today

Calendar

Contacts

Inbox

Tasks

CC or Carbon Copy

Drafts

Attachment

CHAPTER OVERVIEW

This chapter provides an introduction to Outlook 2003. The content focuses on the fundamentals of using the tools in the Outlook program and applying them to a variety of learning activities. The tools, or folders, include the Inbox, Calendar, Contacts, Tasks, Notes, Journal, and Outlook Today. The Show Me section presents instructions on using many of the Outlook tools, for example, to create calendars, to e-mail students and parents, and to create a task list for both teacher and student use. Several Let Me Try student-oriented exercises give specific examples and step-by-step instructions for using Outlook 2003 to accomplish a variety of learning activities. Studying the chapter content and working through the Let Me Try exercises will enable you to use all the tools found in this program.

About Outlook

Outlook is an electronic management system that enables you to keep a calendar, send and receive e-mail, create a list of activities, and maintain an address book. Outlook, in a sense, is an electronic day planner.

You as a teacher can use Outlook for a variety of activities in your classroom. The calendar helps you keep track of appointments with parents, note state testing dates, and even make calendars for parents and students indicating your classroom activities.

How Teachers and Students Might Use Outlook 2003

Teacher Production of Materials

Instruction/Learning	Classroom Management
Create a calender of historical events that happened on calender days.	Create a list of parent contacts via e-mail addresses
Create a contact list of state senators and representatives for the school district for social studies	Create classroom calendars
Create e-mail pen pals with students in other countries	Create a journal of classroom activities and contacts Create appointments for parent/teacher meetings Create a list of contacts for classroom materials, including addresses

Student Production of Materials

Instruction/Learning

E-mail government officials or individuals that are experts in their field asking questions related to materials being studied

E-mail pen pals from other countries to understand the differences and similarities

Create a calendar for the class of important historical events that happened on each school day using the calendar in Outlook

Using the notes section of Outlook create a "quote for the day"

Working with Outlook

The primary purpose of this chapter is to help you become familiar with the fundamental components and features of Outlook 2003 so that you will use them in productive ways in your classes and with your students. To accomplish this objective, we present several examples throughout the chapter that will help you learn the components of Outlook and apply them to your teaching and learning activities. Although the examples here may be specific, the steps and procedures are generic and applicable to a variety of classroom management tasks and learning activities. As you work through the chapter's content, substitute our examples with your own.

A Word About the Outlook Workspace

Unlike other Office programs, Outlook has essentially five different tools that allow you create calendars, list things to do, make appointment lists, send and receive e-mail, and create electronic post-it notes. You have folders that are automatically set up as your Personal Folders along the left side of the screen. These folders include:

- Calendar—your personal calendar
- Contacts—personal contacts
- Deleted items—items you have deleted are stored until permanently deleted
- Drafts—saved e-mail messages you have not finished are stored here temporarily
- Inbox—Where all incoming mail comes in
- Junk E-mail—mail you have designated as junk e-mail is stored here
- Notes—notes to yourself can be stored here
- Outbox—mail waiting to be sent is kept here until it is mailed
- Sent Items—messages sent out are saved here
- Tasks—your to-do list
- Search Folders—contains results of searches you have conducted in your personal folders (the search folders are new in Office 2003; see Figure 7.1)

The Outlook folders do not correspond to folders on your hard drive; their contents are not individual files.

Using the Navigation Pane

The Folder List is really one pane of the Navigation pane, which corresponds to what used to be called the Outlook bar in previous versions of Office. You may modify the size of the Navigation pane by clicking and dragging the thin bar. If you drag it up to shrink the pane, you will see larger buttons on the Navigation pane. If you drag it down, the buttons are replaced by small icons at the bottom of the Navigation pane (see Figure 7.2).

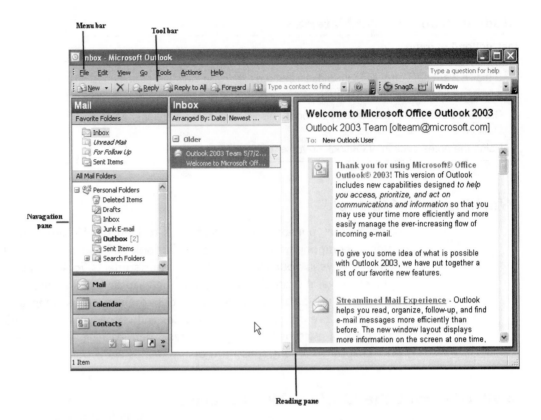

Figure 7.1
Outlook opening screen

Figure 7.2
Changing the size of the Navigation pane

E-Mail Netiquette

Using the Internet for e-mail is different than sending mail using paper and pencil, talking on the telephone, or talking face to face. Keep the following thoughts in mind as you compose e-mail messages:

■ Do not use all UPPERCASE letters in an e-mail message. It is like shouting when speaking.
■ Keep messages short.

- Remember that people other than the individual being sent the message may read the message. The recipient of the message may forward the message to individuals unknown to you.
- Read and be familiar with your school's acceptable use policy. There may be stipulations for the use of e-mail by faculty and students.
- Consider the tone of your messages. With e-mail, you are not personally present, so people cannot note body language to help interpret what you are saying. You may know how you want someone to interpret a message, but you must write it in the manner that conveys your intended meaning.
- Know the individuals to whom you are writing when possible. If you are chatting, lurk (watch in the background) prior to entering into the conversation.
- E-mail is the written word; grammar and spelling count.
- Do not flame other individuals. "Flaming" is what people do when they express strongly held opinions without holding back any emotion.
- Shorthand language used by some individuals includes the following:
  - FYI—For your information
  - IMO—In my opinion
  - IMHO—In my humble opinion
  - BTW—By the way
  - LOL—Laugh out loud
  - FWIW—For what it's worth

Show Me

The Inbox

1. To use e-mail in Outlook, open Outlook 2003. The first time you open Outlook, a wizard appears to help you set up Outlook for your e-mail provider. Click the Start button on the Windows taskbar. On the Start menu, move the mouse pointer over *Programs* and the Programs submenu appears. Move the mouse over *Microsoft Office* and the Microsoft Office submenu appears. Click *Microsoft Outlook* to open the program. *Note:* Depending on how you installed Outlook 2003, the menu items for it may be located in various locations on the Start menu. In most cases, it can be found under *Programs* or under *Programs* within the Microsoft Office folder.

2. To read an e-mail message click on *Mail* along the Navigation pane. Click *Inbox* to view the messages you have received. As you click on the message you would like to read from the Inbox, the message will appear in the Reading pane. All messages in your inbox will be displayed in the Message pane (center pane) and the current message you have selected will be displayed in the Display pane on the right (see Figure 7.3)

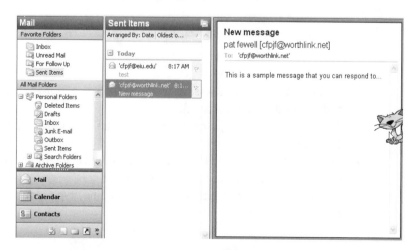

Figure 7.3
Read messages

3. You can double-click on the message to have it appear in the Read pane. You have the ability to forward, reply, reply to all, or delete messages.

Sending E-mail

1. To send a message you must know the e-mail address of the individual you want to contact. *There are netiquette issues you should be aware of when sending e-mail messages* as mentioned previously in this chapter.

2. To send an e-mail, select *Inbox* and then select *New* (see Figure 7.4).

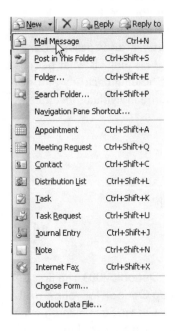

Figure 7.4
Sending new mail

3. The screen shown in Figure 7.5 will appear. Type the e-mail address of the person to whom you are sending the message in the space next to the *To:* line.

Figure 7.5
To recipient of the e-mail

4. If you want to send a message to more than one individual, separate each e-mail address with a semicolon (;).

5. To send a carbon copy of the e-mail to an individual, type that address in the *Cc* space.

6. E-mail messages should have a subject so the recipient knows what the message is about. Type a subject for the message.

7. In the empty screen below the subject line, type your e-mail message (see Figure 7.6).

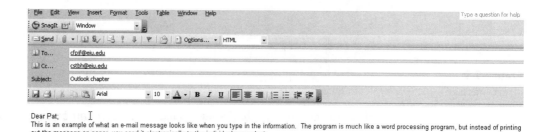

Figure 7.6
E-mail message information

8. Once you have completed your e-mail message, send it. There are options for sending messages. They can be ranked for high importance or low importance, or they can be flagged for follow-up (see Figure 7.7).

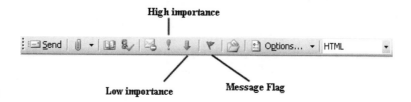

Figure 7.7
Mail sent indicators

9. You can also select Options to make modifications as to the importance of the message, or you could request a response from the recipient (see Figure 7.8).

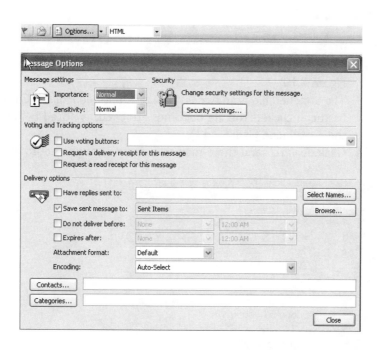

Figure 7.8
Message options

10. Files can be attached to e-mail messages. Attachments might include documents, pictures, and multimedia objects, but the receiving computer must have the software installed to read the attached file. Files can be attached to e-mail messages in several ways. You can click on *Insert* from the main menu bar or click on the Insert File icon or Paperclip icon. To attach a file, click on the Paperclip icon on the toolbar (see Figure 7.9)

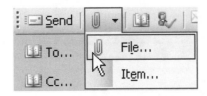

Figure 7.9
Insert message

11. After clicking on the Paperclip icon, a screen immediately comes up for you to indicate the file path to your attachment. Select files that are on any of the drives to which you have access. In Figure 7.10, the attachment is from the floppy drive A: and it is called *Planets. You can find "Planets.mdb" in the "Access" folder in "Examples" on the CD. You can also practice sending attachments with the "Hershey and chip" photograph in the "Outlook" folder on the CD.*

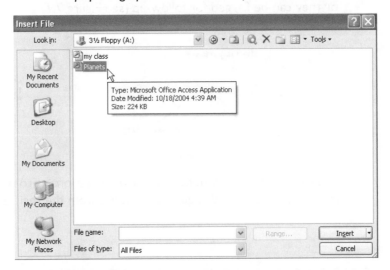

Figure 7.10
Selecting a file to insert

12. Click on the file to highlight it. Double-click the file or click on *Insert* (see Figure 7.10).
13. The attached file is an Access database entitled *Planets*. Once the Insert button has been clicked, the file becomes attached, as noted below the subject line of the e-mail (see Figure 7.11)
14. Click *Send* to send the e-mail message you have created with the attachment.

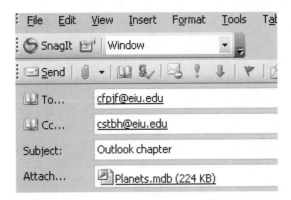

Figure 7.11
E-mail attachment

Replying to and Forwarding Messages

1. When you receive messages, you will want to reply to them. Select a message from your inbox to which you want to reply. Select *Reply* from the toolbar (see Figure 7.12).

Figure 7.12
Responding to an e-mail

2. You could also select *Reply to all*. By doing so, you send a reply not only to the individual who sent you the message but also everyone who received the original message. In this case select *Reply*. Once you click on *Reply*, your e-mail message will look similar to the screen shown in Figure 7.13. The name and e-mail address of the individual who originally wrote your message appears in the *To:* line, and the subject is filled as an *RE* (the title of the original message; see Figure 7.13)

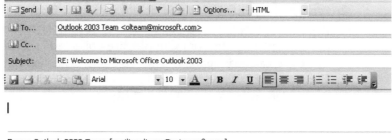

Figure 7.13
Replying to an
e-mail

From: Outlook 2003 Team [mailto:olteam@microsoft.com]
Sent: Friday, May 07, 2004 9:41 AM
To: New Outlook User
Subject: Welcome to Microsoft Office Outlook 2003

3. The cursor appears at the beginning of the text, and you can reply with a copy of your original message at the end of your new message. If you choose, you can highlight and delete the information in the original message. Once you have typed your reply, click *Send* and the message is on its way.
4. To forward a message to another individual, select the e-mail message, then click *Forward*. Notice that instead of the *RE:* in the subject line, the message will now read *FW:* (see Figure 7.14).

Printing E-mail Messages

1. To print an e-mail message, select the message and click on the Printer icon (see Figure 7.15)

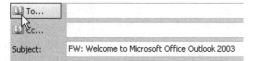

Figure 7.14
Forwarding a message

Figure 7.15
Print icon

2. Or you can select *File* from the Outlook toolbar, then select *Print* (see Figure 7.16).

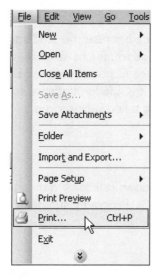

Figure 7.16
Print from File menu

Deleting Messages

1. To delete a message, highlight the message on the Inbox screen. Then click on the Delete icon (see Figure 7.17).

Figure 7.17
Deleting e-mail

2. Periodically, you will want to delete messages from the Deleted items folder (you can retrieve material from the Deleted folder until you empty the folder.) All items you delete from Outlook are collected in this folder, including e-mail messages, calendar appointments, contacts, tasks, and notes.
3. To empty the Deleted Items folder, select *Tools* on the toolbar, then select *Empty "Deleted Items" folder* (see Figure 7.18).

Figure 7.18
Empty "Deleted
Items" folder

LET ME TRY

So far, we have opened Outlook 2003 and created and sent an e-mail message. We responded to an e-mail and reviewed how to forward a message.

Suppose you and your students are studying the federal government. After reviewing what might be included in an appropriate e-mail, have the students write out their e-mail messages for your review. Then send the messages. Some of the e-mail addresses they could use are:

President: president@whitehouse.gov
Vice President: vice.president@whitehouse.gov
First Lady: first.lady@whitehouse.gov

These addresses are good for practice because the students will receive an almost immediate response. These e-mail addresses have what is called a robot response, which notes that an e-mail message has been received that will be read and addressed at a later time. Emphasize that it is a federal offense to make threats by e-mail and that their e-mail messages will be taken very seriously.

Sending E-Mail to the President

1. Click on the Start button on the Windows taskbar. On the Start menu, move the mouse pointer over *Programs* and the Programs submenu appears. Move the

mouse over *Microsoft Office* and the Microsoft Office submenu appears. Click on *Microsoft Outlook* and Outlook 2003 opens.

2. Click on *Inbox.*
3. Click on *New.*
4. Type in the e-mail address for the president: president@whitehouse.gov
5. Type an appropriate subject for your e-mail.
6. Type your e-mail message and sign it.
7. Click *Send* and your message is on its way.

Calendar

1. Another component of the Outlook tools is the Calendar. You can view the calendar as a day, a work week, a full week, or a month. To display the Calendar tool, click on the Calendar icon on the Outlook desktop (see Figure 7.19).

Figure 7.19
Calendar icon

2. To view the different calendar formats, select the views along the toolbar or select *View* from the toolbar, then select the style of calendar you wish to use (see Figure 7.20).

Figure 7.20
Calendar style

3. Select a one-day calendar from the toolbar. The daily appointment displays appointments for the current day. There is a display for the current month (see Figure 7.21).

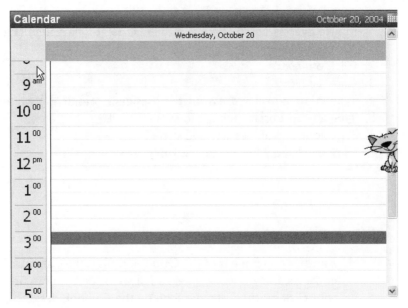

Figure 7.21
One-day calendar

    4. To add an item to the calendar for the day shown, click on the appropriate time and type the information needed, then press Enter (see Figure 7.22)

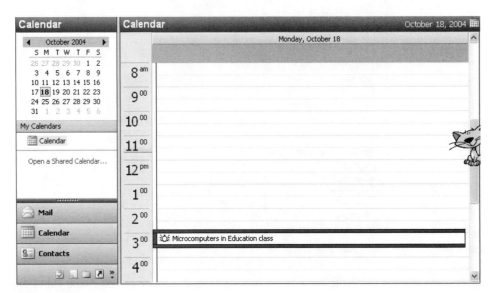

Figure 7.22
Appointment for the day

    5. Once the appointment has been entered, double-click on the appointment and a window appears that allows you to make modifications to the appointment and add information.

    6. Adjust the end time to 5:15 P.M. and close the window, saving your changes. This changes the appointment time (class time) to reflect the new end time (see Figure 7.23).

    7. To display another day of the month, click the date that you would like to select.

    8. To delete an appointment, highlight the appointment and click on the Delete icon or press the Delete key on the keyboard.

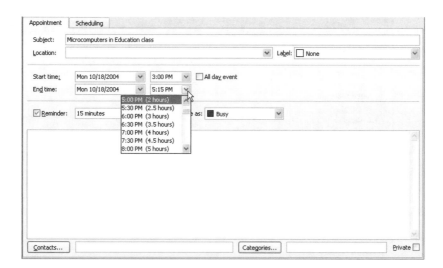

Figure 7.23
Change appoint-
ment time

LET ME TRY

So far we have made an appointment on the current date, modified that appointment, and selected another date. Students can keep their own appointment calendars for class assignments and other activities in which they participate during the school year. Let's set up a day in the student calendar.

1. Open *Outlook*.
2. Click on *Calendar*.
3. Click on a date two weeks from today.
4. Click on the *9:00 a.m.* box.
5. Type in *History test*.
6. Click on the *12:00* box and type *Meet Joan for lunch*.
7. Scroll down the times using the bar along the side of the date until you reach 3:00.
8. Click on *3:00* and drag the mouse to *4:30*; type in *Debate practice*, then press Enter.

Contacts

Outlook Contacts allows you to keep information about friends, family members, colleagues, and students' parents or guardians.

1. Click on Contacts on the Microsoft Outlook screen (see Figure 7.24)
2. If this is your first contact, a screen appears allowing you to double-click on the area to create a new contact.
3. To create a new contact, type information into the Contact display window (see Figure 7.25).
4. Under *Addresses*, select *Home, Business*, or *Other* and identify a preferred mailing address.
5. Each of the fields with an arrow allows for selection of different titles to the field.
6. Once you have typed in the fields, save the contact. Click *File* and select *Save*, or click *Save* and *Close* on the toolbar (see Figure 7.26).

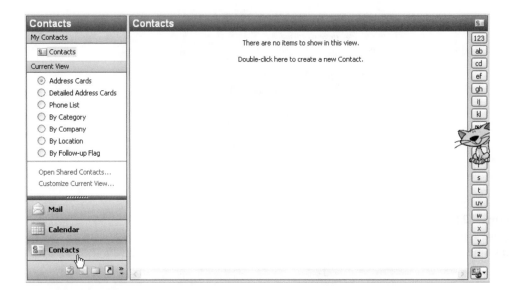

Figure 7.24
Contacts folder

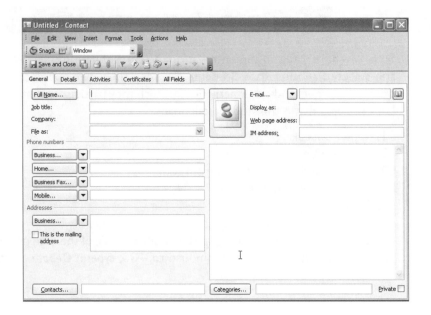

Figure 7.25
Contact window

Figure 7.26
Save and Close

7. If you click on *Save* and *Close,* the window you were just typing in (the individual contact) closes and the list of contacts appears. You can click on the bar of each contact to go to the individual contact information screen (see Figure 7.27).

8. To return to the individual contact screen, click on the gray bar that turns blue. The icons on the toolbar next to the Save and Close icons allow you to create a new contact, print, attach documents, flag this contact for further follow-up, display a map of the address (if you are connected to the Internet), e-mail the contact, and autodial for phone or fax (see Figure 7.28).

9. Click on *Actions* on the Outlook taskbar. A menu drops down. This menu allows you to create a new contact, draft a letter to this contact, and send an e-mail message, among other things (see Figure 7.29).

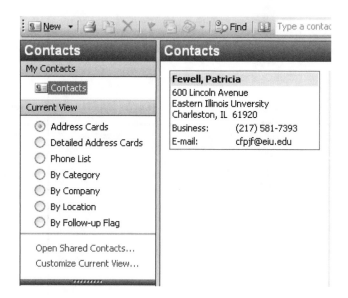

Figure 7.27
Contact list

Figure 7.28
Individual Contact screen icons

Figure 7.29
Actions menu

10. Select *New Letter to Contact.* This launches Microsoft Word and a Letter Wizard that takes you step by step through the process of creating a letter to this contact (see Figures 7.30 and 7.31).

11. You can either continue with the letter or cancel. Close word to return to Outlook.

12. After quitting Word, your Outlook Contact is still on the screen. Select *New Message to Contact.* This takes you to the Outlook Inbox and automatically places the e-mail address for this contact in the e-mail's *To:* line (see Figures 7.32 and 7.33).

Figure 7.30
Letter to contact

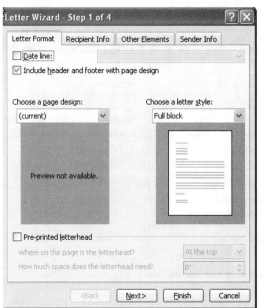

Figure 7.31
Letter Wizard

Figure 7.32
Action list New Messages

Figure 7.33
E-mail from contact actions

LET ME TRY

So far we have opened Contacts and have entered data for one contact. Select one of your students and enter data for that individual. Then write a letter to that student's parents or guardians.

1. Click on *New Contact*.
2. The Contact window appears.
3. Click in an area and type the contact's information that is pertinent to you and/or your class.

4. Click *Save* and then *Close*.
5. The contact information you just typed will appear in the Contact list.
6. Click *Actions*.
7. Click on *New Letter to Contact*.
8. Follow the wizard instructions to create a letter.
9. Click on the Print icon to print the document.
10. Close Word; do not save your letter.

Tasks

Tasks allow you to create an electronic to-do list, including due dates for tasks.

1. Click on the Tasks icon from the Navigation pane. The Task widow will appear (see Figure 7.34).

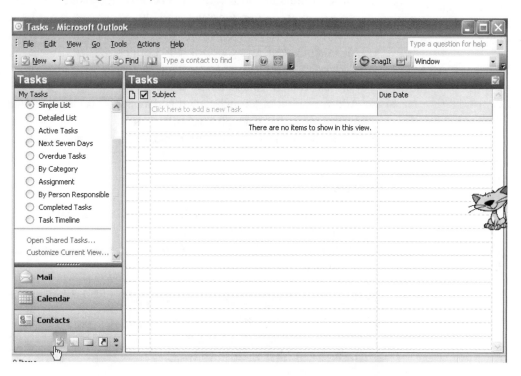

Figure 7.34
Task icon and screen

2. Select *Click here* to add a new Task in the center of the Task read pane. Type the task that you want on the list, and then press Enter. Click on the due date area and insert the date that the task is to be completed by. Once the date is typed, press Enter (see Figure 7.35).

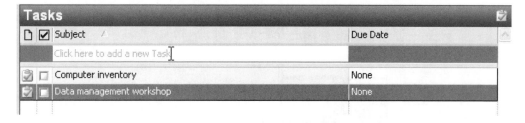

Figure 7.35
Adding tasks

3. After completing a task, click on the box beside the task to mark it as complete. A line appears through the task to note that the task is complete (see Figure 7.36).

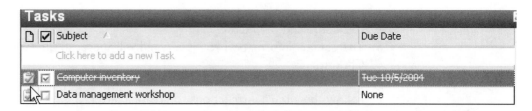

Figure 7.36
Completed tasks

4. To delete a task, click on the checked box next to the item that you want to delete. Click *Delete* on the screen or press the Delete key on the keyboard.

LET ME TRY

So far we have shown you how to make a tasks list. Now you can make a list for your own use.

1. Click on the Start button on the Windows taskbar. On the Start menu, move the mouse pointer over *Programs* and the Programs submenu appears. Move the mouse over *Microsoft Office* and the Microsoft Office submenu appears. Click on *Microsoft Outlook* and Outlook 2003 opens.
2. Click on the Tasks icon or folder, depending on how you have your desktop organized.
3. Select *Click here* to add a new Task.
4. Add your own tasks, including due dates. You may want to begin with committee assignments that have due dates.
5. Click on the Print icon on the toolbar to print your task list.

Notes

1. Outlook Notes are equivalent to small notes that you would make for yourself and have on or around your desk.
2. Click on the Notes icon. A widow appears and you can type the note (see Figure 7.37).

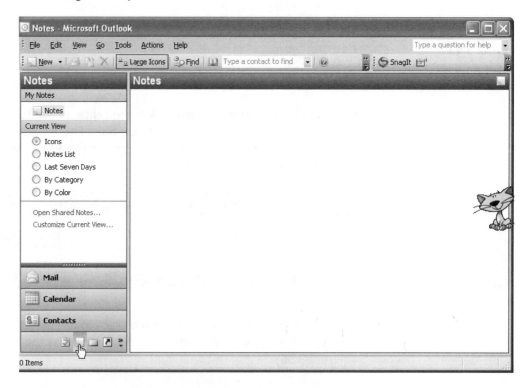

Figure 7.37
Notes icon and screen

10/18/2004 1:14 PM

Figure 7.38
Notes window

3. Select *New* to create a new note. A window appears and you can type the note. The date and time appear at the bottom of the new note (see Figure 7.38).
4. Type the note in the window. When you are finished, click the X in the upper-right corner of the window to close the note.
5. To delete a note, select it, then press the Delete key on the keyboard or click on the delete icon on the toolbar.
6. To open a note after you have created several, double-click on the note you want to open.

LET ME TRY

So far we have shown you how to make notes within the program. Now you can make notes for your own use.

1. Open *Microsoft Outlook.*
2. Click on *Notes.*
3. Click on the new Notes icon on the taskbar.
4. Add your own notes that are now on your computer or your desktop.

Journal

1. Select *Journal* from the icons on the Navigation pane. The Journal in Outlook can be very similar to a journal you may keep in your office. This program monitors activities. Students can use it to record activities that currently may be taking place on a long-term project or program on which they are working.
2. The first time you open Outlook Journal, the screen shown in Figure 7.39 appears. The options allow you to keep track of the contacts or records associated with a student, a particular meeting, or even a thematic unit you may be working on if you have contacts associated with this item. If you do not want to set journal associations with contacts, do not check any of these boxes; simply click *OK.*

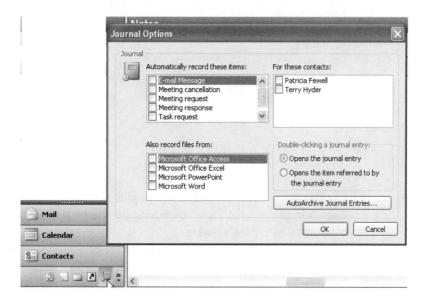

Figure 7.39
Journal options

3. To begin a new journal entry select *Actions* from the toolbar, then select New *Journal Entry* (see Figure 7.40).

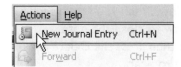

Figure 7.40
Action tab from toolbar

4. After clicking on *New Journal Entry* a window appears and allows you to place information about activities that have taken place today, or any day, by selecting the appropriate date on the calendar in the window (see Figure 7.41).

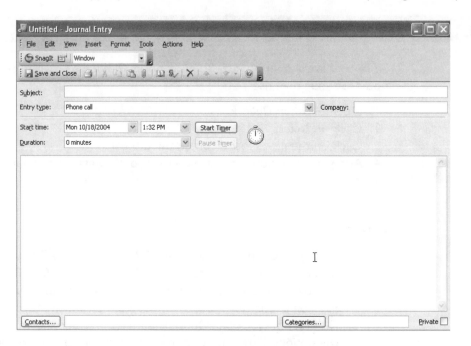

Figure 7.41
New journal entry

5. After entering all of the data you need for the journal entry, click *Save* and then *Close* from the toolbar. This closes the entry and the entry then appears under the date on the journal calendar (see Figure 7.42).

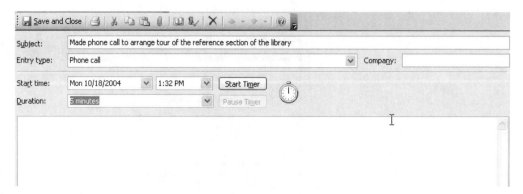

Figure 7.42
Entering information in a journal entry

6. Clicking on the journal entry with a plus beside it allows you to see the information in the journal. Double-clicking on the phone call takes you to the original journal entry for viewing.
7. You can print out the calendar document or the individual journal entries by clicking on the Printer icon on the toolbar.

8. The calendar can be viewed for today, one day, a week, or a month (see Figures 7.43 and 7.44).

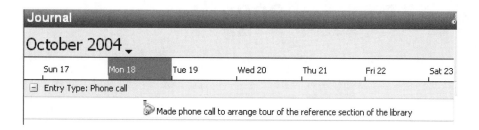

Figure 7.43
Journal calendar

Figure 7.44
Journal calendar
options

A CHALLENEGE USING OUTLOOK 2003

For those of you who would like a challenge beyond the Let Me Try activities presented in this chapter, try the following exercises.

1. Send an e-mail with an attachment.

2. In the address book of the Inbox, create a group for students working together on a project.

3. Have your students create a calendar for appointments, including holidays or official days, and print the calendar.

4. Have your students create a task list for a character in a story they are reading.

TYING IT ALL TOGETHER

In this chapter, we have examined the parts of an electronic date keeper. We created a calendar, a list of contacts, a list of tasks, and worked with e-mail messages. By using all of these tools in conjunction with other components of Microsoft Office, you will be able to maintain your calendar. Your students also will be able to keep information that can be updated, and tasks may be assigned or e-mail messages sent directly to the class.

8 PUBLISHER 2003

CHAPTER OUTLINE

LEARNING OBJECTIVES

At the completion of this chapter you will be able to:

- Start a document from a Publisher template
- Navigate the Publisher workspace
- Resize a textbox in a publication
- Add a frame or artwork to a document
- Cut, copy, and paste in a document
- Preview a document for printing
- Create a new blank Publisher document
- Identify Publisher Design Sets
- Print a publication
- Save a publication

Technical Terms

The following are terms that you will encounter in the chapter and with which you will become familiar:

Independent design elements

Textbox

Frames

Publisher master design set

Chapter Overview

This chapter provides an introduction to Publisher 2003. It focuses on helping you learn Publisher fundamentals and apply them to developing a publication. The Show Me section presents instruction on how to use many of Publisher 2003's tools for creating documents. Let Me Try exercises embedded throughout the chapter give step-by-step instructions for quickly accomplishing tasks presented in the Show Me section. They will also give you opportunities to practice the information presented. Studying the chapter content and working through the Let Me Try exercises will enable you and your students to develop high-quality publications suitable for class reports, presentations, school board meetings, and other educationally oriented activities that call for stylized publications. In addition, you may locate files that correspond to the chapter activities on the accompanying CD-ROM in the Publisher folder under "Examples".

How Teachers and Students Might Use Publisher 2003

Teacher Production of Materials

Instruction/Learning	Classroom Management
Create brochures for supplemental material	Worksheets
Make activity flyers	Field trip permission letters
Make calendars for events within the month	Newsletters for parents
Create learning center materials	Certificates for students
Create project-based materials for class	Create invitations to open house
Activity directions	Create postcards to send home to parents for students "caught being good"

Student Production of Materials

Instruction/Learning
Create newsletters that report about a book
Create a postcard from a country being studied
Develop newsletters about historical topics
Create a resume of a important figure
Develop a business card for yourself
Create a calendar of significant events for the month
Create a banner for a learning center you are creating
Develop an advertisement for a significant scientific invention

About Publisher 2003

Publisher 2003 is a computer application that allows individuals to create, customize, and publish materials. The program may be considered desktop publishing software. Publisher allows you to create a variety of materials. As you open the program there will be a pull-down menu that allows you to choose any of the following items:

Quick Publications
Advertisements
Award Certificates
Banners
Brochures
Business Cards
Calendars
Catalogs
Envelopes
Flyers
Gift Certificates
Greeting Cards
Import Word Documents
Invitation Cards
Labels
Letterhead
Menus
Newsletters
Paper Folding Projects
Postcards
Programs
Resumes
Signs
With Complements Cards
Web Sites and E-mail Design Sets
Blank Publications

Within the listing, once a type of document is selected you can choose a particular template that you would like to use. The items listed allow you to place your own materials within a template that has been designed and included in the program.

There are many ways to use Publisher 2003. You can use the already-created templates to create teacher-made materials for your lessons. Students may use the materials to present information and research not only to the class, but perhaps to parents and outside groups as well. As a teacher you can create materials easily using templates, such as newsletters to send home, calendars of class activities to share with parents, labels for a variety of materials from envelopes to CD, and award certificates for special events for students. The templates presented can be modified to include different pictures and text and to change the layout of the materials. In addition, Publisher allows you to create your own materials without a template using the Blank Publication option, which is in the New Selection portion of the screen when starting the Publisher program. Publisher also allows you to create Web sites and e-mail materials. The Master Design Sets are a series of publications that have the same "look" to them, meaning there is a graphical theme that pervades all of the documents in this set of templates.

As noted, there are a number of possible publications that can be created with Publisher. You will be given an opportunity to learn about some of the processes of creating documents, but the information presented in this chapter will not be exhaustive. Certain templates and processes will not be covered because of space constraints, but the basics of creating documents for your classroom will be addressed and you will become generally familiar with Publisher.

Working with Publisher

Suppose you assign students the task of creating a brochure about a topic within a recent book they read, *HATCHET* by Gary Paulsen. For an example of the completed brochure, see "Hatchet brochure.pub" on the CD. Have the class decide what topics should be in the brochure and the theme of the brochure. Divide the class into several groups that can research the topics chosen to be included in the brochure, write short articles using the information, and find pictures to support the material. One group should work as the design team, taking the articles and pictures and creating the layout of the brochure once the research and writing has been completed. In some respects this process would be similar to a writing circle activity, where each team has individual assignments but also works as a collective group to create a finished product.

This chapter focuses on creating a student-produced brochure based on *Hatchet* and a student-created postcard that the main character in *Hatchet* might have sent. Although the content used here is specific to creating a student brochure, the steps and procedures are generic and applicable to a variety of materials that can be produced using Publisher. Feel free to substitute your own content and modify the materials created in this chapter.

Before developing the document, an orientation to the Publisher workspace and some of its menu functions and tools is needed. When opening Publisher 2003 you have several panes within the screen (see figure 8.1).

Figure 8.1
Publisher workspace

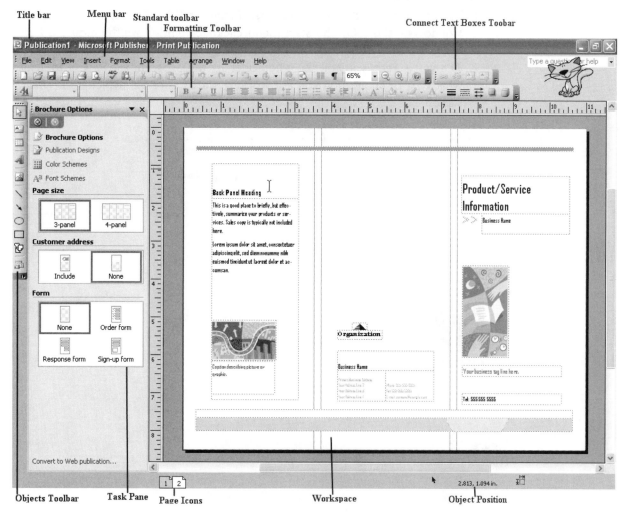

There are several work areas in publisher that may look different than other Microsoft programs. The Objects toolbar contains buttons that allow you to add objects such as pictures or text to a publication. The task pane contains options you can select, such as page size or forms that may be included in the brochure, as well as color scheme options and different publication design options. The Connect Textboxes toolbar contains buttons that allow you to create and work with connected textboxes for text flow. The Page icons allow you to switch between pages in a publication. The Object Position button displays the position of a selected object or the mouse pointer from the left and top edges of the current page in inches.

Show Me

Developing the Brochure

The overall objective of creating the brochure is to allow the students to provide a synopsis of the story, identify the characters within the story, and identify the animal neighbors that Brian encounters. The students will then provide short paragraphs about the animals that Brian has to deal with throughout the book, giving them practice in researching information and writing what they find in their own words.

We will be creating a brochure for the book *Hatchet*. Figures 8.2 and 8.3 show what the finished brochure will look like once you have used Publisher to follow all of the outlined steps.

Opening Publisher 2003

1. To begin creating this brochure, open Publisher. Click the Start button on the Windows taskbar. On the Start menu, click *Programs,* move the mouse pointer over *Microsoft Office,* and click *Microsoft Publisher.*
2. The first screen you will see when opening the program allows you to select what type of publication you are working with. Figure 8.4 depicts the opening screen.

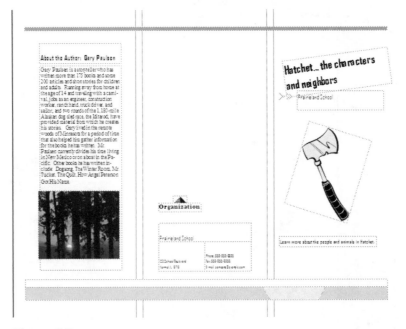

Figure 8.2
Front of the brochure

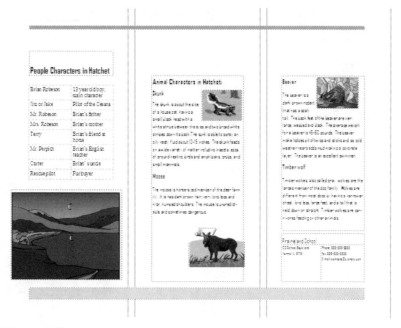

Figure 8.3
Back of the brochure

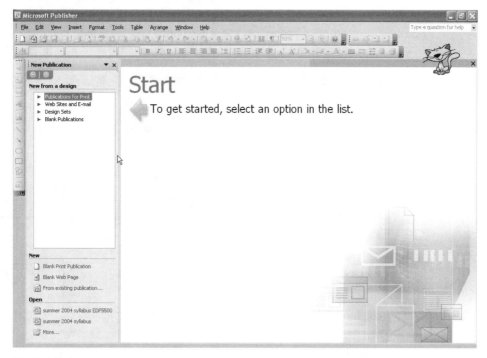

Figure 8.4
Publisher opening screen

Selecting a Template

3. Once you have selected an option from the *New from a design*, the program then produces a listing of templates to select from. This screen will allow you to select brochure as the type of publication for print (see Figure 8.5).

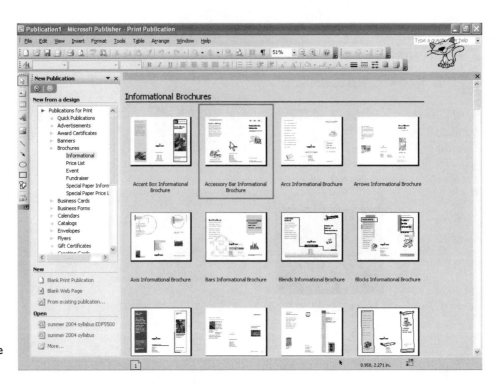

Figure 8.5
Selecting a brochure template

4. In this case we want to select an informational brochure (see Figure 8.6). Select *Arrows Informational Brochure,* the fourth example on the first row, by placing the mouse arrow on the icon. There will be a blue rectangle around the template. Click the right mouse button to select the template (see Figure 8.6).

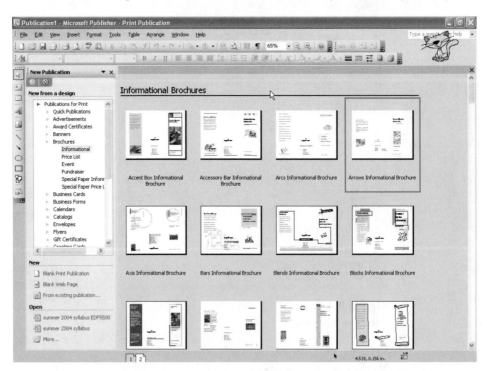

Figure 8.6
Select *Arrows Informational Brochure*

Creating a Brochure

5. Publisher then creates the publication. The first time you create a publication, the *Personal Information* dialogue box appears, asking you to provide information that Publisher will automatically add to your publication. Enter the appropriate information and then click *OK* (Figure 8.7).

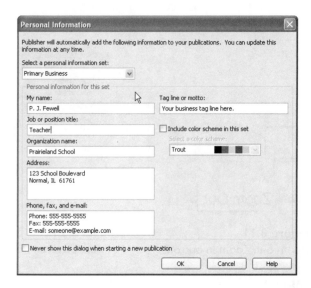

Figure 8.7
Personal
Information

6. You will notice that the individual design elements are noted by a dotted-line box around them. You can modify and/or move any of this information as you create the brochure. The title of the brochure will be "Hatchet . . . the characters and neighbors." Highlight the title of the brochure; you will note that the textbox is activated. Press the Backspace key; this will erase the "Product/ Information" wording and allow you to type in the title (see Figure 8.8). Also, notice that the personal information that you filled in is automatically placed in the brochure. This can be changed if you wish, again by highlighting the text and pressing the Backspace key.

Figure 8.8
Title of brochure

7. You will notice that as you type the title in the textbox there is a green circle above the textbox. This allows you to rotate the text in the textbox. Once you place the mouse pointer over the circle, a curved arrow will appear. After typing in the title, rotate the text just slightly to give an angular effect to the text (see Figure 8.9).

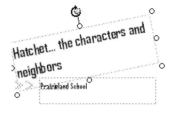

Figure 8.9
Rotating text

8. As you work with the brochure you may want to zoom into the publication by clicking the zoom setting you want to use (see Figure 8.10). You may also zoom in using the buttons on the toolbar (see Figure 8.11). Set the zoom setting at 100% as you work with the brochure more closely.

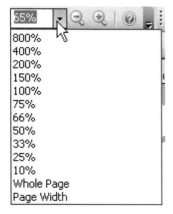

Figure 8.10
Zoom settings

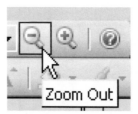

Figure 8.11
Zoom out/Zoom in buttons

Figure 8.12
Insert picture

Importing Graphics

9. As you look on the front part of the brochure, you will want to replace the picture on the front of the brochure with something that relates to the content of *Hatchet.* You may use scanned pictures that students have drawn, pictures from a digital camera, or clip art. If you are going to use art from a source on the Internet, please make sure that it is in the public domain or you will need to obtain permission to use someone else's artwork. In this case we are going to use clip art. Select *Insert* from the toolbar and highlight *Picture from Clip art* (see Figure 8.12).

10. As in the other programs in Microsoft Office, you may use the clip art that comes with the program, or when connected to the Internet you may search the Microsoft Office clip art Web site for additional pictures. Searching for "hatchet" clip art on the Web will produce a number of pictures. Select the designated picture and copy it to the clipboard (see Figure 8.13).

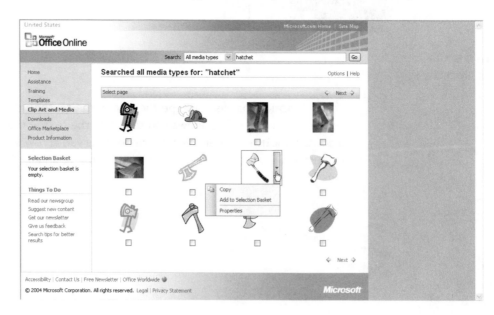

Figure 8.13
Selecting clip art

11. Select the picture in the brochure template by placing the mouse arrow on the picture and clicking the left mouse button when over the picture. This will activate the frame the picture is in and will allow you to select Edit and Paste in the new picture (see Figure 8.14).

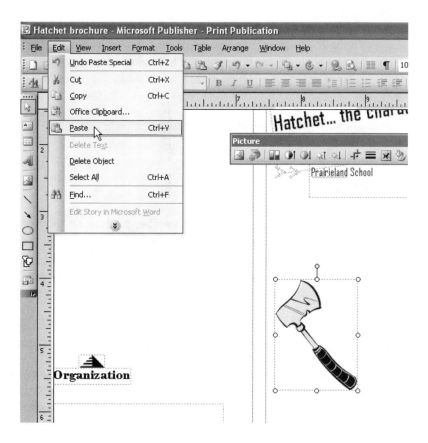

Figure 8.14
Pasting clip art

12. You will want to make the graphic larger and rotate the image a little to make it visually pleasing in the layout of the brochure. To make the picture larger, place the mouse arrow on the picture and click the left mouse button. This activates the "handles" around the picture. Select the upper right-hand circle and hold down the Shift key on the keyboard, at the same time drag the mouse to the upper section of the page and to the right. This allows the picture to be resized in proportion, rather than only in one direction (see Figure 8.15).

13. To rotate the picture, place the mouse arrow over the green circle at the top center of the picture and rotate it slightly clockwise. You may want to literally move the picture over on the section of the page. To do this, click the left mouse button down and hold it, dragging the picture into the location you desire (see Figure 8.16).

Figure 8.15
Enlarging an image

Figure 8.16
Rotating picture

14. The next item on the front of the brochure is the Tag line box. Instead of placing the business tag line, highlight the text and press the Delete key. In place of the business tag line type the following: *Learn more about the people and animals in Hatchet* (see Figure 8.17).

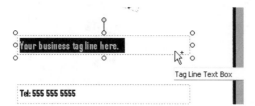

Figure 8.17
Tag line textbox

15. You do not want a telephone number present on the front of the brochure. Using the mouse arrow, click the textbox to activate it and press the Delete key. This will remove the textbox from the brochure.

16. By clicking on the Print Preview icon on the toolbar the brochure should look similar to the screen in Figure 8.18.

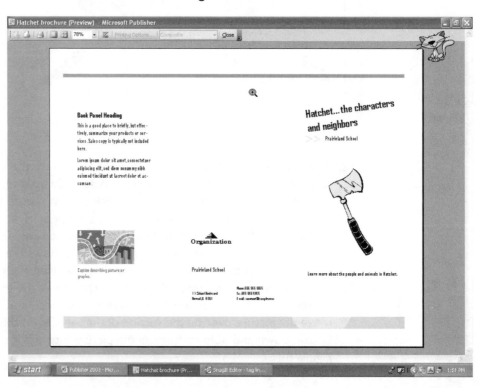

Figure 8.18
Preview screen of brochure

So far we have selected a template for a brochure, changed the title, added a picture, rotated the textbox and the frame for the picture, changed wording in a textbox, and deleted a textbox. Let's practice what we discussed using the following example.

Suppose that your principal has asked you to develop a flyer for the field trip that has been scheduled for the class. See "Zoo trip Flyer.pub" on the CD for an example. Here are the steps for getting started:

1. Open *Microsoft Publisher*.
2. Click *Publications for Print.*

3. Click on *Flyers*.
4. Under *Flyers* click on *Event*.
5. Select the flyer that has "field trip" on it (which is in the second row).
6. The flyer will have your personal information in it if you already entered it previously. Otherwise, you will need to fill in the personal information.
7. Select *Name of Field Trip* by selecting it with the mouse pointer and then clicking the left mouse button.
8. Once the text is highlighted, type *A trip to the Miller Park Zoo.* You will notice that the text resizes to fit within the textbox.
9. Click on the bus picture to activate the frame.
10. Click on *Insert* and select *Picture* and then *Clip art*.
11. In *Search to find the graphic,* click *Search online* and type in *timber wolf.*
12. From the pull-down menu next to the picture select *Copy*.
13. Click *Back to the flyer* and select *Edit* from the toolbar. Select *Paste* and the timber wolf picture will replace the bus.
14. Resize the picture by holding down the Shift key and selecting the upper right-hand circle of the picture until it is an appropriate size for the flyer.
15. Preview the flyer thus far by selecting *Print Preview*.

Adding Content to the Brochure

Now we will add content to the back panel of the brochure.

1. Highlight the Back Panel Heading by clicking in the textbox and dragging the mouse (see Figure 8.19).

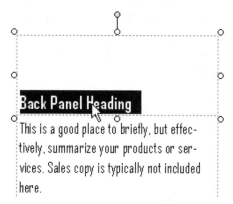

Figure 8.19
Replacing Back
Panel Heading

2. Type in *About the Author: Gary Paulsen.* Resize the textbox by clicking and dragging the circle up toward the top of the page to make the textbox smaller (see Figure 8.20).

Figure 8.20
Resizing textbox

3. Increase the size to match the textbox below the textbox you just typed in. Within this textbox you are going to write a short paragraph about the author. You may use the information presented in the text or do your own research and create your own paragraph (see Figure 8.21).

Gary Paulsen is a storyteller who has written more than 175 books and some 200 articles and short stories for children and adults. Running away from home at the age of 14 and traveling with a carnival. Jobs as an engineer, construction worker, ranch hand, truck driver, and sailor; and two rounds of the 1,180-mile Alaskan dog sled race, the Iditarod; have provided material from which he creates his stories. Gary lived in the remote woods of Minnesota for a period of time that also helped him gather information for the books he has written. Mr. Paulsen currently divides his time living in New Mexico or on a boat in the Pacific.

Other books he has written include: Dogsong, The Winter Room, Mr. Tucket, The Quilt, How Angel Peterson Got His Name.

Figure 8.21
Gary Paulsen bio

4. You will want to remove the picture and material at the bottom of the column. Click on the picture and press the Delete key. Place your cursor in the space by clicking the left mouse button in that space.
5. To replace the picture on the back panel, select *Picture* and *Clip art* from the Objects toolbar (see Figure 8.22).

Figure 8.22
Insert picture from
Objects toolbar

6. As previously done, select *Clip Art on Office Online*. Under the search, type in *forest* and select an appropriate forest picture, then copy the picture. Once the picture is copied, paste it into the space that you just deleted the picture from. You will have to resize the picture to fit in the space. Be aware of where the

margins are for the brochure (shown as a dotted line on the page) to make sure you keep the picture within the designated space. (see Figure 8.23).

Figure 8.23
Forest picture

7. Select *Print Preview* from the standard toolbar to view the outside of the brochure as you have it completed thus far. This will allow you to see what it will look like prior to printing a copy. Click on *Close* to close this window and go back to the work area of the program.
8. To save the publication that we have created thus far, select the Disk icon on the toolbar. It is a good idea to save about every 5 minutes as you work on a project. Select the place that you want to save the publication to, whether it is a floppy disk, hard drive, or other storage device on or within your computer. Name the file something that you can remember and that identifies the project when you try to retrieve it later (see Figure 8.24).

Figure 8.24
Saving a file

9. To start on the second page or the inside of the brochure click on the Page Two icon at the bottom of the page (see Figure 8.25).

Figure 8.25
Selecting page two

10. You now can see the inside, or page two, of the brochure. To place information in the brochure you will start on the leftmost column. In that column you are going to create a table of a list of characters in *Hatchet*. In the textbox containing

Main Inside Heading, highlight the text and type in *People Characters in Hatchet* (see Figure 8.26).

Figure 8.26
People characters

11. In order to make space you will need to delete the information in this column first. Click on each textbox or picture and press the Delete key to remove the items in the column. The textbox will remain—you will have to click on one of the handles to activate the box and then press delete to remove the textbox.

12. Click on the Table icon in the Objects toolbar. Position the mouse in the upper-left corner of where you want the table to be and drag the mouse until the table is the width of the brochure column. Create a table that has nine rows and two columns (see Figure 8.27).

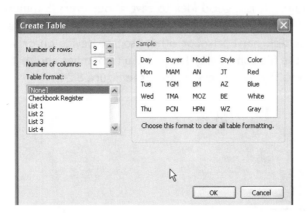

Figure 8.27
Creating a table

13. After typing in all of the characters you discover that there is one extra row in the table. Make sure your cursor is in the row that you want to delete from the table. To delete this extra row, select *Table* from the menu bar and from the drop-down menu select *Delete* and *Row.* This will delete the row the cursor was in (see Figure 8.28).

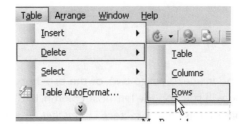

Figure 8.28
Delete row from table

14. From the Objects toolbar select *Picture frame* and *Clip art.* In the clip art section, again select *Clip Art on Office Online,* and under the search, type in *Lake and Landscape.* Select one of the clip art pictures, copy it, and place the picture below the table. Again, you may have to resize the picture in order to have it fit in the space (see Figure 8.29).

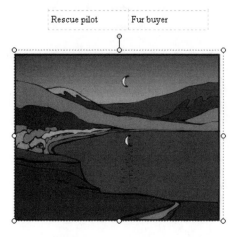

Figure 8.29
Lake picture

15. To see what the column of the brochure you just created looks like, select the Print Preview icon from the standard toolbar. This will allow you to view all of page two of the brochure (see Figure 8.30). After reviewing the page click on *Close* to close the preview page.

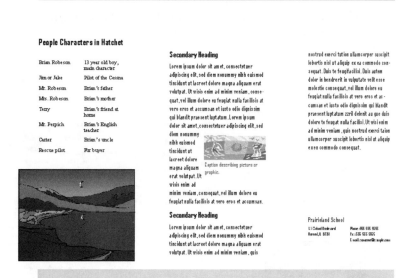

Figure 8.30
Finished column on
Print Preview

16. Columns two and three of the second page will include information about the animals that Brian encounters in *Hatchet.* The students will want to research information and write descriptions of the animals in their own words. The animals to research might include: porcupine, timber wolf, moose, rabbit, snapping turtle, beaver, and skunk. Pictures should be placed with the animals if possible. As you add pictures you may want to format the text around the picture. To do this, click the right mouse button when on the picture and select *Format picture* from the pull-down menu (see Figure 8.31)

17. Select the Layout tab on the Format Picture window that pops up once you have made your selection. Select the tight wrapping style, allowing text and pictures to wrap around in the format (see Figure 8.32).

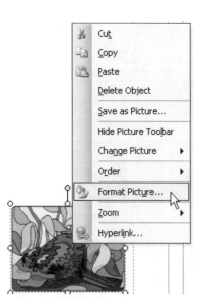

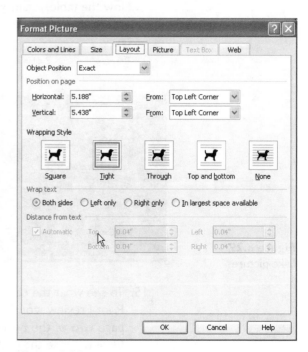

Figure 8.31
Format picture

Figure 8.32
Format picture window

18. The finished second page of the brochure might look like the illustration in Figure 8.33.

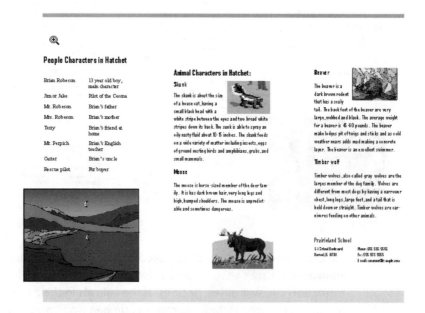

Figure 8.33
Finished second
page of brochure

19. You have finished the brochure and you should save your work.
20. To print your brochure select the Printer icon from the standard toolbar. Or you may select *Print* under the File menu if there is a specific printer that you want the document to be printed on.

Checking Your Publication for Design Problems

1. The Design Checker will find problems such as an image partially off the page or an empty textbox. The checker will not catch every flaw, but it might identify some that you did not catch. It is always a good idea to not only proof the materials, but to have someone else proof them as well.

2. Click on *Tools* and select *Design Checker* (see Figure 8.34).

Figure 8.34
Design Checker

3. The software will prepare a report that indicates where it finds problems (see Figure 8.35).

4. You can select for the program to go to the item where there is difficulty; each identified item has a pull-down menu that will allow you to do so. In that case, the textbox or frame for the picture is made active (see Figure 8.36).

5. When you finish reviewing the design problems, close the Design Checker and save your document if you made any changes.

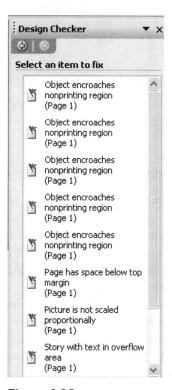

Figure 8.35
Design Checker list of items

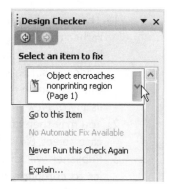

Figure 8.36
Individual Design Checker
pull-down menu

LET ME TRY

Returning to the zoo trip flyer, let's practice what we have discussed.

1. Highlight the textbox that contains "about the field trip." Replace the information with the following: *We will be going on a field trip to Miller Park Zoo, Wednesday, May 5th. The school has chartered buses for us to take, all students and parents who wish to go will ride the bus. We will be leaving from the North parking lot of the school at 8:45 a.m. and will be returning to the same parking lot at approximately 3:30 p.m. Wear school clothing and comfortable shoes, but bring a light jacket in case it is cool in the morning. You will need to bring money for lunch and drinks.*
2. You will have to change the text size to 14 point in order to fit all materials in the space.
3. In the section displaying "when the form needs to be returned," type in *April 20* as the date it must be returned to you.
4. Delete the method of payment sections, leaving the signature line, and replace the information with: *I do give my permission for my child to participate in the Miller Park Field Trip, Wednesday, May 5.*
5. Draw a table box using the Objects toolbar Table icon and place the table between the Name information and the Return Date information.
6. Specify that the table will have two columns and two rows.
7. The information in the table cells is as follows:

Lunch will be $4.00.	If a parent/guardian would like to go the cost of transportation will be $3.00.
All cameras will be the responsibility of the students	If you do wish to participate as a parent in this field trip, please note here: _____ yes, I do want to go on the field trip.

8. Save the flyer and print the flyer out.
9. The finished zoo flyer should look like boxed Figure 8.1.

Creating a Publication from a Blank Document

1. There are occasions when you may wish to start out with a blank publication rather than using a template. You have assigned your students the task of creating postcards that Brian Robeson could have sent while he was stranded in the wilderness. The students will construct the front and back of the postcard. In this case, from the opening screen of Publisher select *Blank Publication* from the listing of *New from a design* (see Figure 8.37).
2. You may then choose what type of new design you would like to create. In this case select, *Blank postcard page* from the listing (see Figure 8.38).
3. Publisher will create a blank postcard, and you will add information and graphics to complete the project. As you start to create the postcard it is always a good idea to do a rough sketch or outline of what you would like the finished product to look like.

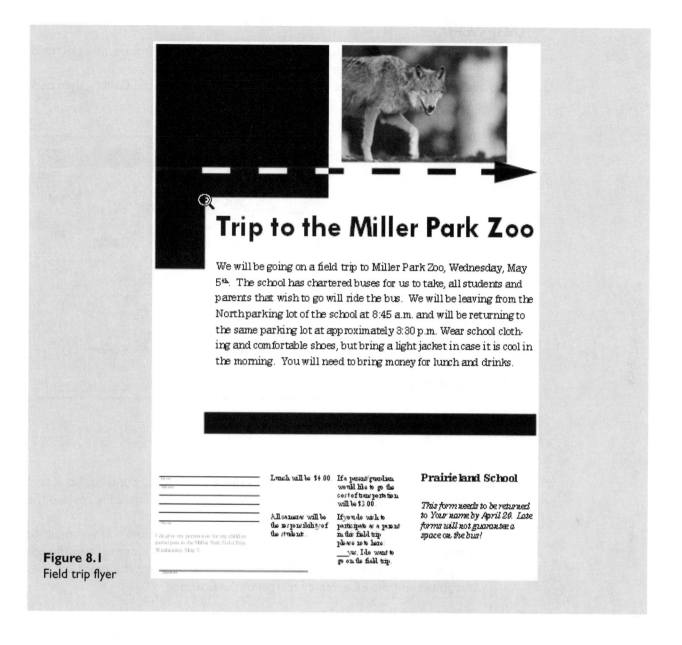

Figure 8.1
Field trip flyer

Figure 8.37
Selecting *Blank Publication*

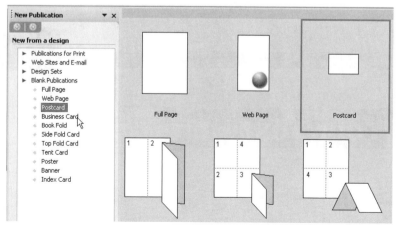

Figure 8.38
Blank postcard

Using WordArt

4. The first part of the postcard you will create will be the front of the postcard. From the Objects toolbar select the WordArt icon (see Figure 8.39).
5. Select a style of WordArt by clicking one of the boxes in the Gallery, then click *OK* (Figure 8.40).

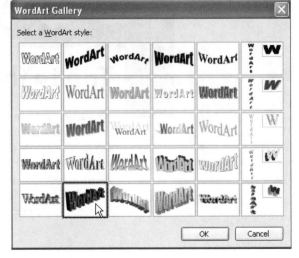

Figure 8.39
Select *Insert WordArt*

Figure 8.40
WordArt Gallery

6. The Edit WordArt window will appear. Where the textbox contains "your text here" type the words *Hampton Airport;* the text will automatically replace the original words. Click *OK* (see Figure 8.41).
7. The WordArt will appear in the workspace of the postcard. You will need to reposition the WordArt by clicking on the WordArt and dragging it to the upper potion of the postcard (see Figure 8.42). Make sure that the WordArt does not go beyond the blue line or margin of the postcard.

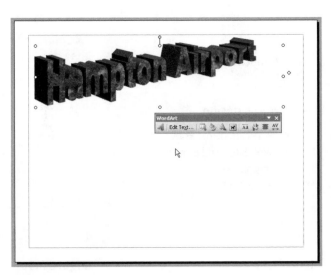

Figure 8.41
Edit WordArt text

Figure 8.42
WordArt on postcard

8. Click on the Clip Art icon from the Objects toolbar. Select a plane picture from the clip art available. Resize the clip art so it covers the entire white area of the postcard (see Figure 8.43).

Figure 8.43
Clip art size of entire postcard

9. From the menu bar select *Arrange* and from the pull-down menu select *Send to Back* (make sure the picture has the circles showing that it is the active portion of the window). See Figure 8.44.

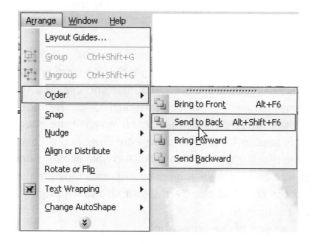

Figure 8.44
Arrange menu

10. This will send the picture into the background and allow the WordArt to show through. Click on Print Preview to see the finished product, which should look like Figure 8.45.

Figure 8.45
Postcard front

11. To create the back of the postcard you will need to add a page to the publication. From the menu bar select *Insert* and from the drop-down menu select *page* (see Figure 8.46).
12. A window will appear asking you how many pages to insert and where to insert them. Select *One page* and *After the current page* (see Figure 8.47).

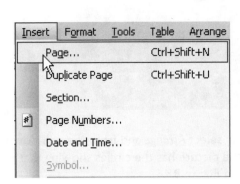

Figure 8.46
Insert new page

Figure 8.47
Insert number of pages

13. A new blank postcard will now appear in the workspace.
14. Select *Textbox* from the Objects toolbar and create a textbox that is approximately one-half the size of the postcard. Click the mouse within the textbox and type the following information: *Hi Terry, We are just getting ready to take off from the Hampton Airport. The plane I am flying in is a Cessna 406, one of the bush planes. The pilot's name is Jim or Jake. A couple of hours and I will be spending the summer with my dad. I will send another postcard as soon as I can. Take care, Brian.* Highlight the text and change the font size to 14 points (see Figure 8.48).
15. Save the publication.
16. Print out a copy of the publication.

Figure 8.48
Writing on the postcard

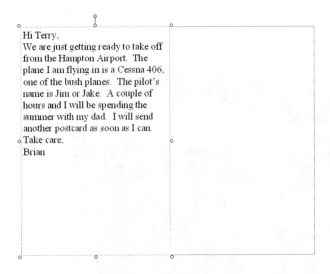

A CHALLENGE USING PUBLISHER 2003

For those who would like a challenge beyond the Let Me Try activities presented in the chapter, try the following exercises:

1. Have students create a newsletter to let their parents and others know what they have been learning and what activities they are interested in learning about.

2. Create a letterhead for the class. Let students design the logo using Publisher.

3. Create a calendar of activities for the month that indicates the various historical activities that may have taken place on each day of the month.

4. Create award certificates for science fairs, history fairs, or good behavior.

5. Have students create a menu that may have been used at a historical event, such as the banquet after signing the Magna Charta.

6. Create business cards for famous people in history, sciences, or literature to allow students to research about these individuals.

7. Create invitation cards for events at school that you might want to invite parents or other dignitaries to attend.

8. Create a Web site that provides additional information for a thematic unit that may be presented in class or added to as the class researches particular topics.

9. Have students create their own resume, or the resume of a famous individual.

TYING IT ALL TOGETHER

In this chapter, we created a brochure using a template for identifying the characters and animals in Gary Paulsen's book *Hatchet*, and we created a postcard that might have been sent by Brian Robeson, the main character of *Hatchet*. In the Let Me Try activity a field trip flyer was created. We saved the publications and printed out the documents created. Publisher provides a variety of publication options. Although this chapter presented many fundamentals to help you get started, there are numerous other components of Publisher 2003 for you to explore.

INTEGRATING OFFICE 2003

CHAPTER OUTLINE

LEARNING OBJECTIVES

At the completion of this chapter you will be able to:

- Copy and paste text from a Word document to a PowerPoint slide
- Place an Excel worksheet into a Word document and a PowerPoint slideshow
- Edit an Excel chart in a Word document and a PowerPoint slideshow
- Embed an Excel worksheet into a Word document
- Link an Excel worksheet to a Word document and a PowerPoint slideshow
- Embed a PowerPoint slide into a Word document
- Run a PowerPoint slideshow from a Word document
- Create contacts in Outlook and export them to Access
- Place Access data into a PowerPoint slide

TECHNICAL TERMS

The following are terms that you will encounter in the chapter and with which you will become familiar:

Document object

Drag and drop

Embed

Insert object

Link to file

Objects

Presentation object

Slide object

Worksheet object

CHAPTER OVERVIEW

Each Office application has a unique purpose and function. The ability to integrate their functionality expands one's capacity to efficiently design and produce materials and to incorporate diverse informational sources and media. Given this capability, it is fitting that an entire chapter of this text should be devoted to approaches to integrating these products. In the Show Me section, you will find instruction on how to develop materials that incorporate PowerPoint slides, Word documents, Excel worksheets, Outlook data, and Access data. The examples presented are only a few of the many options for developing materials. The Let Me Try exercises give step-by-step instructions for quickly accomplishing tasks related to the Show Me section. *In addition, you can locate files that correspond to the chapter activities on the accompanying CD-ROM in the Integration folder under* Examples. *Specifically, you will find a Project log worksheet, a sample proposal, and a proposal slideshow.*

About Integrating the Office Products

As you work with Office, you will undoubtedly encounter situations where you need files or portions of a file created with one application in a file that you created with another application. You may even need to work with one file and from it update, open, or run another file in a different application. For instance, suppose you use Word to create a class newsletter in which you highlight a student project, such as a PowerPoint slideshow illustrating the student's artwork. In Word, you provide a text description of the project as well as illustrations of the slideshow. Because PowerPoint and Word integrate so easily, you are able to select slides from PowerPoint and place them in the newsletter. In addition, if you show colleagues the newsletter you created in Word and they want to view the student project in more depth, you can click on the slide illustration and run the PowerPoint slideshow.

Integrating files across the Office products is extremely useful as you construct teaching and learning materials. It broadens the possibilities for the types of materials you can make and the efficiency with which you can produce them.

Have you ever created a chart and placed it into a document that you planned to distribute to your class of 35 students? Minutes before the class and seconds before clicking the Print button, you notice an error in the chart. Depending on how you made the chart, you may need to open an application, alter chart text and numeric values, prepare the chart for a word processor, and then place and format it. These tasks can be time consuming. Alternatively, by creating the document with Word and the chart with Excel and then linking them, you could quickly modify numeric values in Excel, which would automatically update the Word document and make it ready for printing.

The aforementioned illustration and the examples throughout the chapter present a few approaches to integrating Office programs. As your familiarity with Office deepens, you will no doubt discover inventive ways to employ its integrative capabilities to create interesting and engaging classroom materials and activities.

Working with the Office Products

Suppose you are teaching a basic computer class and assign students to research a topic of interest that relates to an issue discussed in class. Students must create a multimedia project to present their research. You designate teams comprised of three or four individuals. Each team must write a proposal that provides an overview of the topic, a rationale for why it is important to develop the project, project objectives, ideas about how the project will look when it is finished, a projected timeline, and a budget. Since it is important for students to document their work progress, you ask them to maintain a project journal in which they write details about the development process. At a minimum, each time the team works on the project, a team member records the date, time, how much time was spent working, the tasks or what was accomplished, and any thoughts about how the project is progressing.

Over a 4-month period, teams must deliver two 15-minute class presentations. The first, a project proposal presentation, provides an overview of the topic proposal, the development plan, and work already accomplished. During the presentation, teams seek feedback from the class about how to improve the project. After this presentation, teams spend time collecting additional information and materials and developing the project. At the second presentation, teams present the finished multimedia project. When the assignment is complete, students complete a self-evaluation consisting of a written summary of what they learned, an overall evaluation of the finished project, and an assessment of how well members worked together. Your classroom is equipped with a computer and projector so that teams can project their projects onto a screen for the entire class to see.

This chapter focuses on developing materials for the project proposal and the proposal presentation. Using files on the CD-ROM that have already been prepared in Word, PowerPoint, Excel, and Access, you will add material to the project proposal and the proposal presentation. The files needed for this activity are on the CD-ROM in the Integration folder under *Examples*. Although the content used here is specific to creating a project proposal and slideshow, the steps and procedures are generic and applicable to a variety of teaching and learning tasks.

Show Me

The Show Me section is divided into five segments. The first segment presents the following:

- Making a project journal-log in Excel
- Copying and pasting text from Word to PowerPoint
- Inserting PowerPoint slides into Word — copy and paste
- Dragging and dropping a slide
- Inserting objects

Let us suppose that team 1 chooses to create a PowerPoint slideshow that informs the class about how to create Web pages and transfer them to a Web server. The project will also present information about the HyperText Markup Language (HTML). Using an Excel worksheet, team 1 begins by creating a project journal-log (see Figure 9.1). *A sample project log can be found on the CD-ROM in the Integration folder under* Examples. Members set up columns for date, time, hours worked, tasks, and thoughts. Corresponding to the tasks column, they create a column named *Identifier* in which they place codes to help them identify task types. The identifiers are *RSH* for research, *DEV* for development, *ADM* for administrative, and *OTH* for other. When they enter task descriptions, they identify them by one of the four identifiers to help members determine the amount of time spent on different types of tasks.

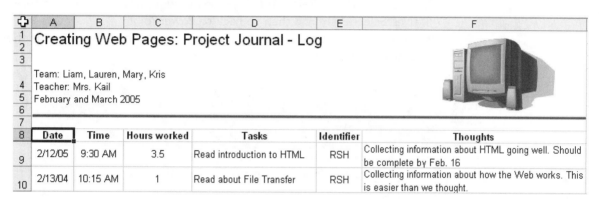

Figure 9.1
Journal-log sample

After making the project journal-log, team 1 creates several PowerPoint slides representative of the finished project. The members also begin developing a project proposal that contains the following sections: Title page, Table of contents, Project summary, Project rationale, Project objectives, Creative strategy (what the project will be like when finished), Project timeline, and Budget. They will use the proposal to guide their development of the PowerPoint slideshow to be delivered at the first (proposal) presentation. That slideshow will include a title slide, project objectives, sample screens (creative strategy), and timeline. In addition, they intend to place slides from the PowerPoint slideshow into the Creative Strategy section of the proposal to illustrate to the teacher (or readers of the proposal) what the finished slideshow will look like.

Copy and Paste Text from Word to PowerPoint

The members of team 1 developed several sections of the project proposal in Word. They also created several sample screens in PowerPoint. In this example, we will use text from the *Objectives* section of the proposal to add to a PowerPoint slide.

1. Open the ProposalSlideShow.ppt PowerPoint file on the CD-ROM in the Integration folder under *Examples* and click on the first slide.
2. Click the New Slide button or select *New Slide* from the Insert menu. If needed, display the task pane by selecting *Task pane* from the View menu.
3. Set the slide layout to *Title and Text.*
4. Open the Proposal.doc Word file in the Integration folder.
5. Locate the *Objectives* section of the proposal and select the text *Objectives.*
6. Click the Copy button.
7. Go back to PowerPoint and click in the Title box of the slide you just inserted. Click the Paste button and the title text should appear (see Figure 9.2).

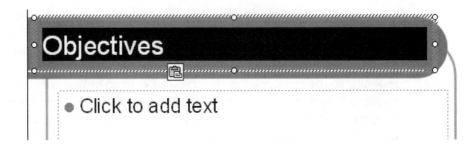

Figure 9.2
Objectives text

8. Return to Word. Below the *Objectives* section heading there are three objectives. Select them and then go back to PowerPoint.
9. Click in the textbox and click the Paste button. The bulleted items should appear (see Figure 9.3).

Objectives

- Present the basics of creating a Web page
- Present the basics of posting a Web page to a Web server
- Present basic HTML tags used to create a Web page.

Figure 9.3
Complete slide

Inserting PowerPoint Slides into Word—Copy and Paste

In this section, we will place two slides from PowerPoint into the *Creative Strategy* section of the proposal. There are several ways to place PowerPoint slides into Word. The easiest method is to copy the slide from PowerPoint and paste it into Word. A slide placed in Word is referred to as a *slide object*.

1. Open the PowerPoint slideshow. In this example, we will open a file named *ProposalSlideShow.ppt*. In the PowerPoint workspace, select the Normal view (select *Normal* from the View menu) and display the slide pane (Figure 9.4).
2. Click the slide that you would like to insert into Word and then click the Copy button (or select *Copy* from the Edit menu). In this example, we want to copy the first slide.
3. Open Word and place the cursor where you would like to insert the PowerPoint slide. We will position both slides in the *Creative Strategy* section of the proposal. The first slide will go after the sentence, *"After the title slide, it will present the objectives of the presentation and information about where the class can view the presentation online."* We will position the second slide at the end of the section.

Figure 9.4
Slide pane

4. With the cursor positioned after the words ". . . *presentation online.*", click the Paste button or select *Paste* from the Edit menu and the slide (slide object) will appear (see Figure 9.5).

Creative strategy (what the project will be like when finished)
Our presentation will open with a title slide that has music playing. After the title slide, it will present the objectives of the presentation and information about where the class can view the presentation online.

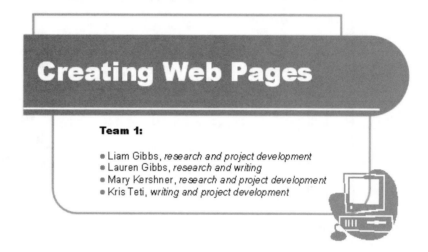

Figure 9.5
Slide pasted

5. Format the slide object by right-clicking on it in Word and select *Format Object* (see Figure 9.6) and the *Format Object* box appears (see Figure 9.7). In this case, we will resize the slide object to 70% of its original size.

Figure 9.6
Format Object menu item

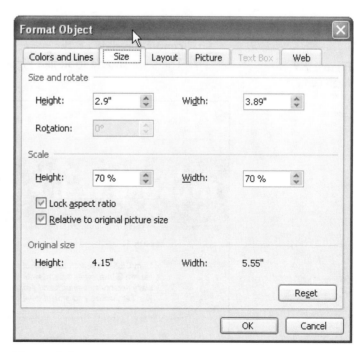

Figure 9.7
Format Object box

6. Click the Size tab and type *70* in the *Height* box. If you have the *Lock aspect ratio* box checked, then the width will automatically adjust. Click *OK* and the slide should be smaller.

7. Place a border around the slide to set it apart from the text. Right-click on the slide and select *Border and Shading* and the *Borders* box appears (see Figure 9.8). Click the Borders tab. In the Preview section of the *Borders* box, click the sides of the image or click the buttons at the left and bottom of the image. Click *OK*.

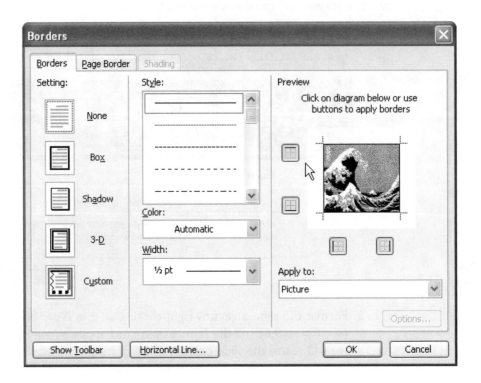

Figure 9.8
Borders box

Figure 9.9
Align center

8. With the slide object selected, click the Align Center icon (see Figure 9.9) to center the slide on the page.

9. The slide should look like Figure 9.10.

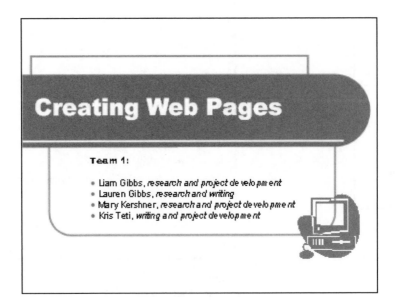

Figure 9.10
Complete slide

10. Place the second slide object into Word. In PowerPoint, click on slide 3 in the slide pane or select one of the slides titled *Storage: Online.*
11. Select *Copy* from the Edit menu or click the Copy button.
12. In Word, position the cursor where you would like to place the slide. In this example, we will place it at the end of the *Creative Strategy* section of the project proposal, after the sentence, *"The presentation will end with a black slide."*
13. Select *Paste* from the Edit menu and the slide object appears.
14. Resize the slide to 70% of its original size.
15. Place a border around the slide to separate it from the text.

Drag and Drop a Slide

Another method of placing a slide object into Word from PowerPoint is to drag and drop it.

1. If possible, position the Word and PowerPoint windows so you can see them both. Right-clicking on the Windows taskbar and selecting *Tile Windows Vertically* arranges the windows so they are both visible.
2. Place the PowerPoint window in the forefront and right-click on the slide that you want to insert into Word. While pressing the right mouse button, drag the slide to its location in Word. When you release the right mouse button, a menu appears (see Figure 9.11). Select *Copy Here* to place the slide object in Word.

Figure 9.11
Menu item

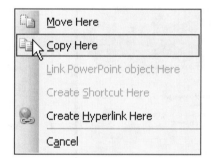

For both the copy and paste and the drag and drop methods, you can edit the slide object by right-clicking on it and selecting *Edit* from the Slide Object menu item (see Figure 9.12). In the edit mode, the Word task pane changes to correspond to PowerPoint's task pane so that you may modify the slide layout,

Figure 9.12
Slide Object menu item

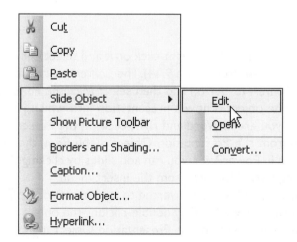

design, and color schemes (see Figure 9.13). The menu items on the Word menu bar also correspond to PowerPoint. You can add and modify clip art, text, and shapes as well as modify the background. You may notice that after you enter the edit mode the task pane disappears. To view it, select *Task pane* from the View menu.

You can also edit the slide in PowerPoint. Right-click on the slide object in the Word document and then select *Open* from the Slide Object menu item. Diagonal lines appear through the slide and PowerPoint opens with the single slide in it. As you edit the slide in PowerPoint, the changes display in the slide object that you placed in Word. To save the slide as a PowerPoint file, select *Save Copy As . . .* from the PowerPoint File menu. This saves the slide as a PowerPoint presentation. As you modify the slide, you do not affect the original PowerPoint file. You will notice that when you choose to edit a slide in PowerPoint, PowerPoint's New Slide menu item and the New Slide button are inactive. This is because we are working with a single slide object and additional slides cannot be added. To add slides to the PowerPoint file, you need to convert it from a slide object to a presentation object.

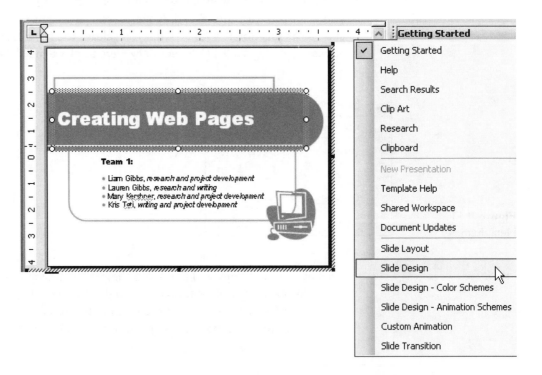

Figure 9.13
Task pane

1. To convert the slide object, right-click on it and select *Convert . . .* from the Slide Object menu item (see Figure 9.14). The *Convert* box appears (see Figure 9.15).
2. Click the *Convert to:* button and then select *Microsoft PowerPoint Presentation.*
3. Click *OK.* The object is now a presentation into which you can add slides. For example, if you are in Word and right-click on the Presentation object and select *Open* from the Presentation Object menu item, the file opens in PowerPoint. When in PowerPoint, you can add slides by clicking the New Slide button or selecting *Insert New Slide* from the Insert menu.

Once a slide object is converted to a presentation, you can run the PowerPoint slideshow from Word by double-clicking the object or by right-clicking on it and selecting *Show* from the Presentation Object menu item (Figure 9.16).

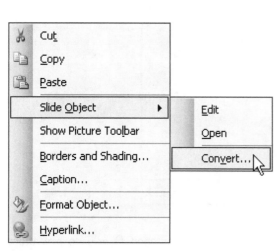

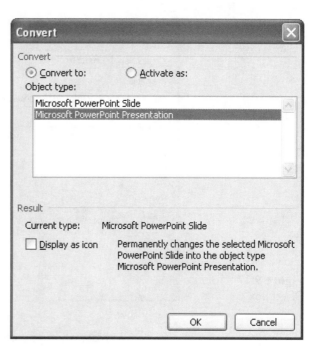

Figure 9.14
Convert slide object

Figure 9.15
Convert box

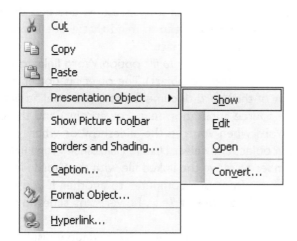

Figure 9.16
Show presentation
object

Inserting Objects

Inserting a Presentation Object and Converting It to a Slide Object

Another method of placing a slide into Word is to use *Insert Object* on the Insert menu.

1. Position the cursor at the location in Word where you want the slide to appear. Select *Object . . .* from the Insert menu and the *Object* box appears (see Figure 9.17).
2. Click the Create from File tab. You will notice on the *Object* box (Figure 9.17) that there is a *Link to file* option. When you insert a presentation object (or any other inserted object) without selecting *Link to file,* a copy of the object embeds into the file. For example, if you insert a PowerPoint presentation entitled *Presentation 1* into Word, Word embeds a copy of that file. Any changes that you make to the file embedded in Word will not affect the original file, *Presentation 1*.

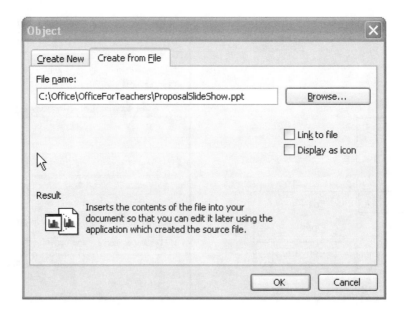

Figure 9.17
Object box

Likewise, when you edit the original file (e.g., *Presentation 1*), you do not affect the copy embedded in Word. Since an object becomes part of the document, it is available as you move the document from computer to computer. For instance, if you move a Word document containing an embedded presentation object to another computer, you can run the slideshow and edit the object if the other computer has PowerPoint. Keep in mind that a document's file size increases when you insert/embed an object.

When you select the *Link to file* option, Word links to the presentation object (or any other inserted object). The object is not embedded—it does not become part of the Word document. After you insert a linked object, you can work in the source application (e.g., PowerPoint) and the changes will be reflected in Word when you run the slideshow or when you right-click on the presentation object and select *Update Link*. Since Word links to the object, you must remember to move the linked file with the Word file when you move the Word document from one computer to another. If you only move the Word document, the linked object (e.g., PowerPoint slideshow) will not run from Word.

3. Click the Browse button and the Browse window displays. Locate the PowerPoint file that contains the slide you want to insert.

4. Single-click on the file (*ProposalSlideShow.ppt*) to select it and click the Insert button on the Browse window.
5. Click *OK*. The first slide of the PowerPoint file displays. In this example, we opened a PowerPoint file named *ProposalSlideShow.ppt* that has several slides. If you want to display a slide other than the first slide, right-click on the presentation object and select *Edit* from the Presentation Object menu item (Figure 9.18).
6. A scroll bar appears on the right side of the presentation object with which you can scroll to another slide (Figure 9.19). After scrolling to the desired slide, click outside the presentation object area to exit the edit mode.

At this point, the presentation object is actually a PowerPoint file that when double-clicked will display the slides in the slideshow. Assuming that we do not need to run the PowerPoint slideshow and we only want to place one slide into Word, we must convert the presentation object to a slide.

7. Right-click on the presentation object and select *Convert...* from the Presentation Object menu item (see Figure 9.20).

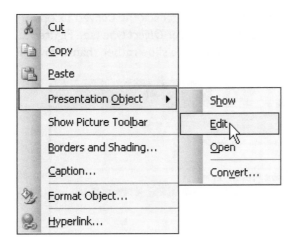

Figure 9.18
Edit presentation
object

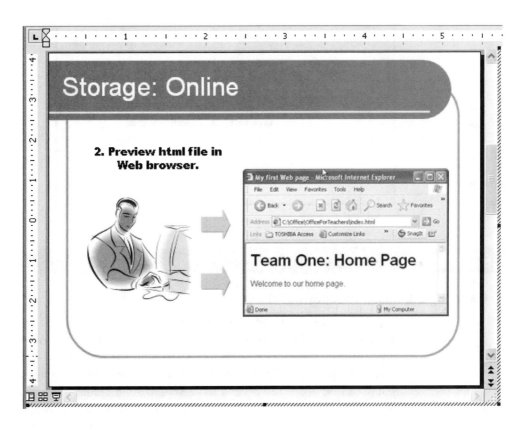

Figure 9.19
Edit mode

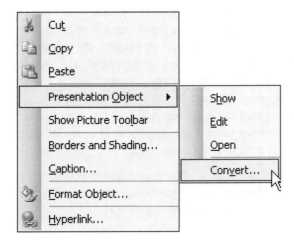

Figure 9.20
Convert object

8. When the *Convert* box displays, click the *Convert to:* option and then click the Microsoft PowerPoint Slide under *Object type* (see Figure 9.21). Click *OK*. The presentation object is now a single slide rather than a PowerPoint presentation file.

Figure 9.21
Convert box

Inserting a Linked Presentation Object

Suppose that you (the teacher) review team 1's proposal prior to the first presentation. You really like the formatting and the slide illustrations within in the document. You ask the group to share the proposal with the class. Team 1 plans to use a computer and projector for the presentation so that everything appearing on the computer can be projected onto a large screen. As a result, the group members decide to insert a presentation object to illustrate what the final project will look like. They can then show the proposal and run their PowerPoint slideshow from Word. During the presentation, the members open up their proposal in Word and discuss the formatting and some key points about the project. When presenting the section containing slide illustrations (the presentation object), they double-click on the object and the slideshow runs, without exiting Word or opening PowerPoint. When they are ready to exit the slideshow, the presenter presses the Esc key and the presentation resumes from the Word document.

The insert object method is an appropriate choice for placing a PowerPoint file into Word. In this example, team 1 can display the PowerPoint slideshow from Word without exiting Word or opening PowerPoint.

1. To insert a PowerPoint file into Word, position the cursor at the location in Word where you want the slide to appear. Select *Object...* from the Insert menu and the *Object* box appears (see boxed Figure 9.1).

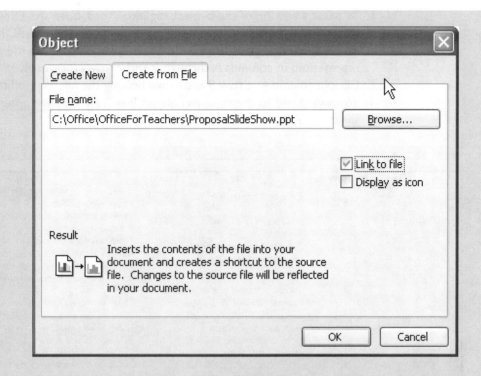

Figure 9.1
Object box

2. Click the Create from File tab.
3. Click the Browse button and the Browse window displays. Locate the Power-Point file that contains the slide you want to insert. In this example, we will insert a PowerPoint file named *ProposalSlideShow.ppt*. Single-click on the ProposalSlideShow.ppt file to select it and then click the Insert button on the Browse window.
4. Click the *Link to file* option on the *Object* box. This enables you to modify the PowerPoint file after inserting it into Word. The changes that you make to the PowerPoint file will be reflected in the inserted object.
5. Click *OK*. The first slide of the PowerPoint file displays.

Running the Linked Presentation Object

6. Run the slideshow by double-clicking on it or by right-clicking on the Linked Presentation object or selecting *Show Link* from the Linked Presentation Object menu item. To exit the slideshow and return to Word, press the Esc key.

This second Show Me section presents the following:
- Copying and pasting the journal-log from Excel into Word and formatting it
- Copying and pasting the journal-log from Excel into a PowerPoint slideshow and formatting it

Paste an Excel Worksheet into a Word Document and a PowerPoint Slideshow

In developing the projected timeline section of the project proposal, team 1 plans to include a sample of the project log. The sample will illustrate the work that the team has completed and it will help justify the budget and projected completion date the team has set. In addition, the team will create a chart that illustrates the time that the members have spent on specific project tasks. We will place these materials in the PowerPoint slideshow.

1. To paste a section of the project log into Word, open the Excel file. In this example, we will open a file named *Project Log.xls* on the CD-ROM. Team 1 would like to show the work that has been completed so far on the project, which is represented in columns A through F and in rows 8 through 19.

2. Click in column A at row 8 and, while holding the left mouse button down, drag downward and to the right to column F at Row 19. The contents of the worksheet should now be selected (see Figure 9.22).

	A	B	C	D	E	F
7						
8	Date	Time	Hours worked	Tasks	Identifier	Thoughts
9	2/12/05	9:30 AM	3.5	Read introduction to HTML	RSH	Collecting information about HTML going well. Should be complete by Feb. 16
10	2/13/04	10:15 AM	1	Read about File Transfer	RSH	Collecting information about how the Web works. This is easier than we thought.
11	2/14/05	2:30 PM	2	Team met and exchanged information about HTML and FTP	RSH	Team members seem to be working well together. Need to get information about Web graphics. Kris and Liam disagree about what needs to be presented and who is going to type proposal.
12	2/14/05	1:15 PM	4	Gather URLs that provide information about Web page design and HTML. Reviewed each page and collected relevant information and shared it with team.	RSH	There are many resources available. It's a bit overwhelming trying to narrow down the information. Liam will help me go through the sites again to determine what we need to include.
13	2/16/05	9:30 AM	1.5	Created first draft of proposal	DEV	Two of us meet and discussed the main topics. Lauren agreed to write the first draft and she will send it to each member for their reactions.
14	2/17/05	12:30 PM	3	Proposal review meeting	DEV	The team met to review the draft proposal. Liam will re-work the goals and objectives, creative ideas and time line section.
15	2/18/05	4:00 PM	3.5	Proposal revision	DEV	The team members had comments on the revised proposal. Lauren will make the revisions and send them to the members by tomorrow.
16	2/19/05	2:15 PM	5	Project outline	DEV	The team met and reviewed the proposal. Liam and Kris will develop an outline of the project. Lauren and Mary will begin to prepare the text of the presentation and identify graphics.

Figure 9.22
Select worksheet content

3. Click the Copy button or select *Copy* from the Edit menu.

4. Position the cursor at the location in Word where you want to place the worksheet. In this example, we will place it in a section of the proposal (see "Proposal.doc" on the CD.) titled *Project timeline*.

5. Click the Paste button or select *Paste* from the Edit menu. The worksheet appears in the Word document. Once the worksheet is placed into Word, it can be modified as a Word table. In this example, the worksheet extends beyond the border of the Word document (see Figure 9.23).

6. To adjust the worksheet, click inside of it and select *AutoFit* from the Table menu and then select *AutoFit to Window* (see Figure 9.24).

7. Set the font style and font size by clicking in the table and choosing *Select* and then *Table* from the Table menu. This action selects the table text. With the text selected, set the font to Arial and the size to 8 points.

Copy and Paste a Worksheet into PowerPoint

We will now add the journal-log sample to PowerPoint and make a new slide to present information about the project timeline.

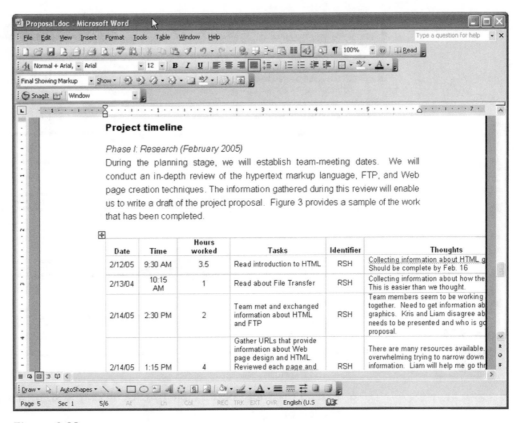

Figure 9.23
Pasted worksheet

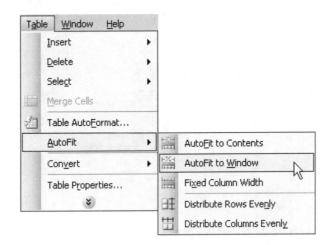

Figure 9.24
AutoFit

1. Open the PowerPoint presentation file *ProposalSlideshow.ppt*. It already contains a *Project timeline* slide. Click on the *Project Timeline* slide.
2. Click the New Slide button. Make this slide a *Title only* slide.
3. Type *Project Timeline* in the title box. Click outside the title box to deselect it.

4. Go to Excel (*ProjectLog.xls*). Since this slide is only a sample of the journal-log, select the contents of the worksheet from cell A8 down to F12. Click the Copy button.
5. Go to the *Project Timeline* slide in PowerPoint. Click in the open area of the slide and click the Paste button. The table should appear (see Figure 9.25).

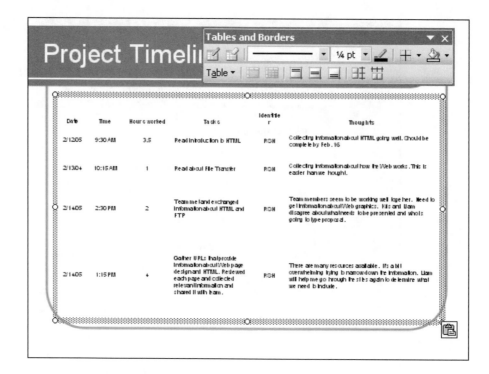

Figure 9.25
Select table

6. Extend the width of the table by clicking on the sizing handles and dragging to the left or right.

7. Place borders around the cells to separate them. Select *Tables and Borders* from *Toolbars* on the View menu. The *Tables and Borders* box displays. With the table selected, set the Border Style to a line, the Border Width to ¼ point, and select *Inside Borders* (see Figure 9.26). The finished slide should look like Figure 9.27.

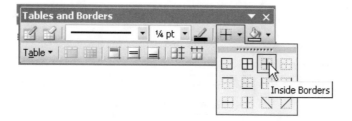

Figure 9.26
Tables and borders

This third section of Show Me presents the following:
- Creating and formatting an Excel chart
- Adding an Excel chart to Word
- Inserting a chart into PowerPoint from Excel

Creating a Chart Illustrating the Time Members Have Spent on Project Tasks

In the proposal as well as in the presentation, the members of team 1 think it is important to illustrate how they have spent their time on the project. We will create a chart that shows how they allocated their time to various tasks and place it in Word and in PowerPoint.

Project Timeline

Date	Time	Hours worked	Tasks	Identifier	Thoughts
2/12/05	9:30 AM	3.5	Read introduction to HTML	RSH	Collecting information about HTML going well. Should be complete by Feb. 16
2/13/04	10:15 AM	1	Read about File Transfer	RSH	Collecting information about how the Web works. This is easier than we thought.
2/14/05	2:30 PM	2	Team met and exchanged information about HTML and FTP	RSH	Team members seem to be working well together. Need to get information about Web graphics. Kris and Liam disagree about what needs to be presented and who is going to type proposal.
2/14/05	1:15 PM	4	Gather URLs that provide information about Web page design and HTML. Reviewed each page and collected relevant information and shared it with team.	RSH	There are many resources available. It's a bit overwhelming trying to narrow down the information. Liam will help me go through the sites again to determine what we need to include.

Figure 9.27
Complete slide

Adding an Excel Chart to Word

In column C of the project journal-log (*ProjectLog.xls*), the members recorded time on task (Hours Worked) and in column E they categorized specific tasks (Identifier). For instance, in Figure 9.28 cell C9 contains *3.5* and cell E9 contains *RSH*. This indicates that members spent 3.5 hours on a research (RSH) task.

	A	B	C	D	E
8	Date	Time	Hours worked	Tasks	Identifier
9	2/12/05	9:30 AM	3.5	Read introduction to HTML	RSH
10	2/13/04	10:15 AM	1	Read about File Transfer	RSH

Figure 9.28
Project journal-log

1. The members would like to chart the time they spent on all tasks so far. In Excel create four column headings: RSH, DEV, ADM, and OTH (see Figure 9.29).

	G	H	I	J
8	RSH	DEV	ADM	OTH
9				

Figure 9.29
Task identifiers

Figure 9.30
AutoSum

2. Click in the cell below the RSH heading and click the AutoSum button (see Figure 9.30). After clicking AutoSum, Excel waits for you to select the cells. Since we have labeled this column as RSH, we only want to select the cells that correspond to the RSH (research) label. Click in cell C9 and drag down to cell C12 (see Figure 9.31). Doing this informs Excel that you want to sum the data in this range of cells. If the cells you want to select are not adjacent, then hold down the Ctr key while clicking and you will be able to select nonadjacent cells.
3. Press the Enter key and the value appears.

B	C	D	E	F		G	
Time	Hours worked	Tasks	Identifier	Thoughts		RSH	D
9:30 AM	3.5	Read introduction to HTML	RSH	Collecting information about HTML going well. Should be complete by Feb. 16		=SUM(C9:C12)	
10:15 AM	1	Read about File Transfer	RSH	Collecting information about how the Web works. This is easier than we thought.		SUM(number1	
2:30 PM	2	Team met and exchanged information about HTML and FTP	RSH	Team members seem to be working well together. Need to get information about Web graphics. Kris and Liam disagree about what needs to be presented and who is going to type proposal.			
1:15 PM	4	Gather URLs that provide information about Web page design and HTML. Reviewed each page and collected relevant information and shared it with team.	RSH	There are many resources available. It's a bit overwhelming trying to narrow down the information. Liam will help me go through the sites again to determine what we need to include.			

Figure 9.31
Selected cells

4. After you add the values for the RSH identifier, click in the cell below the DEV heading. Click AutoSum and select the cells in column C that correspond to DEV (development) tasks.
5. Repeat this procedure for the ADM and OTH identifiers (see Figure 9.32) so that you have summed the hours spent on all tasks.

	G	H	I	J
8	RSH	DEV	ADM	OTH
9	10.5	13	2	2

Figure 9.32
Summed values

6. To chart the data, click the left mouse button and drag across the data headings and the values. In this example, the headings and values are in cells G8 through J9. With the data selected, click the Chart Wizard button or select *Chart* from the Insert menu.
7. From the *Chart Wizard Step 1* box, choose the Pie option on the Standard Types tab and choose the second option under *Chart sub-type:* (see Figure 9.33). Click *Next.*

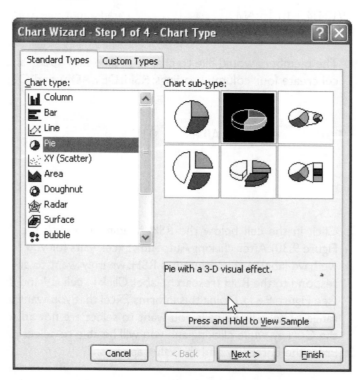

Figure 9.33
Chart Wizard

8. In Step 2 of the wizard, click the Data Range tab and click the Rows option. Click *Next*.
9. In Step 3 of the Wizard, click the Titles tab and add a title (e.g., *Project Work Tasks*) in the *Chart title:* box.
10. Click the Legend tab and deselect the *Show legend* box to remove the legend.
11. Click the Data Labels tab and click the *Category name* and the *Value* boxes (see Figure 9.34).

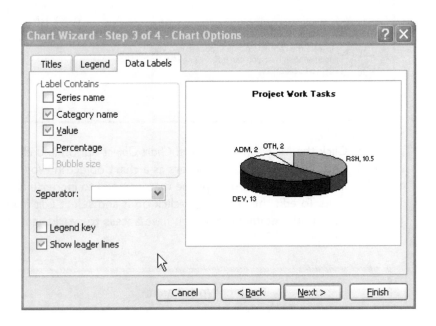

Figure 9.34
Chart Wizard

12. Click *Next*.
13. In Step 4 of the wizard, click the *As Object in (Sheet 1)* option and click *Finish* and the chart should appear (Figure 9.35).

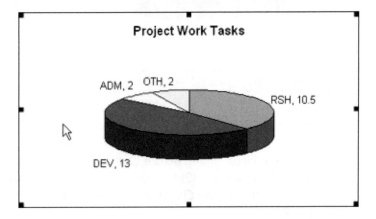

Figure 9.35
Complete chart

14. Click on the chart to select it and then click the Copy button or select *Copy* from the Edit menu.
15. Go to Word and position the cursor where you would like to place the chart. In this example, we will place it in the *Project Timeline* section.
16. Since the team members may need to add more data to the chart, we will paste it as an Excel chart object. From Word's edit menu, click *Paste Special* and the *Paste Special* box appears (see Figure 9.36).

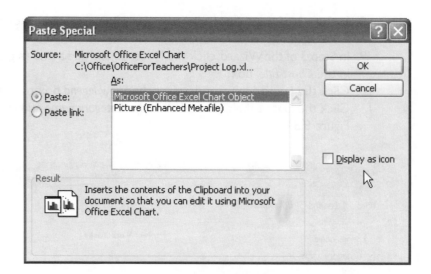

Figure 9.36
Paste Special

17. Click the *Microsoft Office Excel Chart Object* option and click the Paste button.
18. Click *OK* and the chart appears as a chart object in Word.
19. In this example, let us suppose that we need to increase the hours on the OTH tasks. To edit the chart, right-click on it and select *Edit* from the Chart Object item. In the editing mode, you have access to worksheets as well as the chart (see Figure 9.37).

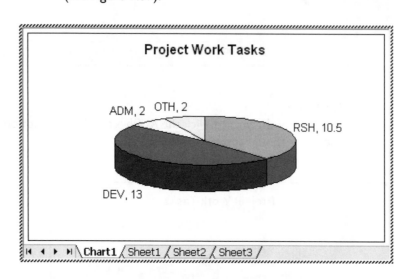

Figure 9.37
Edit mode

20. Click the *Sheet1* tab to view the data sheet.
21. Click in the cell that contains the value for the OTH category and type the number 5 (see Figure 9.38). Before exiting the edit mode, click the *Chart1* tab and then click outside the Object area to exit the edit mode. If you exit the edit mode without clicking the *Chart1* tab, then the worksheet and not the chart will display in Word.
22. The finished chart should look like Figure 9.39.

Inserting a Chart into PowerPoint from Excel

23. Since we made the chart in Excel, we do not need to re-create it in PowerPoint. Open PowerPoint (*ProposalSlideShow.ppt*) and insert a new slide after the last *Project timeline* slide. Make this slide *Title Only* and type *Project Timeline* in the title box.

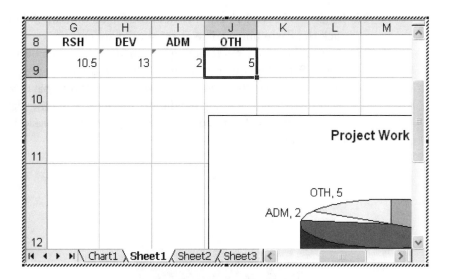

Figure 9.38
Edit mode—Sheet 1

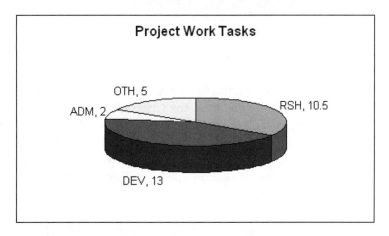

Figure 9.39
Complete chart

24. Open the Project journal-log in Excel.
25. Previously we created a pie chart, which should be in *Sheet1* of Excel (see Figure 9.40). Click on the pie chart and then click the Copy button.

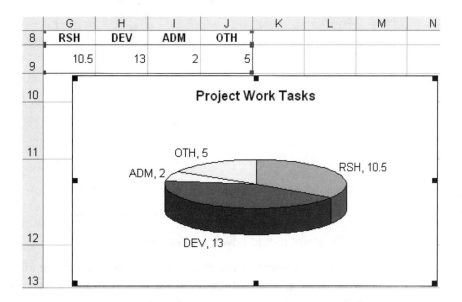

Figure 9.40
Sheet 1

26. Return to PowerPoint and click in the *Project timeline* slide we created and then click the Paste button. The chart should appear.

27. Resize the chart by selecting it and dragging a sizing handle outward (see Figure 9.41). For our purposes, let's resize the chart proportionally by clicking on the sizing handle at the bottom-right side of the chart. While holding the Ctrl key down, drag the sizing handle downward and to the right. The chart resizes in all directions. Resize so that it is large enough to read but it does not overlap the slide borders.

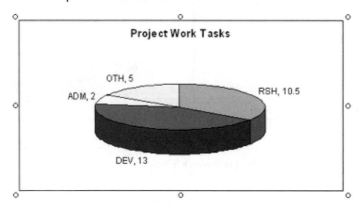

Figure 9.41
Chart sizing handles

28. The chart object has a border around it that we can remove. Right-click on the chart and select *Edit* from the Chart Object menu item.

29. When in the edit mode, select *Selected Chart Area. . .* from the Format menu on the PowerPoint menu bar. The *Format Chart Area* box appears (see Figure 9.42). To remove the border, click the Patterns tab and then click the None button under the Border section. Click *OK*. Exit the edit mode by clicking outside the chart object area.

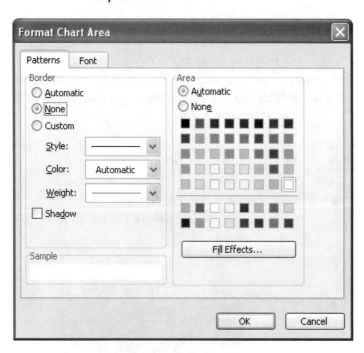

Figure 9.42
Format Chart Area

30. The chart should now look like Figure 9.43.

This fourth segment of the Show Me section presents the following:
■ Embedding a journal-log Excel worksheet as an object in Word
■ Formatting the worksheet object in Word

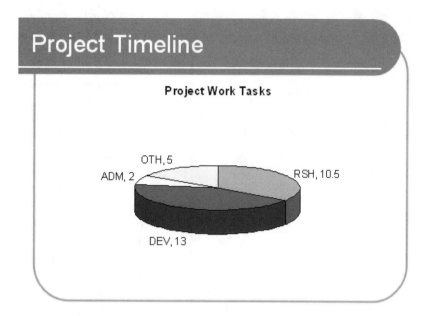

Figure 9.43
Complete chart

Embedding an Excel Worksheet into a Word Document

Team 1 has taken time to develop the project journal-log and so the members intend to place a copy of the entire project journal-log at the end of the proposal (as an appendix) for the teacher to review. In this case, we will embed the worksheet object.

1. With the proposal opened in Word, position the cursor at the bottom of the last page. Create a new page by selecting *Break. . .* from the Insert menu and the *Break* box appears (see Figure 9.44).

Figure 9.44
Insert break

2. Select the *Next page* option under *Section break types*.
3. With the cursor positioned at the top of the new page, select *Object. . .* from the Insert menu and the *Object* box appears.
4. Click the Create from File tab. Click the Browse button and the Browse window displays. Locate the Excel worksheet that you want to insert. In this example, we will insert a worksheet named *Project Log.xls*. Single-click on the Project Log.xls file to select it and then click the Insert button on the Browse window. Click *OK*.
5. The worksheet displays. In this example, it extends beyond the right margin of the Word document. It also extends over two pages. We will set the page orientation to landscape so that all the columns display. Position the cursor on the page containing the worksheet.

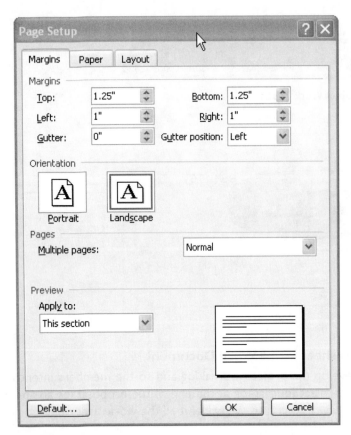

Figure 9.45
Page Setup box

6. From Word's File menu, select *Page Setup* and the *Page Setup* box appears (see Figure 9.45). In the Orientation section of the *Page Setup* box, click the *Landscape* option. In the Preview section, under *Apply to:*, select *This section or Selected Section.* Click *OK*.

7. After you set the orientation, you may notice that the worksheet fits horizontally on the page but it has an empty column(s) and it also extends over two pages (see Figure 9.46). In this example, we first need to make the object smaller so that we can remove empty columns from the display area.

8. Right-click on the worksheet and select *Format Object.* When the *Format Object* box displays, click the Size tab (see Figure 9.47). Enter 6.5 for the height. If you have the *Lock aspect ratio* option selected, then the Width changes automatically.

9. Click *OK* and the object should appear smaller.

10. Right-click on the object and select *Edit* from the Worksheet Object menu item.

11. In the edit mode, you can resize the object window. Go to the bottom-right side of the object and position the cursor over the corner. The cursor changes to a double arrow (see Figure 9.48). While holding the left mouse button down, drag upward and to the left so that the empty rows and columns do not display (see Figure 9.49).

Creating Web Pages: Project Journal - Log

Team: Liam, Lauren, Mary, Kris
Teacher: Mrs. Kail
February and March 2005

Date	Time	Hours worked	Tasks	Identifier	Thoughts
2/12/05	9:30 AM	3.5	Read introduction to HTML	RSH	Collecting information about HTML going well. Should be complete by Feb. 16
2/13/04	10:15 AM	1	Read about File Transfer	RSH	Collecting information about how the Web works. This is easier than we thought.
2/14/05	2:30 PM	2	Team met and exchanged information about HTML and FTP	RSH	Team members seem to be working well together. Need to get information about Web graphics. Kris and Liam disagree about what needs to be presented and who is going to type proposal.
2/14/05	1:15 PM	4	Gather URLs that provide information about Web page design and HTML. Reviewed each page and collected relevant information and shared it with team.	RSH	There are many resources available. It's a bit overwhelming trying to narrow down the information. Liam will help me go through the sites again to determine what we need to include.
2/16/05	9:30 AM	1.5	Created first draft of proposal	DEV	Two of us meet and discussed the main topics. Lauren agreed to write the first draft and she will send it to each member for their reactions.
2/17/05	12:30 PM	3	Proposal review meeting	DEV	The team met to review the draft proposal. Liam will re-work the goals and objectives, creative ideas and time line section.
2/18/05	4:00 PM	3.5	Proposal revision	DEV	The team members had comments on the revised proposal. Lauren will make the revisions and send them to the members by tomorrow.
2/19/05	2:15 PM	5	Project outline	DEV	The team met and reviewed the proposal. Liam and Kris will develop an outline of the project. Lauren and Mary will begin to prepare the text of the presentation.

re 9.46
ized work-

Figure 9.47
Format Object box

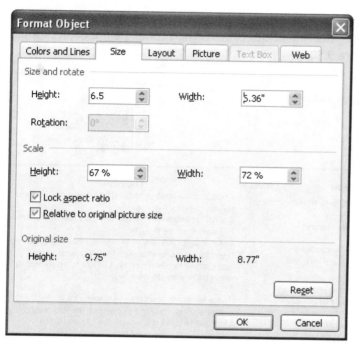

Figure 9.48
Cursor

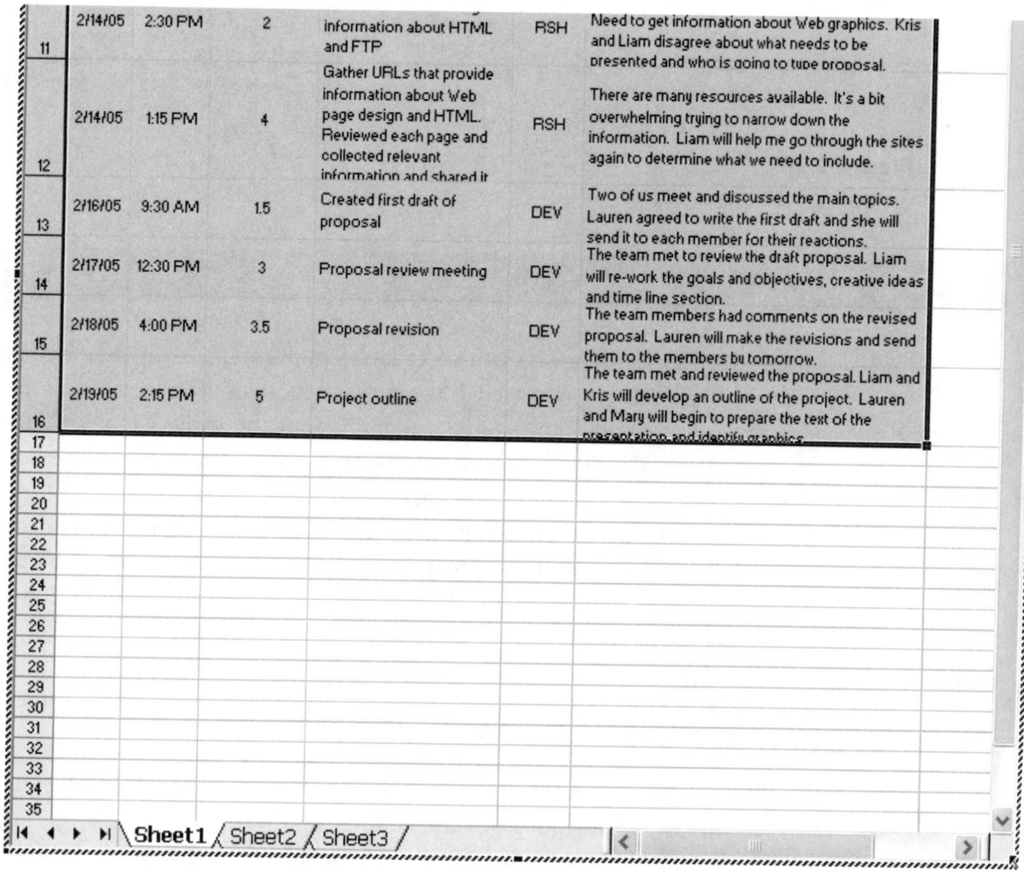

Figure 9.49
Oversized worksheet

12. Exit the edit mode by clicking outside the object area. You may need to increase the object's size using the *Format Object* box. When complete the object should look similar to Figure 9.50.

Creating Web Pages: Project Journal - Log

Team: Liam, Lauren, Mary, Kris
Teacher: Mrs. Kail
February and March 2005

Date	Time	Hours worked	Tasks	Identifier	Thoughts
2/12/05	9:30 AM	3.5	Read introduction to HTML	RSH	Collecting information about HTML going well. Should be complete by Feb. 16
2/13/04	10:15 AM	1	Read about File Transfer	RSH	Collecting information about how the Web works. This is easier than we thought.
2/14/05	2:30 PM	2	Team met and exchanged information about HTML and FTP	RSH	Team members seem to be working well together. Need to get information about Web graphics. Kris and Liam disagree about what needs to be presented and who is going to type proposal.
2/14/05	1:15 PM	4	Gather URLs that provide information about Web page design and HTML. Reviewed each page and collected relevant information and shared it with team.	RSH	There are many resources available. It's a bit overwhelming trying to narrow down the information. Liam will help me go through the sites again to determine what we need to include.
2/16/05	9:30 AM	1.5	Created first draft of proposal	DEV	Two of us meet and discussed the main topics. Lauren agreed to write the first draft and she will send it to each member for their reactions.
2/17/05	12:30 PM	3	Proposal review meeting	DEV	The team met to review the draft proposal. Liam will re-work the goals and objectives, creative ideas and time line section.
2/18/05	4:00 PM	3.5	Proposal revision	DEV	The team members had comments on the revised proposal. Lauren will make the revisions and send them to the members by tomorrow.
2/19/05	2:15 PM	5	Project outline	DEV	The team met and reviewed the proposal. Liam and Kris will develop an outline of the project. Lauren and Mary will begin to prepare the text of the presentation and identify graphics.

Figure 9.50
Complete worksheet object

LET ME TRY

Let us suppose that we want to create a multimedia team research report. We assign team members to research a topic of interest and collect text information, photographs, video, audio, and numerical data about the topic. We use Word to compile the text information; PowerPoint to assemble the photographs, video, and audio; and Excel to organize the numerical data.

We next define tasks for each team member. Assign a student to coordinate the project and integrate the slideshow and worksheet materials in Word. Assign at least one student to develop the PowerPoint slideshow and one student to prepare data and create data charts with Excel.

Linking PowerPoint Files and Excel Files to Word

1. Create a folder to store your files and name it *Team Project*.
2. Create a rough draft of the report in Word.
3. In addition, create drafts of the slideshow and Excel worksheet(s); save the files in the *Team Project* folder with descriptive names.

4. Link the PowerPoint slideshow and Excel worksheets to the Word document. From the Word Insert menu, select *Object*.

5. Click the Create from File tab and locate the PowerPoint slideshow.

6. Click the *Link to File* option and click *OK*.

7. Repeat these steps for the Excel worksheet.

8. Each team member then works on his or her part of the project. As members work on their respective tasks, they must remember to save their files with the same names as used earlier.

9. When the members have completed their tasks, copy the files to the *Team Project* folder. As long as the files' names are identical to the names given earlier, the new (or most up-to-date) files will overwrite the existing (draft) files in the *Team Project* folder.

10. Open the report Word document and the linked objects should be updated.

This fifth segment of the Show Me section presents the following:

■ Creating an e-mail contact in Outlook
■ Exporting contacts to Access
■ Copying and pasting data records from Access to PowerPoint

Creating a Credit Slide: Outlook and Access

Suppose that for the duration of the project the members of team 1 maintained an e-mail contact list in Microsoft Outlook of individuals who assisted them with the project proposal and presentation. As the list developed, they added information in addition to e-mail address, such as phone number, fax number, and address. They would now like to export the list to Access to create a database of experts, which will be a valuable resource for them and their classmates. From the database, they will make a *Credits* slide to give those individuals credit for their assistance.

Creating a Contact in Outlook

1. Open Outlook. Select *Contacts* from the Go menu (Figure 9.51).

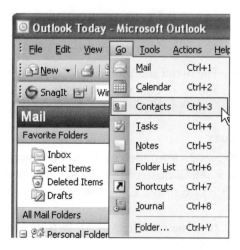

Figure 9.51
Outlook contacts

2. Select *New* from the File menu and then select *Contact* from the submenu (see Figure 9.52).

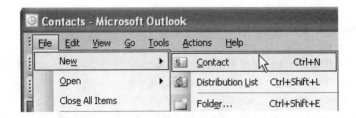

Figure 9.52
Create Outlook
contacts

> 3. An untitled contact box displays. Enter the contact information (see Figure 9.53).

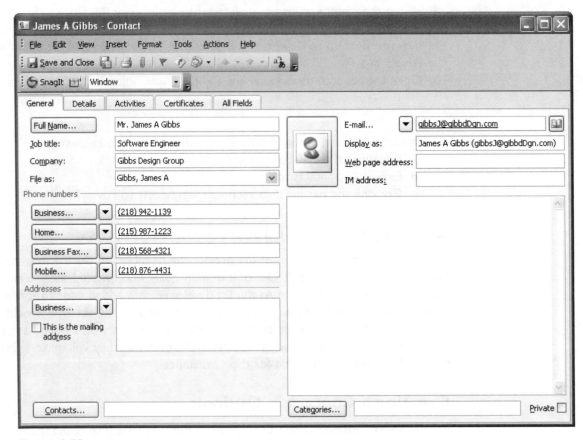

Figure 9.53
Contact information

> 4. Select *Save* from the File menu and then close the Contact window by clicking
>   the Close button. To add more contacts, select *New* and then *Contacts* from the
>   File menu.

Export Contacts to Access

> 5. Select *Import and Export. . .* from the File menu. The Import and Export Wizard
>   displays (see Figure 9.54). Choose the *Export to a file* option and click *Next*.
> 6. The *Export to a File* box displays. Click the *Microsoft Access* option and then
>   click *Next*.
> 7. On the next Export to a File screen, click *Contacts* under *Select folder to export
>   from:* (see Figure 9.55). Click *Next*.
> 8. On the next Export to a File screen, give the file a name and specify a location
>   in which to save it. For this example, we will name the file *Team1 Contacts* and
>   save it in the *My Documents* folder. Click *Next*. The next screen informs you of

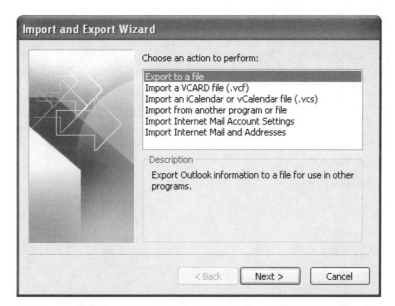

Figure 9.54
Import and Export
Wizard

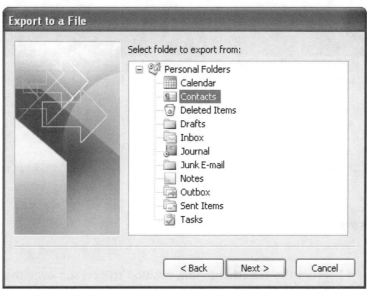

Figure 9.55
Export to File

the action to be taken and *Export "Contacts" from folder; "Contacts"* should be checked. Click *Finish.*

The contacts export to Access and a .mdb file is created with the name you assigned. For example, we named the file *Team I Contacts* and so we will find a file in the My Documents folder named. *Team I Contacts.mdb.*

9. Open Access. From the File menu select *Open* and locate the Team I Contacts.mdb file. You can locate "TeamIContacts.mdb" on the CD. The *Team I Contacts:* database window displays (see Figure 9.56). Under *Objects* on the left side of the window, click *Tables* and then double-click *Contacts table.*

10. From the Access View menu, select *Datasheet view* and the data records display (see Figure 9.57).

Copy and Paste Data Records from Access to PowerPoint

Now that we have created our database, let's copy some of the data records and paste them into PowerPoint to create the credits slide. For the credits slide, we will only need the person's name, company, and department. However, the columns with this information are not adjacent and so we will move them.

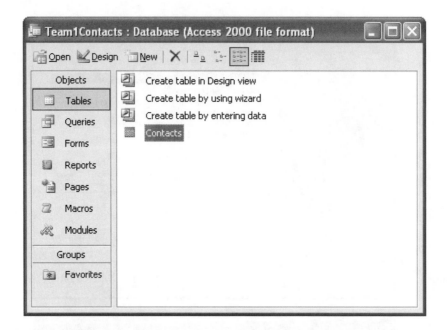

Figure 9.56
Team 1 contacts

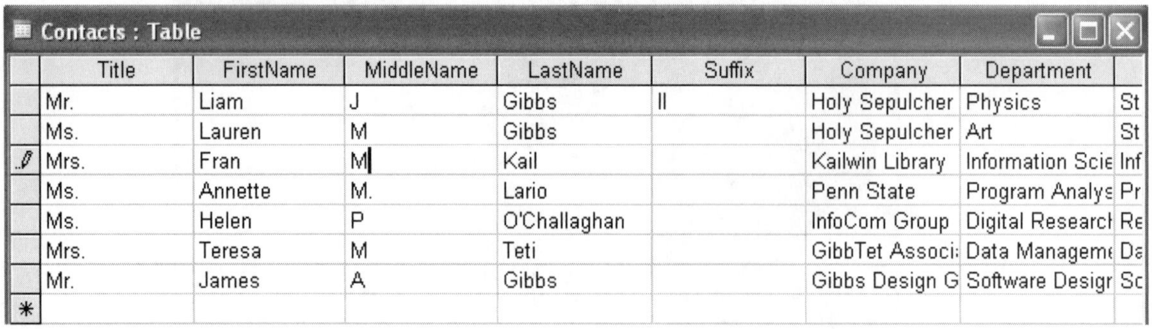

Figure 9.57
Access Datasheet view

	Title	FirstName	MiddleName	LastName	Suffix	Company	Department	
	Mr.	Liam	J	Gibbs	II	Holy Sepulcher	Physics	St
	Ms.	Lauren	M	Gibbs		Holy Sepulcher	Art	St
✏	Mrs.	Fran	M	Kail		Kailwin Library	Information Scie	Inf
	Ms.	Annette	M.	Lario		Penn State	Program Analys	Pr
	Ms.	Helen	P	O'Challaghan		InfoCom Group	Digital Research	Re
	Mrs.	Teresa	M	Teti		GibbTet Associ	Data Manageme	Da
	Mr.	James	A	Gibbs		Gibbs Design G	Software Desigr	Sc

Figure 9.58
Field selector

↓ Company
Holy Sepulcher
Holy Sepulcher
Kailwin Library
Penn State
InfoCom Group
GibbTet Associ
Gibbs Design G

11. From the Datasheet view, position the cursor over the field selector for the *Company* column and the cursor changes to an inverted arrow (see Figure 9.58). Clicking anywhere in the gray title area selects the column.

12. Select the *Company* column and while holding the left mouse button down, drag it to the right of the *LastName* column. Repeat this procedure and move the *Department* column to the right of the *Company* column. The *Contacts: Table* should look like Figure 9.59.

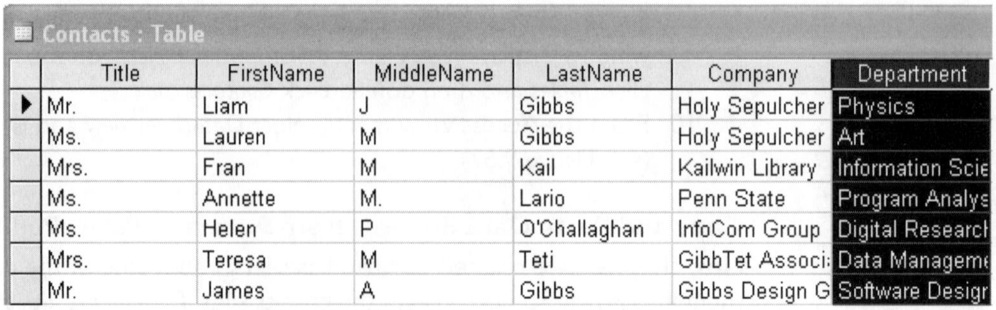

Contacts : Table

	Title	FirstName	MiddleName	LastName	Company	Department
▶	Mr.	Liam	J	Gibbs	Holy Sepulcher	Physics
	Ms.	Lauren	M	Gibbs	Holy Sepulcher	Art
	Mrs.	Fran	M	Kail	Kailwin Library	Information Scie
	Ms.	Annette	M.	Lario	Penn State	Program Analys
	Ms.	Helen	P	O'Challaghan	InfoCom Group	Digital Research
	Mrs.	Teresa	M	Teti	GibbTet Associ	Data Manageme
	Mr.	James	A	Gibbs	Gibbs Design G	Software Desigr

Figure 9.59
Contacts: Table

13. Select the *FirstName, MiddleName, LastName, Company,* and *Department* columns by dragging the mouse over the field selector (gray area with column name) of each column.
14. Click the Copy button.
15. Go to PowerPoint. Click the last side and then click the New Slide button.
16. Set the slide layout to *Title Only.* Type *Credits* in the *Title* box.
17. Click outside the *Title* box to deselect it.
18. Click the Paste button and the Access data should display in the slide. Notice that the title (*Contacts*) of the data table also appears on the slide, which we can delete for this example.
19. Click on the data table to select it. Resize it by holding the Ctrl key down and dragging the bottom-right sizing handle.

    When first clicking on an object, its border changes to a line pattern, indicating that it can be modified. Clicking on the border a second time changes it from a line to a dot pattern. The dot pattern indicates that the contents of the object are selected and that changes (e.g., font size or style) will affect the entire contents of the object.
20. With the table selected (and the border as a dot pattern), set the font size to 14 points and the style to Bold.
21. The table has a border around it that we will remove. Keep the table selected (with the dot-pattern border) and then select *Table* from the Format menu. The *Format Table* box appears.
22. Click the Borders tab and click on the buttons that correspond to the top, left, right, and bottom borders (see Figure 9.60). When you are done, only the borders that separate the cells should display.

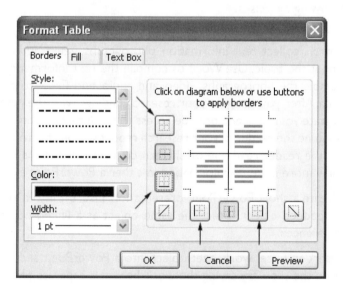

Figure 9.60
Format Table—
borders

23. Click *OK.*
24. We will now center-align the contents of the cells. With the table selected, click the Center Vertically button on the Tables and Border toolbar (see Figure 9.61). When you are done the slide should look similar to Figure 9.62.

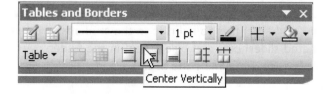

Figure 9.61
Center Vertically

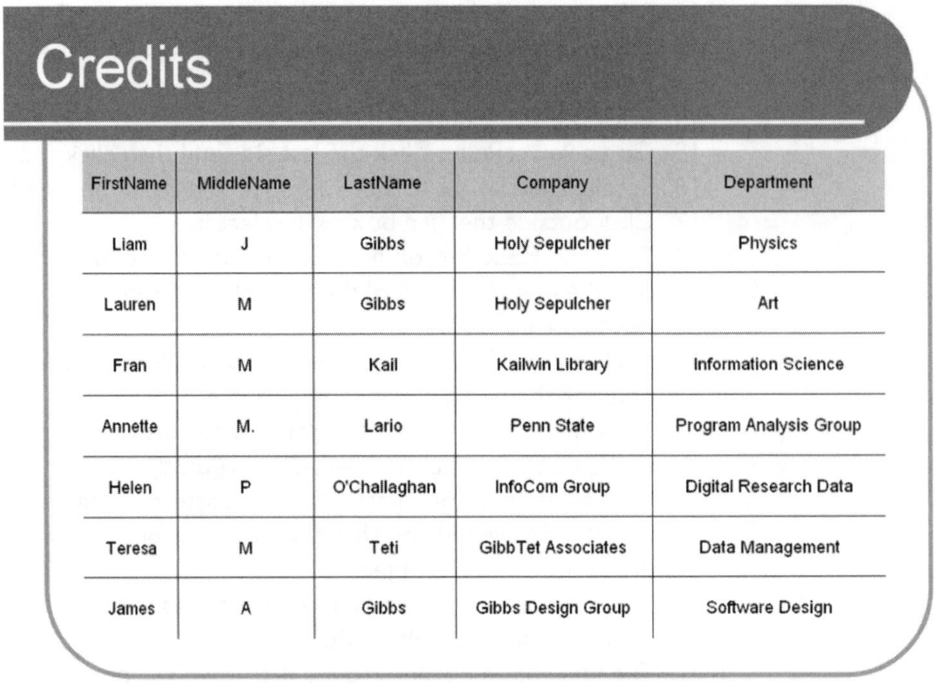

Credits

FirstName	MiddleName	LastName	Company	Department
Liam	J	Gibbs	Holy Sepulcher	Physics
Lauren	M	Gibbs	Holy Sepulcher	Art
Fran	M	Kail	Kailwin Library	Information Science
Annette	M.	Lario	Penn State	Program Analysis Group
Helen	P	O'Challaghan	InfoCom Group	Digital Research Data
Teresa	M	Teti	GibbTet Associates	Data Management
James	A	Gibbs	Gibbs Design Group	Software Design

Figure 9.62
Complete slide

A CHALLENGE INTEGRATING OFFICE

For those who would like a challenge beyond the instructions presented in this chapter, try the following exercises:

1. Create a multimedia research report. Research a topic of interest. In your research, collect text information, photographs, video, audio, and numerical data about the topic. Use Word to compile the text information, PowerPoint to assemble the photographs, video, and audio; and Excel to organize the numeric data. After you compile your research findings with the respective program, integrate your data and provide access to them through one program (i.e., Word). Assume the reader of your research report will be able to view it on a computer. As the reader reads, he or she can click on illustrations (figures and tables) to view more in-depth information in either a PowerPoint slideshow or Excel.

2. Create a short PowerPoint presentation. Insert it into a Word document as an embedded object. Insert the same object as a linked object and compare the differences.

3. Insert an Excel worksheet object into a PowerPoint slide. Enter data and view it on the slide. Try saving the worksheet as a separate file.

4. Create a PowerPoint slideshow that links to two or more presentation objects. Assume that multiple students will each develop PowerPoint slideshows and present them to the class on the instructor's workstation, connected to a computer/video projector. Early in the development process, create a folder to store all the slideshows. Have students create drafts of their slideshows and name them descriptively. Place them in the folder. Create a master slideshow and link all (draft) files to it. Prior to the students' presentations collect all the completed slideshows and place them in the folder overwriting the draft versions of the files, assuming the names are identical.

TYING IT ALL TOGETHER

In this chapter, we used the example of students preparing a multimedia project proposal and presentation. We modified materials in ways that caused us to integrate the Office products. We used several integration approaches including copy and paste, drag and drop, and inserting objects by embedding them in files and by linking to them. In addition, we made a contact list in Outlook and exported it to Access. We then took data records from Access and placed them in PowerPoint. The examples presented in the chapter serve as an introduction to some of the many ways you can use and incorporate the Office programs to work more effectively and efficiently.

WINDOWS

TECHNICAL TERMS

You will encounter the following terms in this appendix:

Desktop

Shortcuts

Taskbar

Start button

Drag and drop

File

Folder

Windows Overview

You access Microsoft Office 2003 through the Windows operating system. This appendix, therefore, provides a basic overview of the Windows XP operating system. It presents some fundamental features of Windows XP that can be used with Office.

A Word About Windows

Before you open and work with any of the Microsoft Office products, it is useful to have a basic understanding of Windows. Windows is an operating system that helps you access, store, and organize information or data on your computer. There are several versions of Windows, such as Windows XP, Windows NT, Windows 98, Windows Me (Millennium edition), and Windows 2000.

As the name *Windows* implies, you interact with programs and files through adjustable rectangular areas, or windows, that appear on your computer screen. Windows has a graphical user interface (GUI). It contains objects (e.g., buttons, icons) through which you access and work with files, folders, and programs. The interface makes working with the computer easy and efficient, and it eliminates the need to type commands that are often confusing.

The Desktop

Typically, when you turn your computer on, the Windows desktop displays (see Figure A.1). The desktop is the work area where you place files and folders. The folders, programs, or files that you open display in rectangular windows on the desktop. Several icons, such as *My Computer,* and *Recycle Bin,* appear that represent applications, files, or system resources (e.g., scanner). To activate these objects, double-click them with the left mouse button. For example, the My Computer icon when doubled-clicked provides access to the contents of your computer and its controls.

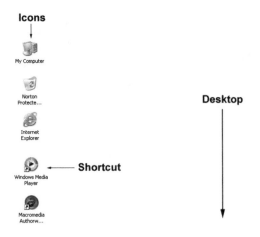

Desktop

Taskbar

Figure A.1
Windows desktop

Figure A.2
Shortcut Icon

Instead of searching your computer each time you want to open a frequently used file or program, you can create a shortcut to it on the desktop. When you double-click the shortcut, the file or program opens. Each Shortcut icon has a small arrow at the bottom-left corner (see Figure A.2) to distinguish it from other icons.

The taskbar is also on the desktop and it contains the Start button. The Start button, located on the left side of the taskbar, is your beginning point to access programs and files. As you open items, a button representing each program displays on the taskbar. You can switch between programs by clicking the appropriate button. In Figure A.3, both Microsoft Word and Excel are open. Clicking either button makes the corresponding application active by bringing the application's window to the forefront on the desktop. Depending on the computer's configuration, icons appear on the taskbar providing access to programs and resources. For instance, the icons appearing on the right of the taskbar in Figure A.3 provide access to audio and network resources. The taskbar can be set to show automatically as the mouse passes over it and hide when the mouse leaves its area. If you do not see the taskbar, pass the mouse over the four sides of the screen and it should appear.

Figure A.3
Taskbar

The Mouse and Windows

The computer's mouse is integral to working with Windows. You use the mouse to select icons, make choices from dialogue boxes and pull-down menus, and move and resize windows.

A typical computer mouse has at least two buttons, the left mouse and right mouse buttons. You use the left mouse button to select and open objects and to resize and position windows. The right mouse button helps open shortcut menus that display commands for a particular object.

You can specify how to choose objects with your mouse. Typically, a single-click with the left-mouse button selects an item and double-click opens it. However, you can change this preference in Windows so that pointing the mouse at an object selects it and single-click opens it. Selecting an object informs Windows that you are going to work with the object in some way, such as opening or moving it. Objects highlight when selected. Figure A.4 illustrates the My Computer object as selected and not selected. The selected My Computer object is on the right side of Figure A.4.

Figure A.4
Icons not selected
and selected

Double-clicking the left mouse button on an object opens it in a window on the desktop. For example, double-click the left mouse button on the My Computer object to open its contents (see Figure A.5).

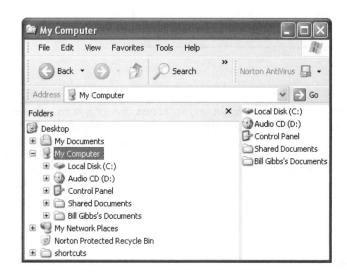

Figure A.5
My Computer

As mentioned, you can set mouse point-and-click options so that pointing to an object selects it and a single-click opens it. To set these options, double-click the My Computer object on the desktop. Select *Folder Options* from the Tools menu (see Figure A.6). The *Folder Options* box appears. Click the General tab and then choose *Single-click to open an item (point to select)* under *Click items as follows.* Click *OK* (see Figure A.7).

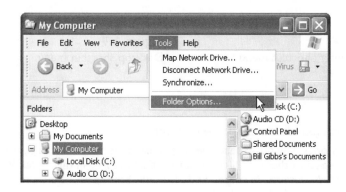

Figure A.6
Folder options

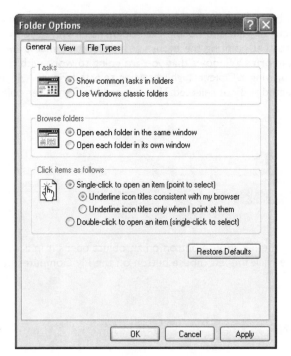

Figure A.7
Folder options: General tab

Shortcut Menus

Shortcut menus can be an efficient way to access files, programs, and system resources, among other things. By positioning your mouse on a folder, an object, the desktop, or the taskbar and then right-clicking, a shortcut menu appears displaying the commands for that object. Right-clicking on *My Computer,* for example, displays its shortcut menu (see Figure A.8). Position your mouse on the desktop, right-click, and the desktop shortcut menu appears (see Figure A.9). Use the Properties option on this shortcut menu to change the computer's desktop colors and background image.

Figure A.8
My Computer shortcut menu

Figure A.9
Desktop shortcut menu

Icons

A typical desktop contains the following features:

My Documents: Windows default storage location for your files (e.g., documents or graphics). Unless you specify otherwise, files are automatically stored in this folder. *My Documents* contains three folders: *My Pictures, My Videos,* and *My Music.* Storing your media (e.g., videos, photographs, music) files in these folders will help you keep them organized.

My Computer: Allows you to see the contents of your disk drives and to access your computer's configuration settings. It contains the A: drive icon, the C: drive icon, the E: drive icon (and icons for any other disk drives you have connected to your computer), and the Control Panel folder. When the A:, C:, or E: drive icons are double-clicked, their contents display on the screen. For instance, double-clicking the C: drive icon displays a list of all the folders, directories, and files contained on the C: drive. By double-clicking the Control Panel, you can access the configuration settings of your computer.

Recycle Bin: Temporarily stores deleted files. All files deleted from the C: drive go first to the Recycle Bin. Only when the Recycle Bin is emptied are the files removed from your computer. You can retrieve files from the Recycle Bin if you deleted them erroneously. If you do not empty the Recycle Bin, your deleted files still occupy disk space. Files deleted from the A: drive (floppy drive) or other external disk drives do not go to the Recycle Bin. They are removed from your computer as soon as you delete them. If you want to delete a file from the C: drive without sending it to the Recycle Bin, hold down the Shift key when you delete it.

My Network Places: Allows you to connect to, find, and share network resources; exchange files and printers; and connect to the Internet.

Windows Media Player: Allows you to play media files, such as musical CDs, and audio and video files.

The Taskbar: As mentioned, the taskbar provides access to opened folders and files and makes switching between them convenient (see Figure A.3).

Start Menu

Click the Start button on the taskbar and the Start menu displays (see Figure A.10). The items on this menu contain most of the things you need to begin using Windows. An arrow to the right of a menu item indicates that more items or submenus are present. When you pass the mouse over the arrow, a submenu appears.

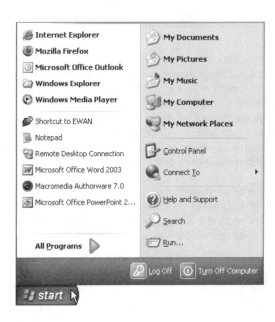

Figure A.10
Start menu

Some of the items on the Start menu are described next. The items on your Start menu may vary somewhat from those presented here because your computer may be configured differently from the one used for the example. The start menu items include:

All Programs: Displays a list of programs that can be opened. To open a program, move the mouse over the words *All Programs* and a submenu appears. When you see the program you want to open in the submenu, position the mouse on it and click.

My Recent Documents: Presents a list of recently opened documents. This item is useful for quickly opening a document without searching for it on your computer.

Search: Allows you to find files and folders located on your computer. You can also search the Internet using this option.

Help: Opens the Windows Help and Support module, which provides information about Windows and many of its features and functions.

Run: Allows you to specify a program to start or a file to open.

Shut Down/Turn Off Computer: Shuts down Windows and turns off the computer. It can also be used to restart the computer or to put it in hibernation mode.

Repositioning and Resizing Windows

As you work in Windows, you will likely open several files or programs at the same time and may need to reposition windows to work efficiently. All windows have a title bar (see Figure A.11) that displays the item's name. You can reposition a window by clicking on the title bar and, while holding the left mouse button down, dragging the window to a new location. You can also activate a window simply by clicking on the title bar.

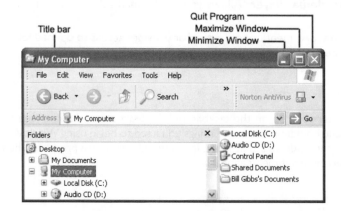

Figure A.11
Window title bar

Title bars contain three buttons on the upper right side. The button on the left reduces, or minimizes, the window. The button in the center enlarges, or maximizes, a window to the full size of the desktop. When the window is enlarged to full screen, the Maximize button changes to the Restore button. Restore returns the window to its original size prior to maximizing it. The button on the right closes the window or program. When you have a program open (e.g., MS Word), clicking the Close/Quit program button exits the program. In addition, right-clicking on the title bar displays a pop-up menu with minimize, maximize, and close/quit options. You can minimize all active windows by right-clicking on a blank area of the taskbar and then selecting *Show the Desktop*.

To make a window larger or smaller, move the mouse pointer to any one of the four sides of the window. The pointer will change to a double arrow. Drag the border to enlarge or reduce the window. A box appears around the window as you resize it (see Figure A.12). Resizing from the bottom-right corner sizes the window proportionally.

Figure A.12
Resizing window

Show Me

Working with Programs and Files

Opening Programs

1. To open a program such as Microsoft Word, click the Start button on the Windows taskbar. On the Start menu, move the mouse pointer over *All Programs* to display the Programs submenu. Move the mouse pointer over *Microsoft Office* to display the *Microsoft Office* submenu (see Figure A. 13).

Figure A.13
Opening MS Word

2. Click *Microsoft Word* to open it. Word opens with a blank untitled document. A button representing Word appears on the taskbar. Depending on how you installed Office 2003, the menu item for it may be located in various locations on the Start menu. In most cases, it can be found under *All Programs* or under *Programs* within the Microsoft Office folder.

Opening Files

There are multiple ways to open a file. In this section, we discuss three methods: (1) opening a file using the application that created it, (2) accessing and opening a file using *My Computer,* and (3) opening a file using *My Recent Documents* on the Start menu.

Opening a File Using the Application That Created It

Using the Start menu, open the application with which you created the file. For example, open a file created with Microsoft Word.

1. Once Word is open, click on *File* and select *Open* (see Figure A. 14). The *Open* dialogue box appears (see Figure A. 15).
2. Use the *Open* dialogue box to locate the file you want to open. If you need to open a file in a different folder, click the down-arrow next to the *Look in* box, then select the disk drive that contains the folder. Once you locate the file, select it by clicking on it one time, then click *Open*. In this example, the file to be opened is Lecture_Week4.doc, and it is in the A_Week1 folder.

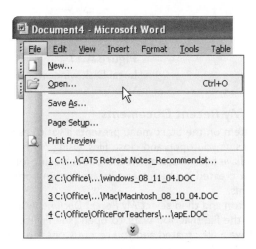

Figure A.14
Open file

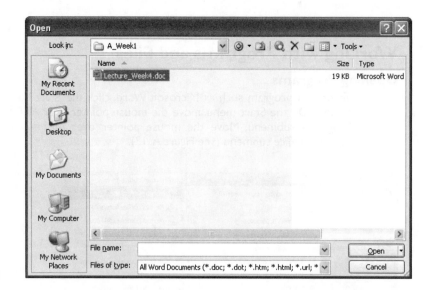

Figure A.15
Open dialogue box

Accessing and Opening a File Using *My Computer*

1. For this example, use the My Computer icon to access and open a file named *Lecture_Week4.doc* located on the local disk, or C: drive, in a folder named *A_Week1*.

   Double-click *My Computer* on the desktop and the My Computer window appears (see Figure A.16). Double-click the drive where the file is located. In this case, the drive is the local disk, or C: drive.

2. In the local disk (C:) window, locate and double-click the A_Week1 folder (see Figure A.17) to open it.

3. In the A_Week1 window, locate the file *Lecture_Week4.doc*. Double-click it and the file opens.

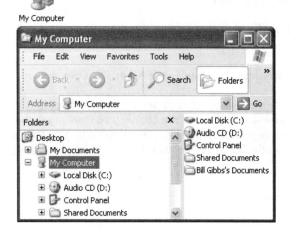

Figure A.16
My Computer window

Figure A.17
Local Disk window

Opening a File Using *My Recent Documents*

The *My Recent Documents* item on the Start menu presents a list of recently opened files. Keep in mind that the list changes as you open and close files. Using *My Recent Documents*, you can quickly open a file that you have been working on without searching for it on your computer or opening the application that created it. The file and its application both open when you open a file with *My Recent Documents*.

1. Click the Start button and then select *My Recent Documents* and a submenu displays.

2. Click the name of the file that you want to open (see Figure A.18). This step assumes that you already have a file created and you recently opened it. In this example, the Microsoft Word file *CMC Research.doc* opens.

Figure A.18
My Recent
Documents

Opening Multiple Programs

When using Windows you can work with several files simultaneously, each of which opens in its own window. For example, you can open Microsoft Word and Excel files and copy and paste data between them. The following steps illustrate how to open multiple programs, switch between programs, reposition and resize program windows, and exchange data between programs.

Opening Programs

1. Click the Start button on the Windows taskbar. On the Start menu, move the mouse pointer over *All Programs* and the Programs submenu appears. Move the mouse over *Microsoft Office* to display the Microsoft Office submenu. Click *Microsoft Word* to open it. Word opens with one blank untitled document. Notice that a button representing Word appears on the taskbar.
2. Open Microsoft Excel and Excel opens with one blank workbook. You now have two programs open, Word and Excel, and each of these programs has one blank file.

Switching Between Programs

1. The Word and Excel documents appear on the taskbar. If you are viewing the Excel document, switch to Word by clicking the Word button on the taskbar. Alternatively, you can switch between programs by pressing the Alt and Tab keys simultaneously (see Figure A.19). Pressing the Tab key repeatedly changes the selection. Release the keys and the selected program becomes active.

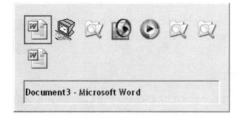

Figure A.19
Program switching
(Alt + Tab)

Repositioning and Resizing Program Windows.

In this example, you can resize the Word and Excel windows and then copy data from Excel into Word.

1. If Word and Excel are open to full screen, restore them to adjust the window size. Click the Restore button at the top right of the window on the Word file. Remember that when a window is full screen the Restore button replaces the Maximize button.
2. Switch to Excel by clicking the button that corresponds to it on the taskbar. Click the Restore button at the top right of the Excel window. *Note:* If, when you restore the Word file, you see Excel in the background, click on Excel's window. This makes Excel active, and it is an alternative to switching between programs using the taskbar. Clicking on windows in the background brings them to the foreground and makes them active.
3. Make either the Word or Excel window active. Resize the window by positioning the mouse pointer at the bottom-right corner of the window. The pointer changes to a double arrow (see Figure A.20). While holding the left mouse button down, drag upwards and to the left.
4. Resize the Word and Excel windows so that they are both visible (see Figure A.21). For this example, assume that you have data in an Excel worksheet (Figure A.21) and you will copy the data to Word. Make the Excel window active by clicking its title bar or by selecting the Excel button on the taskbar. With the Excel window active, select the data in the spreadsheet and copy it.

Figure A.20
Resize window

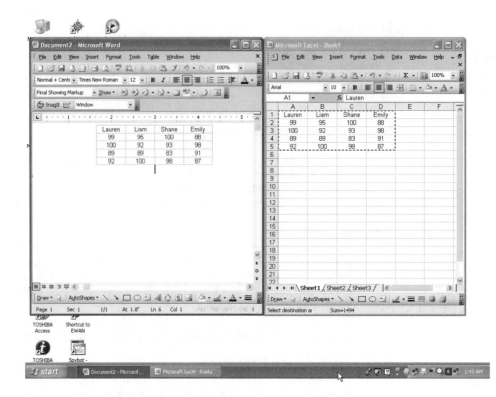

Figure A.21
Resized Word and
Excel windows

5. Make the Word window active by clicking its title bar or by clicking the Word button on the taskbar. Now paste the data from Excel into the Word file.
6. Notice in Figure A.21 that the Word window title bar is darker and the Excel window title bar is a lighter shade. The darker title bar indicates that the Word window is active.
7. To reposition either window, click on the title bar and while pressing the left mouse button, drag the window to a desired location.

Quitting a Program

1. You can quit, or close, a program by clicking the Close/Quit button at the top-right corner of a window (see Figure A.22). The Close button also closes windows associated with folders. In addition, right-clicking on the title bar and selecting *Close* from the shortcut menu closes or quits the program (see Figure A.23).

   When working in a program, you may have multiple documents open. In such cases, there is a main program window and within it individual document windows. Each window has a Close button and each window may appear as a button on the task bar. For example, in Figure A.24, the Excel program window has Minimize, Maximize, and Close buttons, as do the individual document (Book1 and Book2) windows. Note that Book2

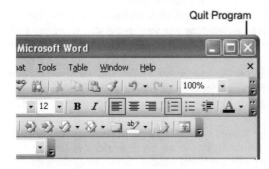

Figure A.22
Close button

Figure A.23
Close program

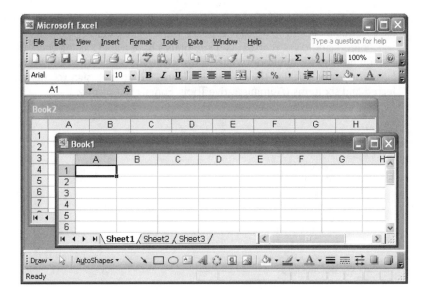

Figure A.24
Multiple document windows

buttons do not display until the book is active. Clicking the Close button on Excel's program window closes Excel and all open documents. Clicking the Close button on a document window closes that document only. Excel and all other documents remain open.

Windows Explorer

Windows Explorer allows you to view and manage files and folders on your computer. When you open Windows Explorer, you get a detailed view of your computer's contents, such as the contents of disk drives, folders, and any connected network drives. You can also manage your files and folders using the Copy, Delete, and Move functions. The view of your computer's contents provided by Windows Explorer is similar to that of the My Computer object but it is more detailed. *My Computer* is best used when working with files in a specific folder. Windows Explorer is better for working with files and folders located in various locations on your computer.

Opening Windows Explorer

To open Windows Explorer, click the Start menu, select *All Programs, Accessories* and then click *Windows Explorer.* An alternative way to open Windows Explorer is by right-clicking *My Computer* on the desktop and selecting *Explorer* from the shortcut menu.

The Explorer Window

Once you open Windows Explorer, the Explorer window appears (see Figure A.25). The left pane of the window displays disk drives and folders on your computer. The right pane displays the contents of the item selected in the left pane. For example, if you single-click a folder on the left side of the screen, its contents display in the pane to the right. In Figure A.25, the *My Documents* folder

Figure A.25
Windows Explorer

is selected and the items contained in it display on the right. You can run a program or open a file by double-clicking it when it appears in the right pane.

Folders and disks that contain subfolders have a +. Clicking the + sign expands the folder list and displays the subfolders. The + sign changes to a − when the list is expanded. You can collapse the list by clicking the − sign. In Figure A.26, the + sign to the left of *Control Panel* is selected and six items (Administrative Tools, Fonts, etc.) display.

Figure A.26
Windows Explorer folder list

The Explorer Toolbar

The Windows Explorer toolbar makes working with files and folders easy. The Explorer toolbar (see Figure A.27) contains buttons to view folders and copy, move, and delete files, among other things. A description of each button follows.

Figure A.27
Windows Explorer toolbar

Back: Takes you back through the most recently visited folders.

Forward: After going back through recently visited folders using the Back button, Forward takes you forward though these same folders.

Up: Moves up the folder hierarchy to the next highest level. For example, Figure A.28 shows the currently selected folder, *My Pictures*. Clicking the Up button moves the folder selection up to the next highest level to *My Documents* (see Figure A.29). When *My Documents* is selected, the files contained within it display in the right pane of the Explorer window.

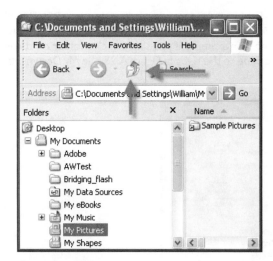

Figure A.28
Up button Example 1

Figure A.29
Up button Example 2

Search: Allows you to search the contents of your computer and all disks connected to it.

Folders: Expands the Windows Explorer display to include more than the selected folder or disk drive.

Within the File, Edit, and View menus, you will find the following options:

History: Presents a list of documents, files, and programs you have viewed in the past few days, hours, or minutes.

Move To Folder: Allows you to move a file to another folder.

Copy To Folder: Allows you to copy a file to another folder.

Delete: Allows you to delete files and folders. Select a file or folder by clicking on it once. Click Delete to send it to the Recycle Bin or to remove it from your computer.

Undo: Allows you to undo the last command you executed. If, for example, you inadvertently move a file to the wrong folder, you can select *Undo* from the Edit menu and the file will be returned to its previous location.

Managing Files: Moving, Copying, Deleting, and Renaming Files

This section explains how to manage files using Windows Explorer.

Moving a File

When moving a file or folder, the object that you want to move is removed from one location (e.g., folder or disk) and placed in another location. Note that the Move command differs from Copy. Copy places a duplicate file in the location of your choice and leaves the original file unaltered.

1. To move a file or folder, open Windows Explorer.
2. Find the file or folder that you want to move and click on it one time to select it. For this example, move the file *Lecture_Week4.doc* from the My Downloads folder to *My Documents*. In Figure A.30, you can see that the My Downloads folder is selected in the left pane. The contents of *My Downloads* display in the right pane, with *Lecture Week4.doc* highlighted.
3. Select *Move To Folder* from the Edit menu and the *Move Items* box displays (see Figure A.31). Select the folder where you want to move the file, which in this example is *My Documents*. Click *Move* and Windows Explorer moves *Lecture_Week4.doc* from *My Downloads* to *My Documents*.
4. Alternatively, you can move files by dragging and dropping them. Using the same example as previously, move *Lecture_Week4.doc* from the My Downloads folder to *My Documents* by dragging and dropping it.

Figure A.30
Moving a file

Figure A.31
Move items

5. Locate and select the Lecture_Week4.doc file. Click on it and, while holding the left mouse button down, drag it to the My Documents folder. The My Documents folder highlights as the mouse pointer approaches it (see Figure A.32). With the folder highlighted, release the mouse button and the file moves to *My Documents*.

Figure A.32
Drag and drop a file

Copying a File

1. The Copy function duplicates a file or folder. Find and select the file or folder that you want to copy. For this example, make a copy of the Lecture_Week4.doc file in the My Downloads folder and place the copy in *My Documents*. In Figure A.33, the My Downloads folder is selected in the left pane. The contents of *My Downloads* display in the right pane, with *Lecture_Week4.doc* selected.

2. Select *Copy To Folder* from the Edit menu and the *Copy Item* box displays (see Figure A.34). Locate and select the folder where you want to copy the file, which in this example is *My Documents*. Click *OK* and Windows Explorer copies *Lecture_Week4.doc* and places the copy in *My Documents*. The original copy of *Lecture_Week4.doc* is still in the My Downloads folder.

3. Alternatively, you can copy files by dragging and dropping them. Using our previous example, we will copy the Lecture_Week4.doc file to *My Documents*. Locate and select the Lecture_Week4.doc file. Press the Control (Ctrl) key and, while holding the left mouse button down, drag *Lecture_Week4.doc* onto the My Documents folder. The My Documents folder highlights as the mouse pointer approaches it. With the folder highlighted, release the mouse button and the file is copied to *My Documents*.

Figure A.33
Copy to Folder option

Figure A.34
Copy Item box

Deleting Files and Folders

There are several ways to delete files and folders, two of which are presented next: (1) using a shortcut menu and (2) using the Delete button.

Using a Shortcut Menu to Delete Files

1. Suppose you want to delete a file named *Lecture_Week4.doc* located in the My Documents folder. Find and select *Lecture_Week4.doc* and right-click it. Right-clicking on a file or folder displays a shortcut menu (see Figure A.35).
2. Select *Delete* and the *Confirm File Delete* box appears (see Figure A.36). Click *Yes* to send the file or folder to the Recycle Bin.

    To remove a file or folder from your computer without sending it to the Recycle Bin, press the Shift key while selecting *Delete*.

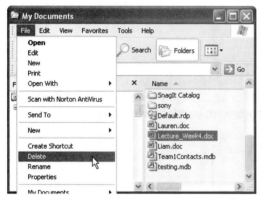

Figure A.35
Deleting files

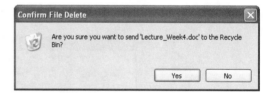

Figure A.36
Confirm File Delete

Using the Delete Button to Delete Files or Folders

3. Another way to delete files or folders is to select the item to be deleted and press the Delete key. The *Confirm File Delete* box appears asking whether you want to send the file to the Recycle Bin. Click *Yes* if you want to remove the file from its current location and place it in the Recycle Bin.

    Remember that files or folders in the Recycle Bin can be recovered. In addition, they take up disk storage space and remain on the computer until you empty the Recycle Bin.

Emptying the Recycle Bin

Windows sends all deleted files and folders to the Recycle Bin before removing them from your computer. Items on removable disks (e.g., floppy disk) are an exception to this fact. Windows removes files or folders on removable disks from your computer as soon as you issue the delete command. They are not sent to the Recycle Bin.

You must empty the Recycle Bin to remove deleted files or folders.

1. Right-click *Recycle Bin* on the desktop and then select *Empty Recycle Bin* from the shortcut menu (see Figure A.37). The *Confirm File Delete* box appears. Click *Yes* to remove the files or folders. Once you empty the Recycle Bin, deleted files are permanently removed from your computer.

Figure A.37
Empty Recycle Bin

Selecting Multiple Files

In the preceding discussion, the examples illustrate moving, copying, or deleting one file at a time. You can also select multiple items at one time to be moved, copied, or deleted.

1. To select multiple items that are adjacent, press the Shift key and click the first and last items. If, for example, you have 14 files that you want to select, press the Shift key and click items 1 and 14. This action selects all items between and including 1 and 14 (see Figure A.38).

Figure A.38
Selecting adjacent items

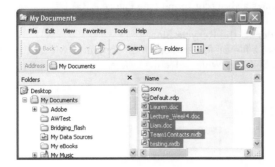

2. When items to be selected are not adjacent, press the Control (Ctrl) key and click the files, folders, or programs that you want to select (see Figure A.39).

Figure A.39
Selecting nonadjacent items

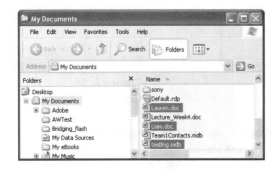

3. You can select numerous files and folders by clicking the left mouse button and, while holding it down, dragging across the items that you want selected.

Renaming a File

1. Right-click the file or folder that you want to rename and select *Rename* from the short-cut menu that appears (see Figure A.40).
2. The file name becomes selected and a blinking cursor appears in the name box. Type a new name and press the Enter key or click outside the name box.
3. Another way to change a file or folder name is to click on the item two times, pausing briefly between clicks. The first click selects the item and the second click makes the name available for editing (see Figure A.41).

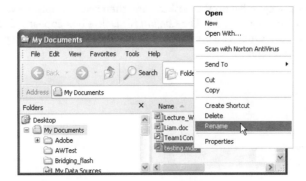

Figure A.40
Rename file

Figure A.41
Rename file, mouse click

Searching for Files or Folders

Search is a useful tool for locating files or folders on your computer and information on the Internet.

1. To locate a file or folder on your computer, click the Start button, then select *Search*.
2. The Search Results screen displays. Click *All Files and Folders*.
3. In the *Search by any or all of the criteria below* box, type the name of the file or folder that you want to locate. For example, typing *Lecture_Week4.doc* obtains the results shown in Figure A.42. If you need to search the contents of files, type the text you are searching for in the *Word or phrase in file* box.

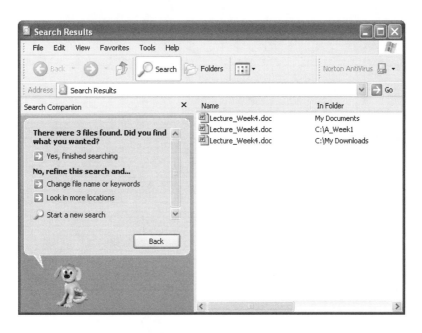

Figure A.42
Search

4. Specify where to search for files or folders by clicking the arrow to the right of the *Look in* box.
5. Begin the search by clicking the Search button. You can stop the search at any time by clicking the Stop button.

Shutting Down Your Computer

You should shut down your computer before turning it off. To exit Windows and turn off your computer, click the Start button and select *Shut Down/Turn Off*. The Shut Down window appears (see Figure A.43). Select *Shut Down/Turn Off*. The Windows session ends and you can turn off your computer.

Figure A.43
Shut down

On the Shut Down window, you will notice several options, including *Restart* and *Stand by/ Hibernate*. *Restart* shuts down the computer and restarts or starts a new windows session. The *Stand by* or *Hibernate* command keeps the computer running on low power.

APPENDIX B

MACINTOSH

TECHNICAL TERMS

The following are important terms that you will encounter in this appendix:

Desktop

Alias

The Macintosh HD

Mac OS

File

Folder

Application

Macintosh Overview

As of this writing, Microsoft Office 2004 is the most current Office version for Macintosh. You access the Microsoft Office products (Word, Excel, Entourage, and PowerPoint) through the Mac OS (operating system). This appendix, therefore, provides a basic overview of the Mac OS X (10.3.3) operating system. It presents fundamental features of the OS and explains how to use them when working with Office 2004.

A Word About MAC OS X

If you purchased Microsoft Office 2004, it may be useful to review a few Macintosh OS X basics to see how the OS works with Office. The Macintosh OS X helps you access Office applications and organize information or data on your computer. You interact with the applications and associated files through adjustable rectangular areas or windows that appear on your computer screen. The operating system has a graphical user interface (GUI). It contains objects (e.g., buttons and icons) through which you access and work with files, folders, and programs such as Figures B.1, B.2, and B.3, showing the different Microsoft Word file, folder, and Word application icons. The interface makes working with the computer easy and efficient, and it eliminates the need to type commands, which are often confusing.

Liam.doc

Figure B.1
Microsoft Word file icon

Applications

Figure B.2
Folder icon

Microsoft Word

Figure B.3
Word application icon

The Desktop

Typically, when you turn your computer on, the desktop displays (see Figure B.4). The desktop is the work area where you place files and folders. The folders, programs, or files that you open display in rectangular windows on the desktop. Several objects, such as *Macintosh HD,* appear on the desktop and represent disks, folders, applications, files, or system resources. To activate these items, double-click on them. For example, the *Macintosh HD* icon when double-clicked provides access to the contents of your computer.

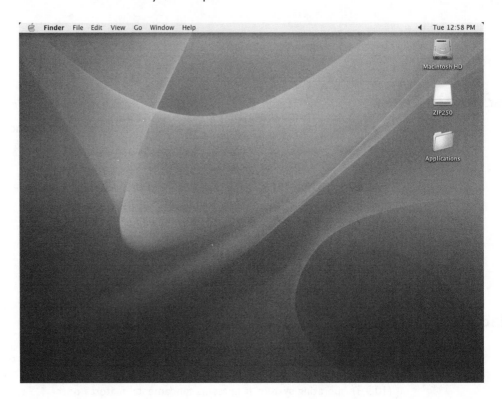

Figure B.4
The desktop

Aliases

A useful item for obtaining quick access to your computer contents is the alias. Aliases on the desktop provide easy access to files and programs. Instead of searching your computer each time you want to open a frequently used file or program, you can place an alias to it on the desktop. When you double-click the alias, the file, program, or disk opens.

Aliases look different from other desktop icons. The icon of each alias has a small arrow at the bottom-left corner and the icon's text is italicized (see Figure B.5).

Figure B.5
Alias icon

You can place an alias on the Desktop to access Office applications. For example, to make an alias, double-click *Macintosh HD* on the desktop and locate the Office applications icons. Click on the icon (e.g., Word) and press the Command key and the letter *L* at the same time. Once the alias is created, drag it to the desktop or to the Dock.

Items on the Desktop

A typical desktop contains the following features:

Macintosh HD: Allows you to see the contents of your computer's hard drive. For instance, double-clicking the Macintosh HD icon opens the Macintosh HD window that displays all the folders or directories and files contained on your computer. You can change the name of the Macintosh HD icon by clicking the icon's name and typing.

Trash: Temporarily stores files that you want to delete. A Trash can icon can be found on the Dock. All files that you intend to delete get sent first to the Trash and only when the Trash is emptied are the files removed from your computer permanently. You can retrieve files from the Trash as long as you have not emptied it.

The Dock: Gives access to frequently used items. Click an item in the Dock and it opens. Minimized documents contract to the Dock. You can add to it by dragging an item over the Dock and dropping it. The Dock is located at the bottom of the screen, but can be moved or resized. The Trash can be found on the Dock.

Desktop menu: The Desktop contains several menu items that help you work with your computer and its files. The items include: Apple, Finder, File, Edit, View, Go, Window, and Help. The desktop menu is located at the top of the screen (see Figure B.6).

Figure B.6
Desktop menu bar

Desktop Menu Items

When working with the Microsoft Office 2004 applications, you will use the desktop menu often. For this reason, each menu item found is reviewed in the next section.

Apple: Allows quick access to system preferences. You can shut down, restart, or put your computer to sleep. Clicking the Apple on the desktop menu bar displays the Apple menu (see Figure B.7). An arrow to the right of a menu item indicates that more items, or submenus, are available. When you pass the mouse over the arrow, a submenu appears.

File: Allows you to perform operations with disks, files, folders, windows, and applications. You can also use the File menu to search the contents of the hard drive and other disks.

Edit: Use the Edit menu to copy and paste when working on the desktop, to select items, or to set desktop preferences.

View: Use the View menu to change the way files, programs, and folders, and information about them, display on your computer screen.

Go: Use Go to access folders, drives, files, and applications on your computer.

Window: Use the Window menu to close or activate windows opened on the desktop.

Help: Use Help to get information about your computer and how to use it. This menu option opens the Help module, which provides information about the Macintosh operating system and many of its features and functions.

The Dock: Located on the bottom of the desktop, the Dock allows you to alternate among all open applications. As you open applications, their icons appear in the Dock. You switch among them by clicking the Applications menu and selecting the item you need. In Figure B.8, both Microsoft Word and Excel are open. Clicking *Microsoft Word* makes it active.

Figure B.7
Apple menu

Figure B.8
The Dock

Selecting Icons

The mouse is an integral component of your computer and it enables you to work with applications such as Office. You can use the mouse to select icons, make choices from dialogue boxes and pull-down menus, and move and resize windows.

You select items by clicking on them one time (single-click) with the mouse and you open items by double-clicking on them. Selecting an item signals the computer that you are going to work with the selected object in some way, such as opening or moving it. Icons highlight when they are selected. For instance, Figure B.9 illustrates the Macintosh HD icon as not selected or highlighted, whereas Figure B.10 shows it selected and highlighted.

Figure B.9
Icon not selected

Figure B.10
Icon selected

Double-clicking an object or icon opens it in a window on the desktop. For example, double-clicking the Macintosh HD opens its contents (see Figure B.11).

Figure B.11
Macintosh HD
Window

Figure B.12 illustrates three Word document icons with three different states of selection: not selected, selected, and selected for renaming. The first item is an unselected icon of a document named *Liam.doc*. The second item is an icon of a selected document named *Lauren.doc;* it was selected by single-clicking the mouse pointer on the icon. The third item is an icon of a document named *Lauren.doc* with its name selected for renaming. If you want to change the name of a file, you could do so by clicking on the icon name, then typing the new name. To select the icon's name, click on the file name rather than the document's icon.

Figure B.12
Word icons

Contextual Menus

Contextual menus can be an efficient way to access and work with files, folders, and windows, among other things. By clicking the mouse pointer on a folder, a file, a window's title, or the desktop and holding the Control (Ctrl) key down, a menu appears displaying the commands for that item (see Figure B.13).

Figure B.13
Contextual menu

Repositioning and Resizing Windows

Often you will have several files or programs open at the same time. To work efficiently, you may want to reposition the document windows. All windows have a title bar (see Figure B.14) that displays the name. You can reposition a window by clicking on the title bar and, while holding the mouse button down, dragging the window to a new location. You can also activate a window by clicking on the title bar or any location within the window.

Figure B.14
Window title bar

Title bars contain three buttons. *Close* closes the active window. *Minimize* makes the window larger or reduces the window to its previous size once it has been enlarged. *Collapse* collapses the window so that only the title bar is visible.

Scroll horizontally in a window by clicking the scroll arrows at the bottom of the window. Scroll vertically by clicking the arrows to the right of the window. You may also move quickly across or up and down a window by dragging the scroll bar.

To make a window larger or smaller, move the mouse pointer over the resize box at the window's bottom-right corner. Drag the border to enlarge or reduce the size of the window. A box appears around the window as you resize it. When resizing a window, dragging diagonally resizes the window proportionally.

Working with Programs and Files

Opening Programs

1. There are several ways to open an application such as Microsoft Word. If you have the application's icon (e.g., Word) on the Dock, click it (see Figure B.15) and the application

Figure B.15
The Dock

opens. In Figure B.15, the Word icon is the fifth item from the right on the Dock.

2. Another way to open an application (e.g., Word) is to double-click the Macintosh HD icon on the desktop, locate the Applications folder, and double-click it. Within *Applications,* double-click the Microsoft Office 2004 folder and then double-click the application's icon.

Opening Files

There are multiple ways to open a file. In this section, we discuss three methods of opening a file: (1) opening a file using the application that created it, (2) accessing and opening a file using the Macintosh HD, and (3) opening a file using *Recent Documents* from the Apple menu.

Opening a File Using the Application That Created It

1. Open the application with which you created the file. For this example, open a file created with Microsoft Word.
2. Once Word is open, click *File* and select *Open* (see Figure B.16). The *Open* dialogue box appears (see Figure B.17).

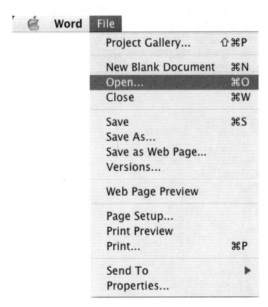

Figure B.16
Open file

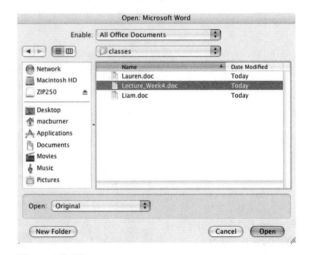

Figure B.17
Open dialogue box

3. Use the *Open* dialogue box to locate the folder or file you want to open. If you need to open a file in a different folder, click the double arrows on the location box (in Figure B.17 the location box has *classes* selected as the current folder), then select the disk drive or folder that contains the item. Once you locate the file, select it by clicking on it one time, then click *Open.* In this example, the file to be opened is *Lecture_Week4.doc,* and it is in the Classes folder. Once it is selected, click the Open button to open the file.

Accessing and Opening a File Using the Macintosh HD

The Macintosh HD can be used to access and open a file named *Lecture_Week4.doc* located on the computer's hard drive in a folder named *Classes.*

1. Double-click the Macintosh HD icon on the Desktop and its window appears.
2. Double-click the folder that contains the file you want to open. In this example, open the file *Lecture_Week4.doc* located in the Classes folder. In the Macintosh HD window,

locate and double-click the Classes folder (see Figure B.18), which opens the Classes window.

3. In the Classes window, locate the file *Lecture_Week4.doc* and double-click it to open the file.

Figure B.18
Open folder

Opening a File Using Recent Items

Recent Items on the Apple menu presents a list of recently opened files and applications. Using *Recent Items,* you can quickly open a file that you have been working on without searching for it on your computer or opening the application that created it. The Recent Items option opens both the file and its application. Keep in mind that the Recent Items list changes as you open and close files.

1. Click *Apple* and then select *Recent Items.* The Recent Items submenu displays.
2. Click the name of the file that you want to open (see Figure B.19). This step assumes that you already have a file created and you recently opened it. In this example, the Microsoft Word file *Lecture_Week4.doc* opens.

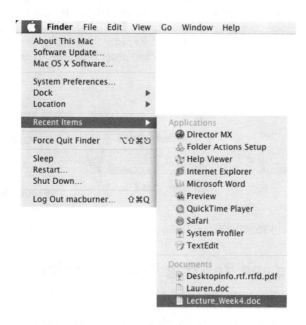

Figure B.19
Recent Items

Opening Multiple Programs

You can work with several files simultaneously, with each file opened in its own window. For instance, you might open Microsoft Word and Excel files and copy and paste data between them. The following steps illustrate how to open multiple programs, switch between programs, and reposition and resize program windows.

Opening Programs

1. Open Word by clicking its icon on the Dock or by accessing it through the Macintosh HD. The Project Gallery appears (see Figure B.20). Click *OK* and Word opens with one blank untitled document.

Figure B.20
Project Gallery

2. Repeat the process (step 1) for Excel. You now have two programs open, Word and Excel, and each program displays one blank document. Both program icons display on the Dock.

Switching Between Programs

1. Use the Dock to switch between Word and Excel (see Figure B.21). If you are viewing the Excel document, switch to Word by clicking the Word icon on the Dock. Alternatively, you can switch between applications by pressing the Command and Tab keys simultaneously. When you press Command and Tab, program icons display on screen indicating the active program (see Figure B.22). In Figure B.22, Word is the active program or the program to be selected. Repeatedly pressing the Tab key changes the selection. Release the key and the selected program becomes active.

Figure B.21
The Dock: Switching between applications

Figure B.22
The Command + Tab: Switching between applications

Repositioning and Resizing Program Windows

In this example, you can resize the Word and Excel windows and then copy data from Excel into Word.

1. If Word and Excel are open to full screen, restore them to adjust the window size. Click the Zoom (expand/contract) button at the top-left corner of the window on the Word file.
2. Switch to Excel by selecting it on the Dock and, if it is full screen, reduce it. *Note:* If you are in Word and see Excel in the background, click on Excel's window. This makes Excel active; it is an alternative to switching between programs using the Dock. When programs are visible, clicking on them in the background brings them to the foreground and makes them active.
3. Resize document windows. Make either the Word or Excel window active. Position the mouse cursor at the bottom-right corner of the window. The cursor changes to an arrow (see Figure B.23). While holding the mouse button down, drag upwards and to the left. A shadowed box displays around the window as it resizes.

Figure B.23
Resizing windows

Resize the Word and Excel windows so that they are both visible (see Figure B.24). If you need to reposition either window, click on the title bar and, while pressing the mouse button, drag the window to the desired location.

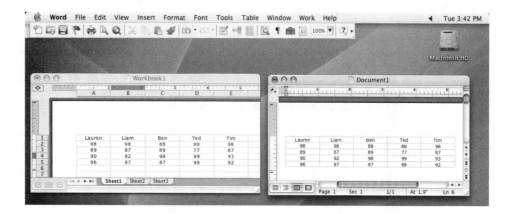

Figure B.24
Resized Word and
Excel windows

4. For this example, suppose you have a data set entered into Excel. Make the Excel window active by clicking its title bar or by selecting the Excel icon on the Dock. With the Excel window active, select the data in the spreadsheet and copy it.
5. Make the Word window active by clicking its title bar or by selecting the Word icon on the Dock. Now paste the data from Excel into the Word file. The data appear in a table within Word. Notice in Figure B.24 that the Word window is darker than Excel's window. The darker shaded window indicates the active program.

Closing a File

1. Clicking the Close button at the top-left corner of a window closes the file. In addition, the Close button closes windows associated with folders.
2. You can also close a file by selecting *Close* from the application's File menu (see Figure B.25). When you close a file, only the active file is closed. The program and any other files remain open.

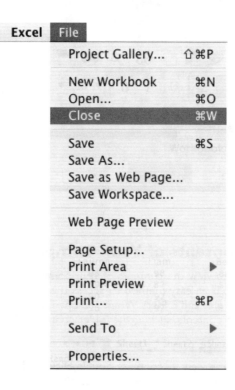

Figure B.25
Close file

3. When working in a program, you may have multiple documents open. In such cases, each document has a window and each window has a Close button. For example, in Figure B.26, Word has two documents open (Document1 and Document2). Clicking the close button on Document2 only closes the Document2 file. The Document1 file remains open.

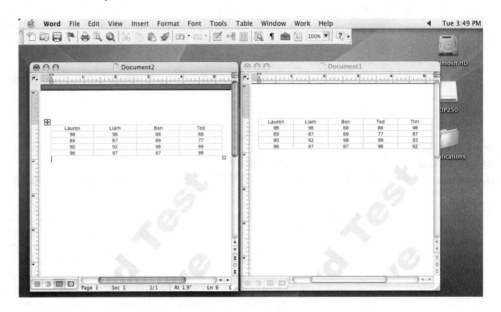

Figure B.26
Multiple document windows

Quitting an Application

To quit a program, select *Quit* from the program's menu (see Figure B.27) or press the Command and Q keys. Quitting a program closes the application (e.g., Word or Excel) and all open files.

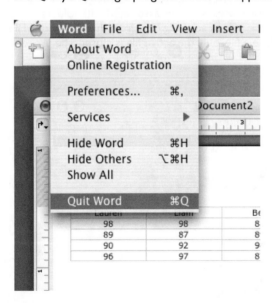

Figure B.27
Quitting an application

Viewing the Contents of Your Computer

Figure B.28
Macintosh HD

There are several ways to view the contents of your computer. Double-clicking the Macintosh HD icon on the desktop is an easy method to access the contents of your computer. It allows you to view and manage files and folders. When you open the Macintosh HD, you get a detailed view of your computer's contents, such as the folder contents, files, and programs.

Opening the Macintosh HD

To open Macintosh HD and view its contents, double-click the Macintosh HD icon on the desktop (see Figure B.28). As an alternative way to open the Macintosh HD from the desktop, you could press the Tab key until the Macintosh HD is selected, then press the Command and the letter O keys.

The Macintosh HD Window

Once you open the *Macintosh HD* window, you will see the programs, files, and folders contained on your computer's hard drive as well as devices (disk drives) connected to your computer. You can view these items in a variety of ways, including lists (see Figure B.29), as icons (see Figure B.30), or as columns (see Figure B.31).

Figure B.29
List view

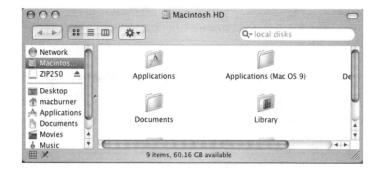

Figure B.30
Icon view

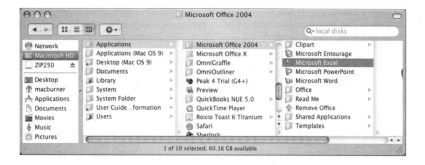

Figure B.31
Column view

You can alter the view (e.g., icon, list, and columns) of window contents by selecting *as Icons, as List,* or *as Columns* from the View menu on the desktop (see Figure B.32).

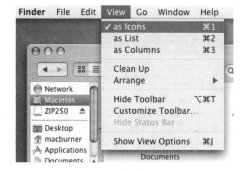

Figure B.32
View menu

Double-click a folder to view its content or, when in the List view, click the arrow to the left of the folder to expand or collapse it. For example, in Figure B.33 the Applications folder was expanded by clicking the arrow to its left. The arrow turns to a downward position. The contents of the Applications folder appear indented under it. In this case, *Applications* contains folders named *AppleScript* and *Art Directors Toolkit 3* as well as other items that are visible in the Macintosh HD window.

From the Macintosh HD window, you can also open files and programs by double-clicking their icons.

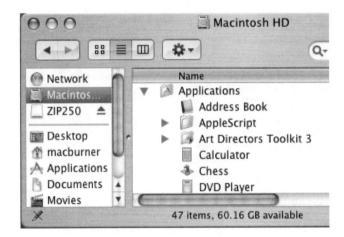

Figure B.33
Macintosh HD
window

Managing Files: Moving, Copying, Deleting, and Renaming Files

This section explains how to manage files with the Macintosh operating system.

Moving a File

When moving a file or folder, you move it from one location (e.g., folder or disk) to another. If, for example, you have a file titled *MyLesson.doc* in a folder titled *Week1*, when you move *MyLesson.doc* from the Week1 folder to another folder, *MyLesson.doc* is no longer in the Week1 folder. The Move command differs from copy. Copy places a duplicate file in the location of your choice. It leaves the original file in place and unaltered.

1. You can move files by dragging and dropping them. To move a file or folder open Macintosh HD by double-clicking its icon on the desktop.
2. Find the file or folder that you want to move and click it one time to select it (see Figure B.34). Figure B.34 shows the List view with *Lecture_Week4.doc* selected.

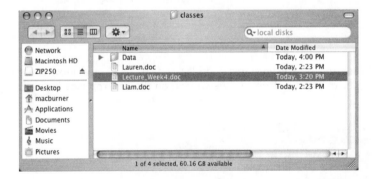

Figure B.34
Moving files

3. In Figure B.34, the Classes folder is open and its contents are displayed beneath it.
4. Move the Lecture_Week4.doc file into *Data* by dragging and dropping it. Click *Lecture_Week4.doc* one time to select it and, while holding the left mouse button down, drag it onto the Data folder. The Data folder highlights as the mouse pointer approaches it. With the folder highlighted, release the mouse button and the file moves to *Data*.

Copying a File

The Copy function duplicates a file or folder. Find and select the file or folder that you want to copy. For this example, make a copy of the Lecture_Week4.doc file in the Classes folder and place a copy of it in *Data*. In Figure B.35, the Lecture_Week4.doc file is selected. From the desktop File menu select *Duplicate* (or press the Command and the D keys) and a copy of the file appears in the Classes folder. Notice that the duplicate file, *Lecture_Week4copy.doc,* appears below the original file in Figure B.35. Now move the duplicate file to *Data* by dragging it on top of the Data folder and dropping it.

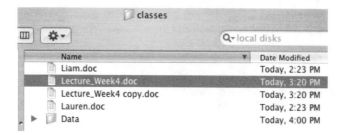

Figure B.35
Copy files

Alternatively, to copy *Lecture_Week4.doc* to the Data folder, you can drag and drop it onto the Data folder while holding the Option key down. This duplicates the file and places the copy inside the Data folder. With this method, *copy* is not appended to the file name.

Deleting Files and Folders

There are several ways to delete files and folders (see Figure B.36), two of which are presented: using the *Move To Trash* option and dragging and dropping files to the Trash.

Figure B.36
Deleting files

Using the Move to Trash Option to Delete Files or Folders

Suppose you want to delete a file named *Lecture_Week4.doc* located in the Data folder. Find and select *Lecture_Week4.doc* and then select *Move To Trash* on the Desktop File menu (see Figure B.36). This command removes the file from its current location and places it in the Trash. Alternatively, once you select the file, you can send it to the Trash by pressing the Command and Delete keys.

Remember that files or folders in the Trash can be recovered or retrieved. In addition, files or folders in the Trash take up disk storage space and only after emptying the Trash are they removed from your computer permanently.

Dragging and Dropping Files to the Trash

Locate the file that you want to delete. Click it once to select it and, while holding the mouse button down, drag the file to the Trash can on the Dock. As the mouse pointer approaches the Trash icon on the Dock, the icon highlights (see Figure B.37). With the Trash icon highlighted, release the mouse and the file is moved to the Trash.

Figure B.37
Trash icon on Dock

Emptying the Trash

All deleted files and folders are sent to the Trash before they are removed from your computer.

1. You must empty the Trash to permanently remove deleted files or folders. Empty the Trash by selecting *Empty Trash* from the Finder menu (see Figure B.38). You can also empty the Trash by pressing the Command, Shift, and Delete keys simultaneously. Another way to empty the Trash is by pressing the Control key while clicking the Trash icon on the Dock.

Figure B.38
Empty Trash

2. An alert box appears asking if you want to remove the items from the Trash (see Figure B.39). Clicking *OK* removes the items.

Figure B.39
Empty Trash alert

Selecting Multiple Files

In the preceding discussion, the examples illustrate moving, copying, or deleting one file at a time. You can also select multiple items at one time to be moved, copied, or deleted.

1. To select multiple items that are adjacent, click the mouse button and, while holding it down, drag across the items that you want to select. After highlighting all the items that you want selected, release the mouse button (see Figure B.40).

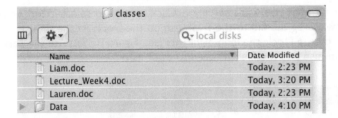

Figure B.40
Selecting adjacent items

2. When items to be selected are not adjacent, press the Command key and click the files, folders, or programs that you want to select (see Figure B.41).

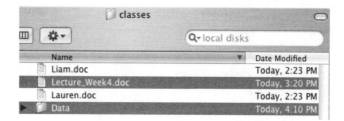

Figure B.41
Selecting nonadjacent items

Figure B.42
Rename file

Renaming a File

Click the file or folder that you want to rename. Click on the item's name rather than on the icon. Clicking the name selects the text. Figure B.42 shows an icon with the text selected. With the text selected, you can edit it or type a new name.

Searching for Files or Folders

Search is a useful tool for locating files, folders, or applications on your computer and information on the Internet.

1. To locate a file or folder on your computer, click the File menu on the Desktop and select *Find*.
2. The *Find* box appears (see Figure B.43).

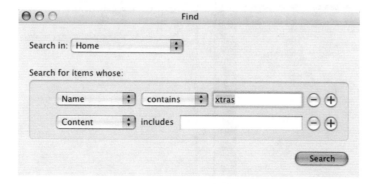

Figure B.43
Search

3. In the *Search in* box type the name of the file or folder that you want to locate. You can search for items by file name or by content.
4. Specify where to search for files or folders by selecting the location with the *Search in* box option.
5. Begin the search by clicking the Search button and the Search Results screen displays. You can stop the search at any time by closing the Search Results screen.

Shutting Down Your Computer

You should shut down your computer before turning it off. To exit the Mac OS system and turn off your computer, click the Apple menu on the desktop and select *Shut Down* (see Figure B.44).

On the Apple menu, you will notice several options, including Restart and Sleep. Restart shuts down and restarts the computer or starts a new session. Sleep keeps the computer running on low power, but it maintains the contents of memory. While in the Sleep mode, touching a key wakes the computer.

The Microsoft Office 2004 and Office 2003 Workspaces

As of this writing, Microsoft Office 2004 is the most current version of Office for the Macintosh. Microsoft Office 2004 for Macintosh includes Word, Excel, Entourage, and PowerPoint. The database program Access is not included. Generally, there is much commonality between the Microsoft Office 2004 applications and the Windows version. The following screens illustrate the

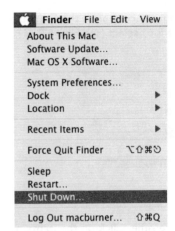

Figure B.44
Shut down

workspaces of three of the Office applications, Word (see Figures B.45 and B.46), Excel (see Figures B.47 and B.48), and PowerPoint (see Figures B.49 and B.50). For each application two sets of screens are presented, one for the Macintosh Microsoft Office 2004 version and the other for the Windows Office 2003. Notice that overall the menu items, toolbars, and workspaces between these versions are similar and that both versions offer many of the same options and features.

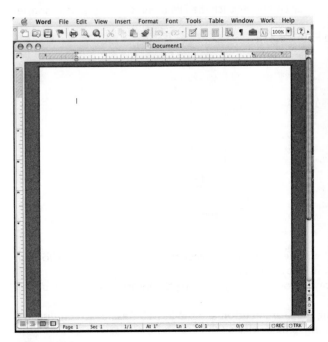

Figure B.45
Office 2004—Word

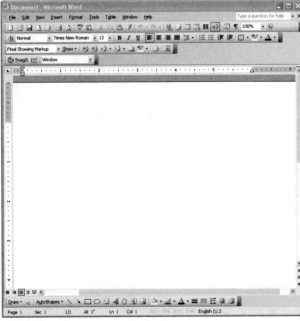

Figure B.46
Windows Office 2003—Word

In many instances, Microsoft Office 2004 and Microsoft Office 2003 offer a variety of methods for accomplishing similar tasks. For instance, you can open a file from within the application (e.g., Word) that created it or you can double-click the file icon on the computer's hard drive (Macintosh HD, My Computer, or C: drive). An understanding of the Mac OS X operating system components, such as the desktop, and knowledge of the varied approaches that it offers for opening and managing files and programs will be beneficial to you when using Microsoft Office 2004.

Figure B.47
Office 2004—Excel

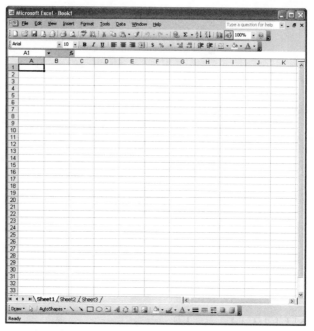

Figure B.48
Windows Office 2003—Excel

Figure B.49
Office 2004—PowerPoint

Figure B.50
Windows Office 2003—PowerPoint

GLOSSARY

Acceptable Use Policies: A set of rules for students, teachers, staff, and administrators that govern the use of school or school district computers, networks, and the Internet.

Alias: A file that provides quick access to frequently used items, such as programs, folders, documents, or disks. An alias is equivalent to a shortcut on the Windows platform.

Application: A software program that performs a specific function or purpose. For example, Word is an application that helps you compose a letter or a report and Excel is an application that helps you analyze data. Word, Excel, and PowerPoint are all applications.

Attachment: A file sent along with an e-mail message. Documents, pictures, and multimedia objects may be sent; the receiving computer must have the software installed to read the attached file.

AutoCorrection: Word has an AutoCorrect options button that allows you to undo automatic corrections or select a different AutoCorrect option.

Calendar: An Outlook folder that keeps track of appointments.

CC or Carbon Copy: An option used to send a copy of an e-mail message to one or more persons.

Cell: A unit in an Excel worksheet column that holds information such as text and numerical data.

Clip Art: Professionally prepared art stored as files that may be inserted in Office applications.

Commands: Tasks that are performed in an Office program, such as Open and Save, and are found in the Office menu bars.

Contacts: An outlook folder that maintains an address book.

Copyright: Laws that regulate and describe the manner in which materials may be used and copied.

Design Templates: Predefined colors, layout formats, and font styles that give PowerPoint presentations and Word documents a specific look.

Desktop: A work area on the computer where you place files and folders. The desktop is the screen that typically displays when you first turn on the computer.

Document Object: A Word document that has been inserted into a file.

Drafts: An outlook folder that stores unsent e-mail messages.

Drag and Drop: A method of moving objects by dragging them with the mouse and dropping them in a desired location by releasing the mouse button.

Dragging: A method of moving objects by dragging them with the computer mouse.

Embed: A method of inserting an object in an Office application file whereby the object embeds or becomes part of the file.

Expanded Menu: A menu format that displays all of the commands in a pull-down list.

Field: In a database, a specific category or location to store information. For example, a field called *first name* could store students' first names.

File: A unit of information produced by a program (e.g., Microsoft Word). For example, a Word document, PowerPoint presentations, and Excel workbooks are files. To organize files, put them in folders.

Floating Toolbars: Toolbars that can be detached from the application window's border, moved, and resized.

Folder: Often referred to as a directory. Computer files or directories are places to store digital work files. Placing work files into folders or directions keeps them organized.

Form: A database object that presents display boxes where information may be displayed or entered. A form usually displays one record at a time.

Formatting: Refers to characteristics (e.g., bold, italic, color, size, type, and so on) applied to text, tables, lists, and documents. In a document, it allows for paragraph formatting or changing columns.

Formula: An Excel expression in the form of a series of numbers or cell references that produces a new value. The formula = (A1 + B1) when placed in cell C1 adds the contents of cells A1 and B1 and places the results in C1. All formulas must start with an equal sign (=).

Frames: A space in Publisher that contains pictures. Pictures may be clip art, a circle, an arrow, a line, or AutoShapes as well as a variety of graphic files such as GIF (graphic interchange format), JPEG (joint photographic experts group), or scanned photographs taken with a digital camera.

Function: Formulas built into Excel (see formula).

Home Page: The first Web document the user sees when entering a Web site.

HTML (HyperText Markup Language):   The computer language used to format Web documents. You can save your Word documents, PowerPoint presentations, and Excel worksheets as HTML documents and put them on the Web.

Hyperlink: Creates a connection between a word or phrase in a document to another document on the computer or to the Internet.

Hypertext Links: Often associated with Web documents but may also be in other files such as PowerPoint presentations. Hypertext links are text and/or pictures that can be clicked to take the user to another screen, Web document, or media object (e.g., video, audio). These screens, documents, and objects may be within the same file, the same Web site, or at a Web site around the world. They are often referred to as hyperlinks.

Inbox: An Outlook folder that stores in-coming (received) e-mail messages.

Independent Design Elements: In Publisher, text and picture portions of a publication that act as independent entities when designing publications.

Insert Object: A method of placing an object or a portion of an object into an Office application file. For example, when a PowerPoint slide is placed or inserted into Word it is referred to as a slide object.

Internet: A large, worldwide network of computers (computing hardware and software) in which the computers communicate with one another.

ISTE (International Society for Technology in Education):   An international organization of educators that developed teaching standards for students and teachers.

Link to File: A method of inserting an object in an Office application file whereby the object is linked to the file. The object does not embed or become a part of the file.

Mac OS: The Macintosh operating system (Mac OS X 10.3.3).

NCATE (National Council for Accreditation of Teacher Education):   A council that developed a set of standards for the accreditation of teachers. NCATE also accredits teacher education organizations.

Objects: A Word document, PowerPoint slide or presentation, Excel worksheet, image, sound, video, etc. are some examples of the files or objects that can be embedded or linked to Office application files. When a file created by a separate application is placed into the Office file, it is referred to as an object.

Outline Tab: One of several view options available for viewing a PowerPoint presentation while it is being developed. The Outline tab presents slides in text outline form.

Outlook Today: Outlook function that displays a summary of the current day's activities.

Presentation Object: A PowerPoint presentation that has been inserted into a file.

Publisher Master Design Set: A set of business publications created in Publisher that contains a consistent color scheme, font scheme, and design. Individuals can choose from 45 Master Design Sets in Publisher 2003. This allows for a consistent look for letterhead, business cards, an brochures.

Queries: Searches in Access that allow users to find specific information in a database, such as who lives in a particular zip code area.

Record: A collection of information about a thing or person (e.g., name, address, phone number, e-mail address, and so on) in a table of an Access database.

Relative Cell Reference: In Excel, a reference to a cell (e.g., C1) that, when used in a formula, changes when the formula is copied to another cell. If cell E1 contains the formula = (C1 + D1) and E1 is copied to E2, then E2's formula changes to = (C2 + D2).

Report: Summarizes Access database information in a document format.

Right-click: On Windows computers, pressing the right mouse button. The computer mouse often has two buttons, a left mouse button and a right mouse button. In most instances the left mouse button is used for selecting menu options, moving objects, and dragging and dropping. The right mouse button when clicked frequency presents menu choices associated with the selected object.

Shortcut Menus: Menus that appear on the screen when you right click an item, display the most frequently used commands.

Shortcuts: Provide quick access to frequently used files and programs. You can place shortcuts on the desktop or in folders. Instead of searching the computer for a file or program, you can create a shortcut to it that opens the file or program.

Slide: A screen that may contain text and content such as pictures, clip art, graphs, tables, diagrams, video, and audio. Several slides make up a presentation.

Slide Object: A single PowerPoint slide that has been inserted into a file.

Slide Show: A PowerPoint view that presents the finished slides of a presentation. In this mode, slides cannot be edited.

Slide Sorter: One of several PowerPoint view options that presents small images of each slide in the presentation. It is useful for seeing the order of all slides. You can copy, paste, delete, and rearrange slides in the Slide Sorter.

Slides Tab: One of several view options available for viewing a presentation while it is being developed. The Slides view presents miniature slides of the presentation.

Start Button: Appears to the left of the taskbar. Clicking *Start* displays the Start menu and provides access to programs, files, help, and search facilities, among other things.

Table: (1) Allows you to display information in a table format in the word processed document. (2) A collection of information in an Access database about a specific topic (e.g., student information, class materials inventory, and so on). A table consists of fields and records. Those may be more than one table in a database.

Task Pane: A window that allows users to work with common tasks, such as opening a new document and formatting text.

Taskbar: Contains buttons that provide access to opened folders and files and make switching between them convenient. Although you can position the taskbar at the top of sides of the screen, it typically appears at the bottom.

Tasks: An Outlook folder that allows the creation of lists of activities.

Textbox: A space that acts as a container for text and can be arranged, reshaped, and created within a publication.

URL: Uniform Resource Locator. Frequently referred to as the address or Web address, such as http://www. duq.edu.

Web Browser: A software application used to view Web content. Some popular Web browsers include Internet Explorer, Netscape, and Mozilla Firefox.

Web Page: A singe Web document that may contain images, text, graphics, video, and audio.

Web Site: A collection of Web documents that may contain images, text, graphics, video and audio.

Windows XP: The Windows operating system. Windows 98, NT, and 95 are earlier versions of the Windows operating system.

Workbook: An Excel spreadsheet file comprised of one or more worksheets. Excel identifies worksheets as Sheet1, Sheet2, Sheet3, and so on. A single workbook may contain numerous worksheets.

Worksheet: A screen in an Excel workbook made up of columns, rows, and cells. Each worksheet may contain as many as 256 columns and 65,536 rows.

Worksheet Object: An Excel worksheet that has been inserted into a file.

World Wide Web: Often referred to as the Web. A collection of information viewed with a Web browser that is available though computing networks.

INDEX